Successes and Failures of Knowledge Management

Successes and Failures of Knowledge Management

Edited by:

Jay Liebowitz

Distinguished Chair of Applied Business and Finance
Harrisburg University of Science and Technology
Harrisburg, Pennsylvania

AMSTERDAM • BOSTON • HEIDELBERG • LONDON
NEW YORK • OXFORD • PARIS • SAN DIEGO
SAN FRANCISCO • SINGAPORE • SYDNEY • TOKYO

Morgan Kaufmann is an imprint of Elsevier

Morgan Kaufmann is an imprint of Elsevier
50 Hampshire Street, 5th Floor, Cambridge, MA 02139, United States

Library of Congress Cataloging-in-Publication Data
A catalog record for this book is available from the Library of Congress

British Library Cataloguing-in-Publication Data
A catalogue record for this book is available from the British Library

ISBN: 978-0-12-805187-0

For information on all Morgan Kaufmann publications
visit our website at https://www.elsevier.com

www.elsevier.com • www.bookaid.org

Acquisitions Editor: Todd Green
Editorial Project Manager: Lindsay Lawrence
Production Project Manager: Mohana Natarajan
Cover Designer: Victoria Pearson Esser

Typeset by Thomson Digital

To all my students and professionals who took my knowledge management courses over the years, and to those organizations that implemented my recommendations for knowledge management over the past two decades.

Contents

CHAPTER 8 Knowledge and Knowledge-Related Assets: Design for Optimal Application and Impact...............113

G.S. Erickson, H.N. Rothberg

CHAPTER 9 Knowledge Management Success and Failure: the Tale of Two Cases 129

S. Larson

**CHAPTER 10 Social Knowledge: Organizational Currencies
  in the New Knowledge Economy** **141**
K.E. Russell, R. La Londe, F. Walters

**CHAPTER 11 Knowledge Management and Analytical
  Modeling for Transformational Leadership
  Profiles in a Multinational Company**...........................**151**
T. Ha-Vikström, J. Takala

CHAPTER 14 Semantic Technologies for Enhancing Knowledge Management Systems 203

V. Sugumaran

Contributors

J. Boyle
NASA Headquarters, Washington, DC, USA

F.A. Calabrese
The International Institute for Knowledge and Innovation (I²KI) IKI-SEA—
Bangkok University, Bangkok, Thailand

Y.E. Chan
Queen's University, Kingston, ON, Canada

S. Earley
Earley Information Science, Inc., USA

J.S. Edwards
Aston Business School, Birmingham, United Kingdom

G.S. Erickson
Ithaca College, Ithaca, New York, USA

B. Filipczyk
University of Economics, Katowice, Poland

J. Gołuchowski
University of Economics, Katowice, Poland

T. Ha-Vikström
University of Vaasa, Vaasa, Finland

E. Hoffman
NASA Headquarters, Washington, DC, USA

C.W. Holsapple
Gatton College of Business, University of Kentucky, Lexington, KY, USA

S.-H. Hsiao
Lawrence Technological University, Southfield, MI, USA

A. Janas
Podhale State College of Applied Sciences, Nowy Targ, Poland

R. La Londe
iTalent Corporation, USA

S. Larson
School of Business, Slippery Rock University, Slippery Rock, PA, USA

N. Levallet
Ohio University, Athens, OH, USA

J.-Y. Oh
Eastern Kentucky University, Richmond, KY, USA

J. Paliszkiewicz
Warsaw University of Life Sciences, Warsaw, Poland

V. Ribière
The Institute for Knowledge and Innovation—Southeast Asia (IKI-SEA), Bangkok University, Bangkok, Thailand

E. Rogers
NASA Goddard Space Flight Center, Greenbelt, MD, USA

H.N. Rothberg
Marist College, Poughkeepsie, New York, USA

K.E. Russell
Wichita State University, USA

V. Sugumaran
School of Business Administration, Oakland University, Rochester, MI, USA

J. Takala
University of Vaasa, Vaasa, Finland

E. Tsui
Knowledge Management and Innovation Research Centre (KMIRC), The Hong Kong Polytechnic University, Hong Kong, China

F. Walters
iTalent Corporation, USA

A.K.P. Wensley
University of Toronto-Mississauga, Mississauga, ON, Canada

Preface

Over the past 30 years, the knowledge management (KM) field has evolved from focusing strictly on capturing knowledge, to moving from "collections" to "connections," to incorporating knowledge assets as part of an organization's intellectual capital strategy. We have seen over the years that the IT codification approach to knowledge management is just one part of the organization's knowledge management strategy, and perhaps the personalization approaches for sharing and collaborating are more impactful in many ways through the use of online communities of practice and other social networking methods. Over the years, we have also witnessed the KM owner in an organization being the CIO, CKO, VP-HR/OD, VP-Strategy, and other senior champions with different slants on the development and implementation of KM strategies in their organizations. Now, as we enter the big data and analytics years, what lies ahead for knowledge management?

To answer this question in the best possible way, I thought it would be most helpful to apply the basic tenets of knowledge management by learning from KM past successes and failures. In this spirit of knowledge sharing, we can learn from others so we don't travel down the wrong paths. This book, with contributed chapters from some of the leading KM authorities, including journal editors of some of the highly ranked KM journals, provides a lens in which we can look at the past, present, and future opportunities facing us in terms of how knowledge management can continue to help organizations achieve their goals.

If you Google "knowledge management" under any job site, you will witness hundreds of knowledge management jobs ranging from librarian roles to technical and managerial roles as applied to leveraging knowledge internally and externally. This seems to suggest that knowledge management has made it into the business mainstream. But, at least from my experience, many organizations don't seem to have enterprise-wide KM strategies. Senior managers and executives also don't seem to talk much about "knowledge management," which may indicate that either KM is already integrated into the fabric of the organization (ie, we don't need to talk about KM, we are already doing it), or KM may not be that important to the organization. Some of the chapters in this book suggest some truths on both accounts. From an academic viewpoint, there are still many conferences worldwide focused on knowledge management, as well as a number of industry-focused KM conferences too.

So, as we look ahead, what can we suggest for the longevity of knowledge management? First, KM must not be siloed and must continue to be an integrative mechanism that bridges across the functional silos in an organization. One of the book chapters mentions that KM should really be interwoven with competitive intelligence (CI) and business intelligence (BI), and perhaps this may be a good way to go as we continue to take advantage of BI and analytics in organizations. Second, KM should really be part of the human capital strategy of organizations. The US federal government has a six-pillar human capital strategy model that has KM and leadership as one of the key pillars. Other organizations should embrace something similar as they build out their enterprise-wide human capital strategy. Third, linkages with the big data, artificial intelligence/machine learning, and analytics communities would be very worthwhile, especially as all these communities face issues with structured and unstructured data. Last, we still are in search, a bit, for the killer app for KM. At first, we thought that KM would be the savior of knowledge capture activities before people left an organization and for building the institutional memory of an organization. Later, the killer app morphed into better ways to increase innovation through sharing and collaboration activities. Now, perhaps the killer app is organizational agility by increasing internal and external organizational effectiveness and responsiveness in competitive environments through KM-related activities. Many organizations are still pondering the key advantage of using KM for their business needs. However, others, through smart search techniques for example, are transforming the way they do work.

Hopefully, this book provides some interesting and insightful perspectives to think about how knowledge management can best be applied in organizations for maximum gains. Through case studies, insights, and research of leading organizations in the field, this book should further illuminate the path of success for organizations to follow in applying KM to meet their strategic goals. With 5–8 international journals focused strictly on knowledge management, the field of knowledge management as a "discipline" can further develop. In the end, we hope that KM will continue to contribute favorably toward organizational success.

I would like to close by thanking the contributors, reviewers, and Morgan Kaufmann/Elsevier for making this book a reality. This will be part of my "knowledge management legacy," and I hope it will be a key reference source for others interested in the field. Without my family's support, this book would certainly never have surfaced, and I thank them for letting me pursue my dreams.

Enjoy!

Jay Liebowitz
Washington, DC

Parameters of knowledge management success

C.W. Holsapple*, S.-H Hsiao**, J.-Y. Oh[†]
*Gatton College of Business, University of Kentucky, Lexington, KY, USA;
**Lawrence Technological University, Southfield, MI, USA;
[†]Eastern Kentucky University, Richmond, KY, USA

INTRODUCTION

The effectiveness of an organization is a function of the resources that it has at its disposal, how those resources are used, and characteristics of the environment in which it finds itself. It is commonly understood that an organization has four basic kinds of resources: human, material, financial, and knowledge. How an organization's knowledge resources are used is a focus of the knowledge management (KM) discipline, which is also concerned with related matters such as the nature of knowledge resources, the interplay between knowledge and the other organizational resources, and the impacts of environmental phenomena on an organization's management of knowledge (and vice versa). Knowledge management success contributes to, or can even drive, an organization's success.

Success and failure are two sides of the "effectiveness coin" and, at the edge, we have gradations where the two meet. At an organization level, two common ways of thinking about effectiveness are *performance* and *competitiveness*—each of which is a way to gauge the outputs emanating from the organization's activities and fourfold assets. Success, then, has occurred when results of organization actions meet criteria for effectiveness, while simultaneously maintaining an alignment with its mission, vision, and values. Failure has occurred when results of organization actions do not meet criteria for effectiveness, or they fall out of alignment with the organization's mission, vision, or values. There are, of course, degrees of success and failure, where the two blend as we assess the organization results. Notice that an output or result can be directed in an inward and/or outward direction.

Performance is concerned with measures of how well something is done relative to criteria established for effectiveness. These criteria may be established by the organization itself (eg, average customer-service representative score in excess of 4.20 on a 5-point scale), or imposed by external forces of its environment (eg, government-mandated miles-per-gallon level for a new vehicle model). From another angle, we can distinguish between performance criteria with an inward orientation (eg, production defect rate of less than 1%) and those with an outward orientation (eg, same-store sales boost of 5% compared to the prior year). Yet another angle recognizes short-run versus longer-run performance criteria (eg, quarter vs annual). No matter the source of criteria, the orientation of criteria, or the temporal scope of criteria, KM can play a role in successfully meeting them.

There are many case studies describing KM initiatives that enhanced the performance of specific organizations in terms of criteria dealing with such features as cost reduction, greater responsiveness, improved processes, new revenue streams, and higher customer loyalty; examples include investigations by Leonard-Barton (1998), Rubenstein-Montano et al. (2001), Smith and McKeen (2003), O'Dell et al. (2003), Wolford and Kwiecien (2003), Oriel (2003), and O'Leary (2008). Each such performance measure can serve as a gauge for assessing the degree of success achieved by a KM initiative.

More directly, and on a larger scale, we can ask whether superior KM can predict superior performance by a for-profit organization as a whole (Holsapple and Wu, 2008a; Zack et al., 2009). For instance, can KM be performed in ways that predict superior bottom-line numbers, such as a firm's earnings per share and other financial ratios? Or, can it be performed in ways that predict superior market performance for the firm, such as price-to-book ratio? There is empirical evidence, based on analysis of archival data, that the answer for each question is "yes" (Holsapple and Wu, 2008b, 2011; DeFond et al., 2010; Wu and Holsapple, 2013). Now the question is: What are the parameters that deserve attention when striving for KM success or superiority? We suggest an answer to this later in the chapter.

Aside from performance, *competitiveness* is another way of looking at an organization's effectiveness. Competitiveness is related to performance in the sense that higher performance is often associated with higher competitiveness. For example, a firm that has superior performance in cultivating supplier relationships may well have an edge over competing firms that are not so well attuned with the organizations that supply its needs. Note that development and maintenance of supplier relationships is a knowledge-intensive endeavor whose success contributes to competitiveness of a purchasing firm (Chen et al., 2015). In other words, how knowledge management is conducted can contribute to an organization's competitiveness (Holsapple and Singh, 2000).

In its most fundamental sense, competitiveness is about survival. As a raw baseline, survival is an indicator of competitiveness (excluding instances where an organization's existence is protected by some external force in its environment). But, as organizations strive to achieve the same thing (eg, high market share, product innovation, excellent customer service, low-cost provider, control of a resource), some fare better than others, in other words, they are *more* competitive. Just as higher performance often leads to higher competitiveness, greater competitiveness can lead to higher performance. Within this reinforcing cycle of organization effectiveness, KM holds a key for success. The extent to which this key works depends on the way it is shaped, designed, and operated relative to features of an organization's fourfold resources (FR), its environing conditions (EC), and its defining principles (DP) embodied in its vision, mission, and values. A knowledge management key that works for one organization may not work so well for another, depending on its fit with the foregoing features.

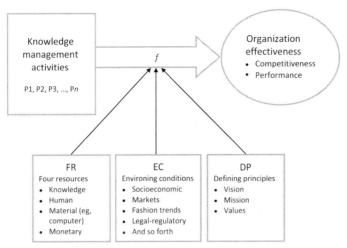

FIGURE 1.1 Organization effectiveness

A starting point for thinking about configuring a KM key to unlock an organization's potential is to identify design parameters that need to be considered. Here, we examine a collection of such parameters that exist independent of any particular organization. Formally, the effectiveness (E) of organization **i** is a function of *n* parameters (P1, P2, …, P*n*), given the state of that organization's resources, environing conditions, and guiding principles:

$$E_i = f(P1_i, P2_i, ..., Pn_i \mid FR_i, EC_i, DP_i)$$

This relationship is visualized in Fig. 1.1.

Collectively, the knowledge management parameters comprise a sort of "control panel" that contains the levers/knobs that every KM initiative needs to consider and properly set (ie, instantiate) to enhance likelihood of success and reduce possibilities of failure. The "proper" settings are with respect to the organization's FR, EC, and DP, which are constraints and enablers for what can be accomplished. As previously explained, E can be regarded in terms of performance and/or competitiveness. In the discussion that follows, we refer mainly to competitive success when examining the KM parameters.

FOUNDATION

As referenced previously, there is ample evidence that an organization can design and perform knowledge management in ways that contribute to its effectiveness. Those "ways" involve particular instantiations for the collection of KM parameters. To understand and appreciate the parameters, some background is needed: a characterization of knowledge and the conduct of knowledge management.

KNOWLEDGE

Renowned cognitive scientist Allen Newell (1982) explains that when a system, be it human-based or computer-based, possesses and can use a representation of "something (an object, a procedure … whatever), then the system itself can also be said to have knowledge, namely, the knowledge embedded in that representation about that thing." Following Newell, we adopt the characterization of knowledge as *that which is conveyed in a usable representation*. A representation is some arrangement in time/space. There are many kinds of representations, including: a physical item (eg, a printed page, document, report), a physical image or movement (eg, animation), spoken words (eg, a conversation, lecture), displayed behaviors (individual or collective), mental patterns or images (eg, a mindset, an idea, a procedure, a rule), digital patterns (eg, files, databases, programs), and so forth.

According to Newell, a representation does not convey knowledge unless it is usable. Usability is the capacity to take action (Sveiby, 1997). The notion of usability implies the existence of processors who do the using, processors that can take the actions. A processor can be human-based, machine-based, or a hybrid. Many, if not most, representations are not usable by some processors; for those processors, the representations do not convey knowledge. Put another way, knowledge does not exist apart from at least one processor that perceives or possesses a representation that it finds to be usable in a circumstance it is facing.

We can consider an organization's knowledge resource in terms of two classes: schema and content (Holsapple and Joshi, 2004). The schematic portion of an organization's knowledge resource does not exist apart from the organization's existence. Indeed, we might say it defines that organization's existence, including purpose (mission, vision), strategy (direction, path), culture (shared assumptions, norms, beliefs), and infrastructure (roles, relationships, regulations). If an organization ceases, so does its purpose, strategy, culture, and infrastructure. In contrast, the content portion of an organization's knowledge resource can come and go. It has an existence independent of the organization in which it is found. The content knowledge resource is comprised of participants' knowledge and the knowledge conveyed in/by artifacts. The former is knowledge belonging to a processor (eg, from human mental representations or computer digital representations); it also belongs to the organization, but only insofar as the processor functions as a participant in the organization. In contrast, an artifact is an object that has no innate knowledge-processing capability (a document, for instance), yet is (or holds) a representation of knowledge that may be usable to at least one knowledge processor in the organization.

There are degrees of usability based on a hierarchy of qualities: clarity, meaningfulness, relevance, and importance (Holsapple and Whinston, 1996). Meaning requires clarity, relevance requires meaning, importance requires relevance. When a processor, confronting some task, sees levels of these qualities for a specific representation as being high, then the usability of that representation for that task is high (ie, the knowledge it conveys is of high utility). When a processor perceives levels of the qualities as being lower, then the representation is less usable and knowledge it conveys is of less utility for the task at hand. From a bird's–eye view, usability of a particular representation by a particular processor is influenced by the fit between the representation and processor, the action/task being attempted by the processor, and the environment within which the action is to take place.

Three main types of knowledge are descriptive, procedural, and reasoning knowledge (Holsapple and Whinston, 1996). Descriptive knowledge characterizes (ie, describes) the nature of some world—be it historic, current, expected, hypothetical, or speculative (eg, a narrative or portrayal). Procedural knowledge is a step-by-step specification of how to do something (eg, an algorithm). Reasoning knowledge tells us what conclusion is acceptable when a given circumstance exists (eg, a set of rules). A processor has these three types of knowledge at its disposal for use in recognizing and solving problems, as it seeks competitive advantage or superior performance. A processor operates with them when striving to find opportunities, challenges, disturbances, threats, and other problems. It also operates with the three types of knowledge when striving to cope with what has been recognized and to solve open problems—all in the interest of greater organization (or individual) effectiveness.

CONDUCT OF KNOWLEDGE MANAGEMENT

The conduct of KM within an organization involves an integration of *knowledge* (ie, conveyed by usable representations), *processors* that operate on that knowledge, and *processes* that organize the actions of processors and availability of knowledge. As we shall see later, the parameters P1, P2, … Pn are concerned with the operations that processors perform and the processes that guide and influence them. The conduct of KM can be seen as episodic, with each episode involving some collection of processors executing some configuration of operations on available knowledge resources, triggered by the intent to satisfy a knowledge need or opportunity, subject to schematic constraints and a variety of influences. The outcome of a successful episode is that learning has occurred —by virtue of the sensed need being satisfied or opportunity being examined.

What kinds of needs can arise in an organization's quest for effectiveness? One clue to answering this comes from the analytics field, where we find the SPED taxonomy of problems (Holsapple et al., 2014): sense-making problems, prediction problems, evaluation problems, and decisional problems. Solving any of these kinds of problems is a knowledge-intensive effort, suggesting a SPED taxonomy for recognizing and solving problems in knowledge management episodes: sense-making episodes, prediction episodes, evaluation episodes, and decisional episodes.

Now, when it comes to using KM to implement an organization's competitive strategy, what can an organization do in its conduct of knowledge management to gain an edge relative to its competitors? Based on the foregoing discussion, several possibilities emerge:

- Build and maintain a superior knowledge base available to its processors—superior in the sense of relevance, importance, volume, variety, currency, organization, accuracy, and security.

- Develop a superior processor base—superior in the sense of a suitable mix of human and machine processors that can squeeze high value out of available knowledge resources.
- Devise superior processes—superior in the sense of excelling in deployment and coordination of knowledge processors, in making knowledge resources available, and in learning from experiences.
- Integrate the utilization of a knowledge base, processors, and processes for superiority in episodes of:
  - Sense making
  - Predicting
  - Evaluating
  - Decision making

Each checkmark suggests a KM aspect that may be worthy to audit, searching for deficiencies or underperformance relative to competitors. Each also suggests a focal point for experimentation with creative ways that may result in greater success for the organization.

As for the SPED episodes, each involves a KM process that applies some mix of descriptive-procedural-reasoning knowledge and some assortment of knowledge processors to deal with the problem of making sense of a situation, making a prediction for a situation, making an evaluation of a situation, or making a decision about addressing a situation. In the interest of organization effectiveness, we should strive for episodic effectiveness—both within individual episodes and across the interplay among an organization's knowledge-managing episodes. Episodic effectiveness can be examined from two angles: outcome and process. In the effective conduct of KM, efforts are mustered to succeed in producing superior outcomes via superior processes.

SUPERIORITY AND THE PAIR MODEL

Knowledge-chain theory holds that KM can be practiced in ways that contribute to competitiveness; further, it advances the PAIR model of competitiveness, which identifies four directions in which KM can contribute: productivity, agility, innovation, and reputation (Holsapple and Singh, 2001). In pondering "superiority" of KM outcomes or processes, the PAIR model is suggestive of four dimensions to consider:

- productivity, which refers to a ratio of acceptable output to expended input
- agility, which refers to a combination of alertness with response ability
- innovation, which refers to invention and adoption
- reputation, which refers to perceived degree of dependability, integrity, and quality

Each of these is a potential avenue toward competitiveness. That is, in its quest for success, an organization can build its competitive strategy around one or more of these four dimensions and attune its knowledge management conduct toward implementing that strategy. As an example, an organization's competitive strategy may be to have superior agility relative to its competitors—expanding its customer base by

Table 1.1 A PAIR Examination of KM Process and Outcome

	Productivity	Agility	Innovation	Reputation
KM process	Productivity of a process that makes sense, predictions, evaluations, or decisions about a situation	Agility of a process that makes sense, predictions, evaluations, or decisions about a situation	Innovativeness of a process that makes sense, predictions, evaluations, or decisions about a situation	Reputability of a process that makes sense, predictions, evaluations, or decisions about a situation
KM outcome	Knowledge that aids an organization's productivity	Knowledge that aids an organization's agility	Knowledge that aids an organization's innovativeness	Knowledge that aids an organization's reputation

cultivating a high alertness to emerging customer needs and preferences while also developing and executing fast responses.

Both process and outcome of a KM episode (or KM initiative involving multiple episodes) can be examined in terms of the PAIR dimensions. This results in the eight cases shown in Table 1.1. The top row distinguishes between a productive process (eg, lean or efficient), an agile process (eg, rapid awareness and response for disruptions), an innovative process (eg, deviates into new approaches), and a reputable process (eg, adheres to high standards of rigor, integrity, dependability, and quality). KM process-superiority along any one (or several) of the PAIR dimensions can be regarded as a kind of KM success and, all else being equal, translates into a higher competitive standing for the organization.

The bottom row in Table 1.1 is concerned with the effects of a KM process on the state of an organization's knowledge. It distinguishes between knowledge that allows or fosters higher productivity for the organization (eg, less waste, higher production rate, less cost per unit, greater efficiency), higher agility for the organization (eg, better able to cope with disturbances, recognizing them early and responding to them rapidly), higher innovativeness for the organization (eg, better able to develop and apply new ideas), and higher reputation for the organization (eg, boost perceptions of organization as being trustworthy, ethical, and a provider of quality goods and services). Superiority of KM outcomes along any one (or several) of the PAIR dimensions can be regarded as a kind of KM success and, all else being equal, translates into a higher competitive standing for the organization.

PARAMETERS

If a knowledge management process, within or across episodes, can be an important aspect of organization effectiveness, then it behooves us to understand the kinds of components that can serve as building blocks for constructing that process. Generally, a *process is a systematic arrangement of activities* for making something.

In the KM case, we are making knowledge that satisfies a need for a sensible account of a situation, for a prediction about a situation, for an evaluation of a situation, or for a decision concerning a situation. What are these activities—these basic classes of components—that can be integrated into a KM process? This is an important question because its answer reveals parameters that can be set, instantiated, tailored, or adjusted in search of KM success for a given resource bundle (FR), a set of definitional principles (DP), and the environing conditions (EC).

The answer we examine here borrows from the knowledge chain theory, which identifies nine classes of KM activity (Holsapple and Singh, 2001). We contend that each serves as a parameter (P1–P9) in the organization effectiveness equation. Five of them are first-order activities, meaning that each operates directly on a knowledge resource, manipulating it in a fashion that is functionally distinct from the other four knowledge chain activities. The five are:

- P1—*Knowledge acquisition*: an activity in which a processor(s) identifies knowledge in the organization's environment, captures it, and makes it available in a suitable representation for transference to other KM activities. The knowledge source may require some compensation or commitment from the processor as a condition for identification and/or capture.
- P2—*Knowledge assimilation*: an activity in which a processor(s) alters an organization's knowledge resources, resulting in learning. The alteration may be additive, eliminative, revisionary, or a restructuring of how the resources are organized. The processor filters, screens, and cleans the knowledge being assimilated. Assimilation includes targeting which knowledge resources are to be altered (eg, those of a community of processors vs a central repository), structuring knowledge into representations appropriate for the targets, and transferring these representations to their targets.
- P3—*Knowledge selection*: an activity in which a processor(s) identifies knowledge within an organization's existing base of knowledge resources, captures it, and transfers it in a suitable representation to a KM activity that needs it. The organization may require some kind of security clearance by the processor as a condition for identification and/or capture.
- P4—*Knowledge generation*: an activity in which a processor(s) derives or discovers knowledge in the context of existing knowledge resources and transfers this generated knowledge in an appropriate representation to an appropriate activity. The generation results are problem definitions or problem solutions—with the problems belonging to the classes of sense making, prediction making, evaluation making, and decision making. The processor relies on available selection and/or acquisition activities to furnish the knowledge it needs. Procedural and/or reasoning knowledge is especially important in guiding or driving the generation activity. The processor also relies on its own innate skills for creating, synthesizing, analyzing, assembling, and organizing.
- P5—*Knowledge emission*: an activity in which a processor(s) projects some portion of an organization's knowledge, through an appropriate representation,

into a targeted element(s) of its environment. The activity of emitting knowledge occurs subject to security constraints. The target may provide some compensation or make some commitment to the organization as a condition for emitting knowledge.

When considering how to make an organization more effective, the foregoing parameters suggest five levers that are in play. For any specific organization, there is considerable flexibility in the treatment of the five activities. For instance, which processors are involved in which activities, when, and in what episodes? What processor roles are machine-based, which are human-based, and which are hybrid processors? What protocols regulate the flows of knowledge and behaviors of processors assigned to implement one of the activities? Answers to such questions amount to settings or instantiations for parameters P1–P5. Some will lead to greater success for a KM initiative than others.

We do not advocate a particular setting for any of the five parameters, as the settings are situation-specific. For a given set of resources (knowledge, human processors, machine processors, financials); a given environment; and a set of defining vision, mission, and values; a "good" instantiation of an activity may be "poor" under different circumstances. Here, the emphasis is on drawing attention to, and systematically characterizing, the activities that must play out in knowledge work. Their instantiations may be left to serendipity or they may be intentional, studied, and adjusted over time—with an objective of learning those that are more likely to lead to high levels of organization performance and competitiveness.

In addition to the five foregoing parameters, there are four second-order activities. Primarily, these function as managerial influences on the conduct of knowledge management within and across KM episodes. They are concerned with shaping KM processes and securing efforts from processors engaged in the knowledge work. They are more managerial activities than those of the first order, which are more focused on manipulating knowledge in various ways. The second-order parameters are:

- P6—*Knowledge measurement*: an activity wherein a processor(s) gauges the state of knowledge management within an organization. Specifically, it takes measurements (quantitative and qualitative) of the organization's
  - knowledge resources
  - knowledge processors
  - first-order activities
  - second-order activities
  - knowledge management episodes
  - overall conduct of knowledge management

  These measurements form a scorecard, indicating where an organization is and has been with respect to knowledge management.
- P7—*Knowledge control*: an activity wherein a processor(s) strives to ensure that needed knowledge resources and processors are available in sufficient quality and quantity for executing other KM activities, subject to security requirements

being satisfied. Because an organization's resources are not unlimited, it may not be possible to have all processors and all knowledge that could conceivably be needed, in which case, the control activity strives to maintain a workable mix in the volatile face of dynamic situations. Results of knowledge measurement are instrumental to the exercise of knowledge control and, in turn, track the effects of knowledge control activity.

- P8—*Knowledge coordination*: an activity wherein a processor(s) manages dependencies among the nine KM activities, the knowledge resources, the knowledge processors, KM processes, and KM episodes. Whereas the knowledge control activity strives to ensure proper availability (realizing there can be some shortages or deficiencies due to resource constraints), the coordination activity is concerned with the connections among what actually are available. It can be regarded as dealing with mappings such as the assignment of specific processors to specific instances of KM activities, of a sequence of these activities to an episode, of particular knowledge and an arrangement of episodes to a process, and so forth. It can also be regarded as establishing current infrastructure (ie, defining the roles that processors play, the authority and communication relationships among those roles, and the regulations that govern processor behaviors).

- P9—*Knowledge leadership*: an activity wherein a processor(s) strives to create circumstances that allow or encourage other knowledge processors to be highly effective in accomplishing the organization's knowledge work. Just as knowledge coordination is concerned with the infrastructure for knowledge work, knowledge leadership is concerned with the culture for knowledge work. Aligned with an organization's vision, mission, and values, the processor(s) engaged in knowledge leadership develops a culture conducive to extracting maximum efforts from the organization's knowledge processors. The processors become imbued with an attitude that knowledge work is vital to the organization's success. To facilitate this, the knowledge-leadership activity can create experiences for KM processors that lead to a joint conviction that there are superior ways to handle knowledge management and that all processors need to participate in discovering or creating them.

As with the first five parameters, there is considerable flexibility in treatment of the four additional parameters. For example, one instantiation of the knowledge coordination parameter may involve a market mechanism for making processor assignments, whereas an alternative may rely on applied heuristics, and yet another on prioritized resource allocation. Or, for the knowledge control parameter, the preferred instantiation may differ, depending on whether the processor is human or computer-based. Or, for the knowledge measurement parameter, criteria for assessing processor performance can vary. How the second-order activities are instantiated in an organization will contribute to establishing the "way" in which it performs KM. This "way," in turn, affects the degree of success for KM initiatives.

Because settings for second-order parameters are likely specific to the "givens" of the situation faced by a firm (recall the equation for E), we do not advocate a particular setting for any of them. For a given set of resources (knowledge, human processors, machine processors, financials), a given environment, and a set of defining vision, mission, and values, an instantiation of a second-order activity that is "good" for one organization may be "poor" for another. As with the first-order parameters, our emphasis is on drawing attention to, and systematically characterizing, second-order activities that must play out in knowledge work. Their instantiations may be left to serendipity or they may be intentional, studied, and adjusted over time—with an objective of learning those that are more likely to lead to superior levels of organization performance and competitiveness.

CONCLUSIONS

Summarizing, there is evidence from many anecdotes and scholarly studies that knowledge management can be performed in ways that predict superior organization competitiveness or performance. What are those ways? One might be to assemble a superior set of computer-based and human knowledge processors. Another might be to assemble a superior base of knowledge resources. Here, we investigate another possibility: perform knowledge management activities in a superior way. A starting point is to identify the classes of KM activities that are operative regardless of the organization, its array of processors, its resource portfolio, or its environment. Here, we describe a collection of nine generic activities, each one of which can be instantiated in multiple ways. Thus, each of the nine serve as a parameter for a conditioned function that indicates the degree of organization effectiveness.

The parameters provide a mental framework for thinking about the relationship between success and the conduct of knowledge management. The nine parameters form a checklist for auditing how KM is being done in an organization, for systematically formulating new KM initiatives, for studying how to improve an organization's practice of KM, and for avoiding blind spots in a search for avenues to KM success. By calling attention to the nine parameters, we seek to stimulate and provoke research into enumerations of feasible instantiations for each, effects of such instantiations on KM success, and prudence of instantiation alternatives in varying conditions.

Ultimately, this may lead to a "playbook" that recommends what instantiations are well suited for the conditions in which an organization finds itself.

REFERENCES

Chen, L., Ellis, S., Holsapple, C., 2015. Supplier development: a knowledge management perspective. Knowl. Process Manage. 22 (4), 250–269.

DeFond, M.L., Konchitchki, Y., McMullin, J.L., O'Leary, D.E., 2010. Does superior knowledge management increase shareholder value? American Accounting Association Annual Meeting, San Francisco, August 2010.

Holsapple, C.W., Joshi, K.D., 2004. A formal knowledge management ontology: conduct, activities, resources, and influences. J. Am. Soc. Inform. Sci. Technol. 55 (7), 593–612.

Holsapple, C., Lee-Post, A., Pakath, R., 2014. A unified foundation for business analytics. Decis. Support Syst. 64, 130–141.

Holsapple, C.W., Singh, M., 2000. The knowledge chain. In: Proceedings of the Annual Conference of the Southern Association on Information Systems. Atlanta, Georgia, March 2000.

Holsapple, C.W., Singh, M., 2001. The knowledge chain model: activities for competitiveness. Expert Syst. Appl. 20 (1), 77–98.

Holsapple, C.W., Whinston, A., 1996. Decision Support Systems: A Knowledge-Based Approach. West Group, St. Paul, MN.

Holsapple, C.W., Wu, J., 2008a. In search of a missing link. Knowl. Manage. Res. Pract. 6 (1), 31–40.

Holsapple, C.W., Wu, J. 2008b. Does knowledge management pay off? In: Proceedings of the Hawaii International Conference on System Sciences, January 2008, Waikkoloa, HI.

Holsapple, C.W., Wu, J., 2011. An elusive antecedent of superior firm performance: the knowledge management factor. Decis. Support Syst. 52 (1), 271–283.

Leonard-Barton, D., 1998. Wellsprings of Knowledge: Building and Sustaining the Sources of Innovation. Harvard Business Press, Boston.

Newell, A., 1982. The knowledge level. Artif. Intell. 18 (1), 87–127.

O'Dell, C., Hasanali, F., Hubert, C., Lopez, K., Odem, P., Raybourne, C., 2003. Successful KM implementations: a study of best-practice organizations. Handbook on Knowledge Management, vol. 2. Springer, Berlin, Heidelberg, pp. 253–287.

O'Leary, D.E., 2008. Evolution of knowledge management towards enterprise decision support: the case of KPMG. Handbook on Decision Support Systems, vol. 2. Springer, Berlin, Heidelberg, pp. 581–608.

Oriel, S.L., 2003. From inventions management to intellectual capital management at the Dow Chemical Company: a 100+ year journey. Handbook on Knowledge Management, vol. 2. Springer, Berlin, Heidelberg, pp. 489–500.

Rubenstein-Montano, B., Buchwalter, J., Liebowitz, J., 2001. Knowledge management: a US social security administration case study. Gov. Inform. Q. 18 (3), 223–253.

Smith, H.A., McKeen, J.D., 2003. Knowledge management in organizations: the state of current practice. Handbook on Knowledge Management, vol. 2. Springer, Berlin, Heidelberg, pp. 395–410.

Sveiby, K.E., 1997. The New Organizational Wealth: Managing & Measuring Knowledge-Based Assets. Berrett-Koehler Publishers, San Francisco.

Wolford, D., Kwiecien, S., 2003. Driving knowledge management at Ford Motor Company. Handbook on Knowledge Management, vol. 2. Springer, Berlin, Heidelberg, pp. 501–510.

Wu, J., Holsapple, C.W., 2013. Does knowledge management matter? The empirical evidence from market-based valuation. ACM Trans. Manage. Inform. Syst. 4 (2), 1–23.

Zack, M., McKeen, J., Singh, S., 2009. Knowledge management and organizational performance: an exploratory analysis. J. Knowl. Manage. 13 (6), 392–409.

Why are companies still struggling to implement knowledge management? Answers from 34 experts in the field

V. Ribière*, F.A. Calabrese**

*The Institute for Knowledge and Innovation—Southeast Asia (IKI-SEA), Bangkok University, Bangkok, Thailand; **The International Institute for Knowledge and Innovation (I²KI) IKI-SEA—Bangkok University, Bangkok, Thailand

INTRODUCTION
THE STATE OF KNOWLEDGE MANAGEMENT

Knowledge management has now been around for more than 20 years. The book *Managing Knowhow* by Karl Erik Sveiby (1987), followed by the article "Brainpower" by Thomas A. Stewart (1991) in *Fortune* magazine, can be considered the first sparks of KM. A series of three books by Karl Wiig followed in 1993, titled Knowledge Management Foundations: Thinking about Thinking - How People and Organizations Represent, Create and Use Knowledge" (Wiig, 1993). These were followed in turn by the classic books of Nonaka and Takeuchi (1995), Davenport and Prusak (1998), and the first *Knowledge Management Handbook* by Liebowitz (1999). During the period between 1995 and 2000, organizations started seeking knowledge management practices, and the academic literature gained notable momentum. Prusak (2001), explaining the origins of KM, stated "knowledge management is not just a consultants' invention but a practitioner-based, substantive response to real social and economic trends including globalization (complexity), ubiquitous computing, and the knowledge-centric view of the firm." The academic interest in KM evolved rapidly at the outset of the 21st century and shows a steady decline over the past 10 years, as depicted by the number of Google searches containing the keywords "knowledge management" (Fig. 2.1). Looking at the trend evolution by region (not displayed in this chapter but available in Google trends), we can also see a shift of interest from the Western to the Eastern worlds, with a large amount of activity in India, South Africa, and Asia.

Practitioners' surveys have also shown a corollary decline of interest in KM. The biannual Bain & Co Management Tools and Trends surveys did not mention knowledge

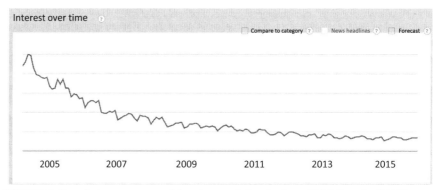

FIGURE 2.1 Knowledge management Google search trends since 2004 (Google, 2015)

management in the 2013 and 2015 editions (Rigby and Bilodeau, 2013, 2015). Looking back at the evolution of KM usage and satisfaction between the years 1996 and 2010 (Fig. 2.2), we can see that the usage trend over the 14 years averages 42%, and the satisfaction is 3.61 out of 5, with a general increase over the last several years. This does not indicate that "KM is dead," as some have posited, but it does show that organizations no longer perceive KM as one of the top priorities.

Interestingly, if we consider the KM academic literature from 1994 to 2014 by focusing on the number of scholarly and peer-reviewed publications containing the keywords "knowledge management," we see a continuous increase of publications, (Fig. 2.3) indicating many researchers are still actively seeking to better understand

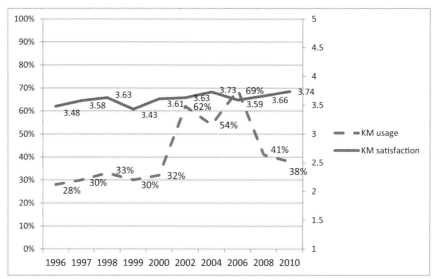

FIGURE 2.2 Knowledge management trends based on Bain & Company Management Tools & Trends Surveys (1996–2011) (Rigby and Bilodeau, 2009, 2011)

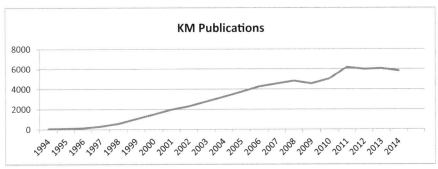

KM Publications

FIGURE 2.3 Number of academic publications with the keywords "knowledge management"

the remaining KM issues. Furthermore, KM conferences still attract appreciable numbers of practitioners and academics each year.

Even after 20 years of its "birth," KM is still not a mainstream process for organizations. Why are organizations still struggling to implement knowledge management, despite the huge amount of literature and conferences on the topic and despite numerous successful case studies and lessons learned? That is the question we asked 34 experts in the field, and we share our findings with you in this chapter.

ORIGINAL SOURCE MATERIAL KNOWLEDGE BASE

The source data foundation for this chapter represents a unique collection of opinions by 34 active academics, researchers, and practitioners in the world of knowledge management. Many have been teaching, writing, and practicing KM for more than 20 years. In total, 3% (1) are strictly KM academics; 18% (6) are KM practitioners; and the majority, 79% (27), act as both academics and practitioners. Most of them will have immediate name recognition for international KM organizations. However, to facilitate the merits of their stated opinions, they are listed (Table 2.1) by title, name, organization, and native or current country of domicile, which usually reflects where they have spent/are spending their careers. They represent 12 countries from all the 5 continents.

The capture media for their remarks is a series of video recordings named IKI-Talks (http://ikitalks.iki-sea.org), recorded by the Institute for Knowledge and Innovation – South East Asia (IKI-SEA), Bangkok University, Bangkok, Thailand. The participants constitute an International Visiting Faculty for IKI-SEA's Research PhD Program in Knowledge and Innovation Management, now in its fifth year. The recordings were created during the period 2012–2014 as original responses to a six-question interview series and have never been published.

The material for the present chapter focuses on question 6, which seems most appropriate for this book chapter since it asked the KM experts:

"Why do you think companies are still struggling to implement knowledge management and innovation management?"

Table 2.1 Names of the 34 KM Experts Interviewed

Title	First Name	Last Name	Organization	Country
Ms	Mary	Adams	Smarter-Companies	USA
Dr	Debra	Amidon	Entovation	USA
Dr	Vittal	Anantatmula	Western Carolina University	USA
Dr	Kate	Andrews	Knowable	Australia
Dr	Aurilla Aurelie	Arntzen	University College of Southeast Norway	Norway
Mr	Steve	Barth	Hitachi	USA
Dr	Denise	Bedford	Georgetown University	USA
Dr	Alex	Bennet	Mountain Quest Institute	USA
Dr	Francesco	Calabrese	International Institute for Knowledge and Innovation	USA
Dr	Valerie	Chanal	University of Grenoble	France
Dr	Nancy	Dixon	Common Knowledge Associates	USA
Dr	Rivadávia	Drummond de Alvarenga Neto	HSM Educação Executiva	Brazil
Dr	Jean-Louis	Ermine	The Knowledge Improvement Project and Telecom Business School	France
Dr	Rudy	Garrity	American Learnership Forum	USA
Dr	John	Girard	Middle Georgia State University	USA
Dr	Annie	Green	Seed First, LLC and GWU	USA
Dr	Michel	Grundstein	Grundstein Consulting	France
Dr	William	Halal	George Washington University	USA
Dr	Peter	Heisig	University of Applied Sciences Potsdam	Germany
Dr	Thierry	Isckia	Telecom Business School	France
Dr	Johann	Kinghorn	Stellenbosch University—Centre for Knowledge Dynamics and Decision making	South Africa
Mr	Patrick	Lambe	Straits Knowledge	Singapore
Dr	Eunika	Laurent Mercier	Institute FR Bull, EPITA, Innovation3D	France
Dr	Steve	Newman	ARES Corporation and GWU	USA
Mr	Geoff	Parcel	Practical KM	UK
Dr	Vincent	Ribiere	Institute for Knowledge and Innovation Southeast Asia— Bangkok University	Thailand
Ms	Waltraut	Ritter	Knowledge Dialogues	Hong-Kong
Dr	Arthur	Shelly	Organizational Zoo	Australia
Dr	Manasi	Shukla	Institute for Knowledge and Innovation Southeast Asia— Bangkok University	India
Dr	David	Snowden	Cognitive Edge	UK

Table 2.1 Names of the 34 KM Experts Interviewed (*cont.*)

Title	First Name	Last Name	Organization	Country
Dr	Michael	Stankosky	George Washington University	USA
Mr	Ron	Young	Knowledge Associates Cambridge Ltd	UK
Mr	Tom	Young	Knoco	UK
Dr	Suzanne	Zyngier	University of Melbourne Business School	Australia

The recordings have been transcribed at different times by various IKI-SEA staff over this period, and some of the most recent transcriptions have focused solely on question 6 to support this chapter.

RESEARCH METHOD

The coauthors of this chapter have undertaken oversight activity to ensure the translation and consistency of interpretative license by listening to all of the interviews and verifying the merits of the verbatim transcripts. Each coauthor has then independently selected and documented his interpretation of content intention by each interviewee response and extracted key phrases. The individual interpretations of each coauthor were compared and discussed to generate a final document that lists findings grouped by themes.

In parallel, the transcripts were analyzed by a text mining tool (QDA Miner—WordStat 7) to extract keywords and their cluster. The result of the text mining tool was used as an additional validation mechanism.

The results of this winnowing research analysis method and software tool manipulation were used to suggest emergent themes of opinions leading to the recommended results of the "expert" cadre. The themes are presented in the next section of this chapter, followed by some researched and summarized current literature opinions all compared to the cadre's base reference materials used by the coauthors to project the future status of acceptance and incorporation for KM integral to the inner workings of organizations.

KEY FINDINGS
DATA ANALYSIS

As previously explained, the researchers extracted from the 34 interviews 111 key reasons why the knowledge experts believed that organizations are still struggling with knowledge management. The 111 key reasons were grouped into 7 main categories:

- culture
- measurement/benefits

- strategy
- organizational structure
- governance and leadership
- IT-related issues
- lack of KM understanding/standards

The subsequent tables are extracts from interviews that support each theme.

Culture (13)	Measurement/Benefits (16)
Cultural issues	Difficult to measure KM
Culture incompatibility	KM benefits take time to appear (companies are not patient enough)
Don't consider workers as knowledge workers	KM is not a quick fix
Hard to create a knowledge sharing/creating environment	KM must show value and ROI
Hard to motivate people to share knowledge	KM takes time
Human collaboration and knowledge transfer only work well on small scales	Knowledge needs to build over time
Knowledge cannot be demanded of employees	Lack of maturity
Knowledge should be embedded in the business itself and the mind and thinking of employees	Lack of usefulness
Lack of appreciation for KM	No time to contemplate and reflect (Eastern philosophy)
Lack of trust	Organizations are short-term focused
Need for cultural change	Organizations are too much after direct, quick, tangible results (Western philosophy)
	ROI not immediately visible
Need for four enabling conditions—social behavior issues, cognitive issues, structure issues and information, and communication issues	
Turf protection	Short-term focus versus long-term focus
	There should not be a need to justify KM
	Trying to measure success of KM through KM metrics (should be org metrics)

Strategy (13)	Organizational Structure (18)
KM is only perceived as a nice thing to have	People and companies still rely and operate on the old industrial age model
KM and innovation will help companies compete and not perish	Business plans are obsolete
Organizations don't have a clear understanding of why they implement KM	Change is needed
KM is not for every organization; it should not be forced on them	Complacency

Strategy (13)	Organizational Structure (18)
KM is not addressed at the strategic level	Current approaches to KM forces people in the wrong models and modes
KM not fully aligned with business strategy	Should move from benchmarking to benchlearning
KM is not perceived as a priority (not critical, only nice to have)	KM execution is weak
KM was fashionable	KM has to be nurtured to grow and contribute to the organization
Lack of strong rationale to implement KM	Management still focuses on control rather than cultivate, accelerate, support, and facilitate
Organizations have not used an organizational learning approach (where time is needed and accepted)	Managers look for status quo more than for change
To do KM requires improved learning and not every organization is a learning organization	Need for enabling contexts "Ba"
KM cannot be add-ons to an organization, it must quickly become an integral part of the organization	Need for new ways to manage
	Organization must adapt to KM needs
	People are not educated/prepared for the world as it exists today
	Resistance from traditional organizations and structures
	Still bureaucratic management structures

Governance and Leadership (12)	IT-Related Issues (14)
KM is at risk since it's often sponsored/driven by one hypermotivated person	Document-centered approach doesn't work for KM
KM is assigned to a unique KM department that has to make it happen	KM focuses on technology rather than on people
Focusing on external/consultant help and support rather than growing it from within	Initial disappointment of IT tools' capabilities
Heavy reliance on consultants	KM focus should be on human/social aspect and not on technology
KM has to make friends and partner with other support activities	Lack of integration between available people and technologies
KM is currently not part of management role	Lack of integration between management and IT approaches
KM needs more awareness and endorsement at the strategic level	Need to change KM paradigm from technological approach to managerial and sociotechnical approach
KM requires governance, encouragement, measurements	Oversimplistic IT understanding of knowledge
KM should not be a particular department or position	Overselling of IT systems
Lack of leadership commitment	Too much original focus on IT

Governance and Leadership (12)	IT-Related Issues (14)
Need for inside KM advocates and supporters Too often KM reports under CxOs, and doesn't have its own CKO	Too much emphasis on mechanisms to enable knowledge sharing KM should focus on people not technology (still misconceptions) Difficult for humans to manage knowledge transfer on a large scale (using IT)

Lack of KM Understanding/Standards (25)
"Managing knowledge" is easier to understand than "knowledge management"—wording matters Academics have not agreed on a definition, it creates confusion and rejection Ambiguity in KM terms and definitions Confusion between information and knowledge Confusion/lack of agreement about what KM is in a commonly accepted framework Organizations declared victory on KM too early KM concept not always clear to companies KM has to be more precise and more proven KM is presented as something too complicated Lack of common KM definition Lack of executive understanding of what intangibles are and how to manage them Lack of understanding of what KM really is Lack of understanding on how to implement KM No need to call it KM No unified validated process for KM Organizations do not understand the nature of knowledge in KM Organizations don't get KM Organizations fail to understand that knowledge management is about augmentation of human intelligence Organizations think KM is easy to do Oversimplification of complexity by simple models Should start and focus on organizations' problems Solutions to sharing knowledge are simpler than people expect Some companies jumped too fast into KM without knowing what it was Superficial understanding of KM complexity Too much time/focus on trying to define KM

TEXT MINING ANALYSIS

The 34 transcripts were analyzed with a text mining tool (QDA Miner—WordStat 7). The 34 transcripts were composed of 254 sentences and 6411 words. Combined, they represent 1 h of audio recordings. The output of the system is a list of keywords ranked by frequency of occurrences. The system was set to only display keywords that occurred eight or more times in the transcripts. Table 2.2 presents 22 keywords that were extracted.

Table 2.2 Automatically Extracted 22 Keywords From 34 Transcripts

Keywords	Frequency	% Shown	% Processed	% Total	No. Cases	% Cases	TF • IDF
KM	102	20.00	5.60	1.59	25	75.76	12.3
Organization	87	17.06	4.78	1.36	21	63.64	17.1
Knowledge	51	10.00	2.80	0.80	21	63.64	10
People	39	7.65	2.14	0.61	22	66.67	6.9
Management	27	5.29	1.48	0.42	12	36.36	11.9
Work	21	4.12	1.15	0.33	8	24.24	12.9
System	17	3.33	0.93	0.27	8	24.24	10.5
Time	17	3.33	0.93	0.27	10	30.30	8.8
Understand	17	3.33	0.93	0.27	11	33.33	8.1
Technology	15	2.94	0.82	0.23	7	21.21	10.1
Information	14	2.75	0.77	0.22	8	24.24	8.6
Human	12	2.35	0.66	0.19	6	18.18	8.9
Business	10	1.96	0.55	0.16	6	18.18	7.4
Change	10	1.96	0.55	0.16	9	27.27	5.6
Implement	10	1.96	0.55	0.16	7	21.21	6.7
Return	10	1.96	0.55	0.16	3	9.09	10.4
Share	10	1.96	0.55	0.16	7	21.21	6.7
Strategic	9	1.76	0.49	0.14	5	15.15	7.4
Benefit	8	1.57	0.44	0.12	3	9.09	8.3
Learning	8	1.57	0.44	0.12	5	15.15	6.6
Support	8	1.57	0.44	0.12	5	15.15	6.6
Tool	8	1.57	0.44	0.12	5	15.15	6.6

If we map 21 keywords (not including KM) to the 7 themes previously created, we can see that they match perfectly:

1. Culture
   a. people
   b. human
   c. change
   d. share
2. Measurement/benefits
   a. time
   b. return
   c. benefit
3. Strategy
   a. business
   b. strategic
   c. learning (organizational)
4. Organizational structure
   a. organization
   b. work
   c. implement
   d. support
5. Governance and leadership
   a. management
6. IT-related issues
   a. system
   b. technology
   c. information
   d. tools
7. Lack of KM understanding/standards
   a. knowledge (versus information)
   b. understand

The software tool also allowed a clustering analysis to suggest how the keywords link and are related to each other as presented in Fig. 2.4.

The cluster shows when keywords are used together. For example, if we look at the top cluster, *change* and *time* are linked since respondents often mentioned that the changes required for KM do take time. *KM* is implemented at the *organizational* level, and *knowledge* is in *people*. *Management* can manage *people* (and their *knowledge*) to implement *KM* in the *organization* as a *system*, but it requires *time* and *change*, and this is a not a very well *understood* process.

In the middle cluster, we can find the main issues linking back to the main pillars of KM, *human* (people), *technology* and *information,* and *work* (processes). The lower cluster refers more to issues related to the *implementation* of support and *tools* for knowledge *sharing.*

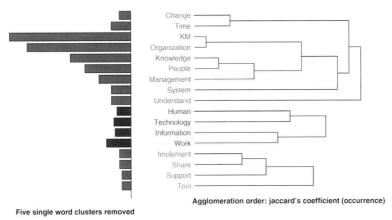

Five single word clusters removed

FIGURE 2.4 Cluster of main keywords

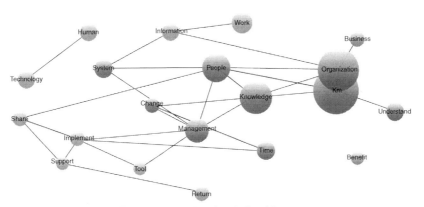

FIGURE 2.5 Mapping of main keywords and their relationships

Fig. 2.5 is another visual representation that displays the 22 keywords and their relationships. The size of the circle is proportional to the keyword frequency, and the thickness of the line that links the keywords represents how strongly these concepts are related.

DATA INTERPRETATION

What can we learn from all these findings? We have noted that the combinations of data/information displayed by Table 2.2, Fig. 2.4, and the blue–red–green "mega clusters" in Fig. 2.5 offer opportunities for multiple inquisitive discussions but have chosen to proceed on a direct path to our themes structure. So let's first interpret and summarize the findings for each of the seven main themes that emerged from our study:

Culture

The people aspect of KM has been, and will always remain, the difficult part of KM. If we agree that knowledge is only available in the minds of people, then managing knowledge indirectly means managing people. Culture can be defined as:

> "A pattern of shared basic assumptions that the group learned as it solved its problems of external adaptation and internal integration, that had worked well enough to be considered valid, and therefore, to be taught to new members as the correct way to perceive, think and feel in relation to those problems."
> (Schein, 1992, 1999)

Some organizational cultures are more or less friendly to knowledge-sharing behaviors. Our respondents mentioned possible *incompatibilities*[a] between KM expected behaviors and the organizational culture. We believe that by nature, and in general, people have no problem sharing knowledge, but other cultural issues often become a barrier, like lack of interpersonal *trust* and *lack of appreciation for KM* (no recognition or *motivation*), and we all know that *knowledge cannot be demanded of employees. KM should be embedded in the structure of business itself and the mind and thinking of employees.* As previously mentioned in the "structure theme", it is not easy to create a *knowledge-sharing/creating environment.* Ba environments, where knowledge sharing and learning take place, work well with small groups since *human collaboration and knowledge transfer work well on small scales,* but on a larger scale things become more difficult. A need *for cultural change* is often expected, but changing a culture is a difficult and long process. Evolving the culture or slowly encouraging people to change their behavior might be a better strategy. Currently, the use of gamification approaches seems to increase the motivation of employees to share knowledge. A recent KM APQC (2015) survey reveals that more than half (54%) of the 482 companies they interviewed said that gamification will impact their programs either in 2016 or within 3 years. Leadership and management styles (Ribière and Sitar, 2003) (Calabrese 2000 and 2009) also need to adjust to consider employees as *knowledge workers.* Sensitivity to four enabling conditions—social behavior issues, cognitive issues, structure issues, and information and communication issues—is suggested in culture change.

Measurement/benefits

Measuring the value/benefits of KM! *Do we really need to justify KM?* This has been a continuous question and problem. As Deming (1993) said "If you can't measure it, you can't manage it." In fact, it looks like based on a recent article from John Hunter (2015), Deming might also have added "There are many things that cannot be measured and still must be managed. And there are many things that cannot be measured [yet] managers must still make decisions about [them]." This is the aspect that we believe a lot of organizations are missing regarding KM. Based on our respondents' opinions, it is *difficult for organizations to measure the benefits/ROI/value of KM and*

---

[a]We used italics for the terms/answers provided by the respondents during the interviews.

without them, budgets and resources are not easily dedicated or renewed for KM. In general, KM *takes time to show value* and benefits, and many organizations do not want or cannot wait for a long period to see that value. Companies are *not patient enough*, they are *looking for quick fixes*, they are *short-term focused* and look for *direct, quick, tangible results (Western philosophy). Organizations should take time to contemplate and reflect (Eastern philosophy).* Another important issue raised by the respondents is that in fact there should not be some specific metrics/knowledge process improvement to measure KM value/benefits. KM is a supporting process that helps organizations to innovate and deliver on their goals faster, better, and cheaper. *So organizational metrics* should be used, rather than specific KM metrics.

Strategy

Like the early days of information technology, *KM was not often addressed by organizations at the strategic level* but rather as a tool at the operational level. KM is too often *perceiveived as a nice thing to have/do* and *not as priority*, and as soon as budgets are reduced or other priorities emerge, KM is deferred or stopped. Some companies engaged in *KM because it was fashionable* or because their competitors did it and not because they were strongly convinced of its value, and *neither did they have a strong rationale to implement it.* So *KM sustainabilty* is at risk for organizations who *don't have a clear understanding of why they chose to implement* it. Consequently a lot of organizations embark on KM *without a clear KM strategy,* or with a *KM strategy that is not aligned with the business strategy,* even ignoring suggested models to integrate the two (Stankosky, 2005). The KM strategy and the business strategy should be coupled together. *KM cannot be an add-on to an organization, it must quickly become an integral part of the organization.* For instance, what kind of competencies will the organization need 3–5 years from now to achieve its goals? The strategic gap between what the organization knows today and what it will need to know tomorrow is directly linked to a knowledge gap that a KM strategy can help to manage (Zack, 1999). Our respondents also mentioned that *organizations have not used an organizational learning approach (where time is needed and accepted).* Organizational learning is the process of creating, retaining, and transferring knowledge within an organization, so it can learn from its experience (successes and failures). Once again, organizational learning can only happen if there is a strong push for it from the top, so strategy is key. *KM and innovation will help companies compete and not perish.*

Organizational structure

A lot of organizations still have *bureaucratic management structures* and still *use industrial age approaches to management.* But those *business plans are obsolete!* Creating a knowledge-sharing culture in such an environment is not an easy task; *change is needed,* as are *new ways to manage.* As previously described, KM strategies are often nonexistent resulting in weak *KM execution* or *forcing people into the wrong models and modes (destructive).* Organizations are by nature resistant to change and live in complacency, so KM efforts can evaporate over time. Organizations also have a tendency to benchmark their KM efforts and best practices. Unfortunately, what works for KM in one organization might not work well in others; the culture and context are always different. Organizations should *move from benchmarking to benchlearning.*

Governance and leadership

KM governance is often an underestimated success component of KM, but the sustainability of KM relies on it heavily. *KM requires governance, encouragement, and measurement* (previously discussed). Here is a definition of KM governance from Zyngier and Burstein (2012):

> *"KM governance confirms, through development of KM policies, the alignment of KM with the value proposition and strategy of the organization. KM governance assumes setting up explicit and transparent access conditions to organizational knowledge: quality and maintenance procedures; decision-making processes; and means for resolving KM obstacles. KM governance holds authority and is the mechanism that delegates authority and consequential responsibility. Hence KM governance is also concerned with authority and its delegation."*
> *(Zyngier and Burstein, 2012)*

Often the KM governance is not clear and employees don't know who is responsible for it. *KM is currently not part of the management role.* Sometimes, *KM is assigned to a unique KM department that has to make it happen. Too often KM reports under a CxO and doesn't have its own CKO. KM should not be a particular department or position,* it should be everyone's job! But in order to reach this level of embeddedness and decentralization, *KM needs more awareness and endorsement at the strategic level*; too often *organizations lack leadership commitment [to KM]. There is a need for inside KM advocates and supporters; KM has to make friends and partner with other support activities. KM is at risk since it is often sponsored/driven by one hypermotivated person. Heavy reliance on consultants (external/consultant help and support) is also a risk, rather than growing it from within.*

IT-related issues

Information technology issues are often blamed for the failure of KM, but one has to realize that IT is also what spurred KM at the start. Without advanced collaborative and supportive technologies the KM movement could have never started and grown so fast. Yes it is true that at the early stage of KM in the mid 1990s, there was *too much original focus on IT.* The *overselling of IT systems,* as knowledge management systems, seemed to be the magic solution for KM. But organizations became rapidly *disappointed by IT tools' capabilities,* and they realized that it was an *oversimplistic IT understanding of knowledge;* for us IT can only manage information, and knowledge is the human capability to take effective action (Bennet and Bennet, 2008). Whatever comes out of our brain becomes information and only then can IT help to capture, store, and share it. So *KM should focus on people/social aspects and not so much on technology (still misconceptions),* since technology is just an enabler.

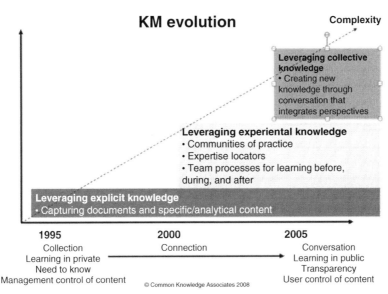

FIGURE 2.6 The three eras of knowledge management (Dixon, 2010)

Respondents recognized that there is still some *lack of integration between available people and technologies as well as a lack of integration between management and IT approaches.* So there is a need to *change the KM paradigm from a technological approach to a managerial and sociotechnical approach. A document-centered approach doesn't work for KM,* it just represents the codification approach to KM with little or no emphasis on the personalization approach (Hansen et al., 1999). This is reflected by the d*ifficulty for humans to manage knowledge transfer on a large scale (using IT).* The KM evolution graph (Fig. 2.6) from Nancy Dixon (Dixon, 2010) helps to better understand the evolution of KM and, indirectly, the evolution of IT tools to support it.

Fortunately, for the past 5–10 years new generations of IT tools—social networks—started to facilitate the integration of codification and personalization approaches, and they became a user-friendly and fun way to seamlessly share "knowledge." Enterprises 2.0 platforms are slowly entering the enterprise world and should facilitate knowledge sharing, particularly when they are associated with gamification approaches that will "reward" and "encourage" employees to share and reuse knowledge.

Lack of KM understanding/standards

The last emerging theme is the one that was the most mentioned by the KM experts interviewed as a key reason because of which organizations still struggle to implement KM. It is related to *the lack of understanding of what KM really is* or is not. After 25 years of practice and research in this field, one might think that the concept of KM should be clear for everyone—not so! *Academics have not agreed on a definition,* consequently *it creates confusion and rejection. Organizations don't understand KM and the nature of knowledge; the KM concept is not always clear to companies; KM has to be more precise and more proven; KM is presented as something too complicated!* Consequently there is a *lack of understanding on how to implement KM since there is no unified, validated process for KM, nor is there a commonly accepted framework.* In contrast, one of the interviewed experts said that *too much time [has been] spent on trying to define KM.* From a practitioner point of view, trying to agree on a unified definition of knowledge and KM seems fruitless. Debates about the definition of knowledge started in the time of Greek philosophers. One has to accept that there are different points of view and that we should pick the definition that best reflects our needs and context. At the core of it, *organizations fail to understand that knowledge management is about augmentation of human intelligence.*

Our respondents suggested one of the reasons why everyone is still struggling with KM was the *oversimplification of KM complexity by simple models and a superficial understanding of KM's complexity.* In addition, *organizations thought KM was easy to do and some companies jumped too fast into KM without knowing what is was,* and some *declared victory on KM too early! There is also a lack of executive understanding of what intangibles are and how to manage them.*

A way to overcome these problems could be to identify the KM process as *"managing knowledge,"* which is easier to understand than *"knowledge management"*— *wording matters! Organizations should start by focusing on an organization's problems* and seeking how related KM activities could help solve them. *Solutions to sharing knowledge are simpler than people expect.*

COMPARATIVE ANALYSIS WITH PREVIOUS STUDIES

Without conducting an exhaustive review of the literature, we will now compare our findings from the recent literature on KM successes and KM failures. Based on her literature review, Weber (2007) identified 15 main reasons (Table 2.3) why KM systems fail.

After analyzing 10 case studies of failure in knowledge management (KM) systems and projects, Akhavan and Pezeshkan (2014) identified 26 main critical failure factors (Table 2.3).

Based on five KM failure case studies, Chua and Lam (2005) identified 19 main failure factors that they grouped in four distinct categories of KM failure factors: technology; culture; content; and project management (Table 2.3).

Based on the mapping (Table 2.3) of the three selected researches to our seven main themes, we can see that the themes emerging from our study not only match other research findings but also expand their scope. A "knowledge" category is often present in KM success/failure studies, where if the knowledge is of poor quality, not well organized, or not well maintained it will affect its usage and transfer. We

Table 2.3 Comparison of Various Findings Regarding Causes of KM Failures Mapped Against Our Seven Main Themes

Our 7 Themes	Weber (2007) 15 Factors	Akhavan and Pezeshkan (2014) 26 Factors	Chua and Lam (2005) 19 Factors
Culture	• KM approaches may fail when they are designed without input from all stakeholders • KM approaches may fail when users are afraid of the consequences of their contributions • KM approaches may fail when they do not promote collaboration	• Lack of KM-oriented culture in organization • Resistance against the change in organization • Inability of KM team for distinguishing organizational relations • Lack of knowledge sharing because of knowledge speculation • Wrong perceived image of KM • Lack of sufficient involvement of workers • Lack of conflict management • Unfamiliarity of workers with KM tools • Lack of required relation among workers • Inefficient reward system	Human and organizational behavior • Politics • Knowledge sharing • Perceived image • Management commitment
Measurement/benefits	• KM approaches may fail when they are not able to show measurable benefits • KM approaches may fail because users do not perceive value in contributing	• Project cost • Not measuring and evaluating the KM project result	
Strategy	• KM approaches may fail when they do not integrate humans, processes, and technology.	• Lack of efficient strategy for development and rollout	
Organizational structure	• KM approaches may fail when they attempt to create a monolithic organizational memory. • KM approaches may fail when they are outside the process context	• Inappropriate members of KM team • Lack of detailed planning and timing for KM project • Lack of separate and sufficient budget for KM	Management of KM initiative • User involvement • Technical and business expertise • Conflict management • Rollout strategy • Project cost • Project evaluation • Involvement of external consultants

(Continued)

Table 2.3 Comparison of Various Findings Regarding Causes of KM Failures Mapped Against Our Seven Main Themes (*cont.*)

Our 7 Themes	Weber (2007) 15 Factors	Akhavan and Pezeshkan (2014) 26 Factors	Chua and Lam (2005) 19 Factors
Governance and leadership	• KM approaches may fail due to lack of leadership support • KM approaches may fail when they do not enforce managerial responsibilities	• Lack of commitment and support of top management for KM • External consultants' weakness in business knowledge and organizational relation	
IT-related issues	• KM approaches may fail when they store knowledge in unrestricted textual representations • KM approaches may fail when they rely on inadequate technology • KM approaches may fail when they ignore impediments to knowledge transfer • KM approaches may fail when they do not properly oversee the quality of stored knowledge	• Nonconformities between current systems and new systems • Improper technical infrastructure • Overreliance on technology • Weak usability of KM system • Inappropriate knowledge structure • Irrelevant knowledge with inappropriate flow and stream	KM infrastructure, tools, and technology • Connectivity • Usability • Over-reliance on KM Tools • Maintenance costCharacteristics or properties of the knowledge itself • Coverage • Structure • Relevance and currency • Knowledge distillation
Lack of KM understanding/standards	• KM approaches may fail when contributors do not know the ideal specificity of knowledge	• Lack of top managers' familiarity with aspects of KM projects • Not clarifying the KM result relation to routine tasks	

decided to group knowledge–related issues in the IT category, since as explained earlier, we believe knowledge is only in the head of employees and that everything else is information (codified knowledge).

Recently, Thomas Davenport (2015), the author of one of the first books on KM (Davenport et al., 1998; Davenport and Prusak, 1998), was interviewed by the *Wall Street Journal* on the topic: Whatever happened to knowledge management? For Davenport, the main reasons why KM has faded is because:

- It was too hard to change behavior.
- Methods to improve knowledge flow were mostly ignored.
- Everything devolved to technology.
- It was time consuming to search for and digest stored knowledge (Google has helped kill KM).
- KM never incorporated knowledge derived from data and analytics.
- The focus of knowledge-oriented projects has shifted to incorporating it into automated decision systems.
- Big data and analytics are now much more the focus.

> *"If you believe in knowledge management — and you should — perhaps in your organization you can avoid the pitfalls I have listed and allow the idea to thrive. And if you favor a different idea and want it to survive over the long term, don't hitch a complicated set of behaviors to technology alone. Don't embrace a vendor for your concept that doesn't care much about your idea. And if another notion that's related to yours comes along and gains popularity, don't shun it, embrace it."* (Davenport, 2015)

Once again the explanations provided by Davenport are perfectly aligned with our findings.

CONCLUSIONS

Based on the interviews of 34 international KM experts, we were able to identify some of the main reasons why organizations are still struggling to implement knowledge management. Seven main categories of reasons emerged from our study: culture, measurement/benefits, strategy, organizational structure, governance and leadership, IT-related issues, and lack of KM understanding/standards. Among our findings, the concept of time was revealed to be a key factor. Organizations often do not have or take the time to wait for a new KM practice to show its value. Benefits are expected to appear quickly because the focus is often on the quarterly basis and rarely on the long term. Organizations seldom take the time to reflect on their KM activities and lessons learned, and these attributes provide KM programs enough time to show their strong value.

The objective of this chapter was not to provide general solutions for problems that reflect the current issues. The intent is to provide awareness of these issues to help organizations better address them going forward. There is no single solution for the KM "issues." Every organization has different cultures, objectives, and contextual environments, but a lot of lessons learned from the past 20 years can be used to address most of these issues of embedding management of knowledge within the organizational structure. As Lambe (2011) clearly demonstrated, the KM literature has a tendency to forget about past research findings by focusing on the recent ones, and we have provided that menu.

To conclude on a positive note, KM is not dead and never will be! Knowledge will always be one of the key resources for organizations, and those that have been able to properly manage its flow and retention have received major benefits. In a recent survey of the American Productivity Quality Consortium on KM priorities for 2015, 61% of respondents said they feel positive or very positive about the future strategy and direction of their organizations' KM programs and efforts. The level of effectiveness of their current KM programs and efforts to achieve their stated goal still has room for improvement, since a little more than 1 in 3 survey participants rated their organizations' KM programs as effective or very effective (vs. somewhat effective, slightly effective, or not at all effective).

The top three 2015 priority goals for the surveyed organizations (520) were:

1. enabling sharing and collaboration within and across team units
2. promoting a knowledge-sharing culture
3. capturing content and explicit knowledge

Big data and analytics ranked first as the main technology they expected to be incorporated into or have an impact on their organization's KM tools and approaches. The Google trend analysis (Fig. 2.7) supports the trend that big data interest has surpassed KM interest since 2014. Our question is: Will there still be talk about big data in 2036, 20 years from now? If you absorb this chapter, perhaps you will assist us as part of a future trend analysis for 2036.

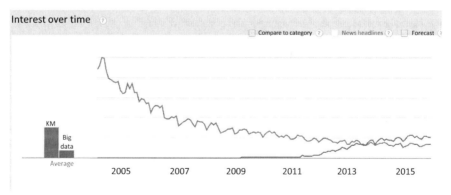

FIGURE 2.7 Knowledge management interest versus big data Google search trends since 2004 (Google, 2015)

ACKNOWLEDGMENTS

The authors deeply thank all 34 KM experts who agreed to be interviewed for the IKI Talks series and who shared their experience and wisdom with us. Feel free to watch their videos online at http://ikitalks.iki-sea.org.

REFERENCES

Akhavan, P., Pezeshkan, A., 2014. Knowledge management critical failure factors: a multi-case study. VINE 44 (1), 22–41.

APQC, 2015. 2015 Knowledge Management Priorities. APQC, Houston, TX.

Bennet, D., Bennet, A., 2008. The depth of knowledge: surface, shallow or deep? J. Inform. Knowl. Manag. 38 (7), 405–420.

Calabrese, F.A., 2000. A suggested framework of key elements defining effective enterprise knowledge management programs. Doctoral dissertation.

Calabrese, F.A., 2009. In Search of Knowledge Management Pursuing Primary Principles, xxv Table 1 Representative current additional pillar "descriptors."

Chua, A, Lam, W, 2005. Why KM projects fail: a multi-case analysis. J. Knowl. Manag. 9 (3), 6–17.

Davenport TH, 2015. Whatever happened to knowledge management? Wall St. J. Available from: http://blogs.wsj.com/cio/2015/06/24/whatever-happened-to-knowledge-management/

Davenport, T., Prusak, L., 1998. Working Knowledge. How Organizations Manage What They Know. Harvard Business School Press, Boston, MA.

Davenport, TH, De Long, DW, Beers, MC, 1998. Successful knowledge management projects. Sloan Manage. Rev. 39 (2), 43–57.

Deming, W.E., 1993. The New Economics for Industry, Government, Education. The MIT Press, Cambridge, Massachusetts, USA.

Dixon, N., 2010. The three eras of knowledge management—summary. Available from: http://www.nancydixonblog.com/2010/08/the-three-eras-of-knowledge-management-summary.html.

Google, 2015. Google trends. Available from: https://www.google.com/trends.

Hansen, M.T., Nohria, N., Tierney, T., 1999. What's your strategy for managing knowledge? Harv. Bus. Rev. 77 (2), 106–116.

Hunter J., 2015. Myth: If you can't measure it, you can't manage it. Available from: http://blog.deming.org/2015/08/myth-if-you-cant-measure-it-you-cant-manage-it/.

Lambe, Patrick, 2011. The unacknowledged parentage of knowledge management. J. Knowl. Manag. 15 (2), 175–197.

Liebowitz, Jay, 1999. Knowledge Management Handbook. CRC Press Inc., Boca Raton, FL.

Nonaka, Ikujiro, Takeuchi, Hirotaka, 1995. The Knowledge Creating Company. Oxford University Press, New York.

Prusak, L., 2001. Where did knowledge management come from? IBM Syst. J. 40 (4), 1002–1007.

Ribière, V, Sitar, AS, 2003. Critical role of leadership in nurturing a knowledge-supporting culture. Knowl. Man. Res. Pract. 1 (1), 39–48.

Rigby, D., Bilodeau, B., 2009. Management Tools and Trends 2009. Bain & Company, Boston, MA.

Rigby, D., Bilodeau, B., 2011. Management Tools and Trends 2011. Bain & Company, Boston, MA.

Rigby, D., Bilodeau, B. (2013). Management Tools and Trends 2013 Bain & Company, Boston, MA.

Rigby, D., Bilodeau, B., 2015. Management Tools and Trends 2015. Bain & Company, Boston, MA.

Schein, E.H., 1992. Organizational culture and leadership, second ed. Jossey-Bass, San Francisco.

Schein, E.H., 1999. The corporate culture survival guide. Jossey-Bass, San Francisco.

Stankosky, M.A., 2005. Creating the Discipline of Knowledge Management: The Latest in University Research. Elsevier Butterworth-Heinemann, Boston.

Stewart, T.A., 1991. Intellectual capital is becoming corporate America's most valuable asset and can be its sharpest competitive weapon. The challenge is to find what you have—and use it. Brainpower, Fortune Magazine. Available from: http://archive.fortune.com/magazines/fortune/fortune_archive/1991/06/03/75096/index.htm

Sveiby, K.E., 1987. Managing Knowhow. Bloomsbury, London.

Weber, R.O., 2007. Addressing failure factors in knowledge management. EJKM 5 (3), 333–346, www.ejkm.com.

Wiig, K.M., 1993. Knowledge Management Foundations: Thinking About Thinking – How People and Organizations Represent, Create and Use Knowledgevol. 1Schema Press, Texas.

Zack, M.H., 1999. Developing a knowledge strategy. Calif. Manage. Rev. 41 (3), 125–145.

Zyngier, S., Burstein, F., 2012. Knowledge management governance: the road to continuous benefits realization. J. Inform. Technol. 27 (2), 140–155.

REAL knowledge and the James Webb Space Telescope: success and failure coexisting in NASA[a]

3

E. Hoffman*, J. Boyle*, E. Rogers**

*NASA Headquarters, Washington, DC, USA; **NASA Goddard Space Flight Center, Greenbelt, MD, USA

INTRODUCTION

How can organizations and practitioners best leverage project knowledge and knowledge services to achieve success and avoid failures in an unforgiving modern complex project environment?

Based on research, experiences, and conversations across public, private, government, industry, academia, and professional organizations, practitioners say it is increasingly difficult to bring ideas to fruition and projects to successful completion. One study found that only 56% of strategic initiatives meet original goals and business intent in surveyed project organizations and also reported that 48% of projects that are not highly aligned to organizational strategy succeed (Project Management Institute, 2014). NASA collaborated with Aviation Week and industry leaders on the second annual Young Professionals study and discovered that the top frustration of the under-35 workforce was bureaucracy and politics, and that there is no time to innovate and create (Anselmo and Hedden, 2011). Within NASA itself, a review of three major internal studies found that one common thread leading to success is better assessment of early concepts to assure the program/project and the organization have common assumptions and expectations.

Over 30 years of experience at NASA suggests that significant improvements can be gained through a focus on the capture and flow of project knowledge in terms of organizational, individual, and team project factors within an organizational systems perspective. For NASA, knowledge involves the unique requirements, solutions, and

---

[a]Disclaimer: This material is based upon work supported with resources and the use of facilities at the National Aeronautics and Space Administration (NASA), Office of the Chief Knowledge Officer and is available as open source information and may be used by external individuals and organizations with proper author citation.

Successes and Failures of Knowledge Management
2016. Published by Elsevier Inc.

expertise shared across individuals, teams, projects, programs, mission directorates, and centers, often defined as codified knowledge (scientific knowledge, engineering and technical knowledge, and business processes) and know-how (techniques, processes, procedures, and craftsmanship), presenting the classic dichotomy of explicit and tacit knowledge where Polanyi (1966) first said of tacit knowledge, "we can know more than we can tell."

There are also other relevant types of knowledge that play a significant role, such as that in a social context. In one example, Neffinger and Kohut (2013) emphasized the importance of perceptions of strength and warmth in interpersonal and team environments and how an optimal balance of these characteristics informs social situations. A better understanding of the social context of project knowledge can serve as a basis for improved prioritization and a more pragmatic approach to problem solving. Organizational disregard for this type of knowledge can lead to project failures such as those in the NASA Challenger and Columbia Shuttle disasters (Hoffman and Boyle, 2013), where the technical root causes were investigated but the underlying causes were poor team communications and lack of organizational learning.

The driving motivation concerning knowledge for NASA is ultimately achieving success. Complexity works against this success, and it can take many forms:

- Confusing, vague, poorly defined priorities, strategies, lines of authority, governance, policies, roles and responsibilities, and support, characterized by iterative reorganizations, constant budget changes, constant resource level adjustments, a proliferation of administrative burdens, and endless requirements.
- A proliferation of customers, stakeholders, and strategic partner interfaces at multiple levels of interest, involvement, and responsibility.
- Technical complexity and system integration issues within and across multiple disciplines and multiple systems.
- Increased data and information amount and availability for process input, throughput, and output.
- Multiple overlapping, conflicting, and outdated processes and procedures that involve multiple points of contact distributed across multiple organizational levels and across multiple oversight and advisory entities, characterized by competing priorities, strategies, lines of authority, governance, policies, roles and responsibilities, and support requirements.

Complexity drives a rapid pace of change that impacts organizational social, technical, strategic and administrative systems. Davenport and Prusak (1998) recognized this when they defined future success in terms of organizations that know how to do new things well and quickly. The shelf-life of products and services is increasingly shortened, requiring a management methodology that is flexible and adaptable across the operational and strategic contexts to accommodate change, yet rigorous enough to ensure that progress continues toward goals and objectives in the most efficient and effective way possible. Project management (PM) is a discipline often applied to achieve this flexibility and adaptability, thus handling the knowledge requirements for projects to better perform under these increased burdens makes sense. For NASA, a project knowledge systems perspective best addresses handling complexity within an environment of increasingly constrained resources.

How are these barriers and complications originating from multiple sources of complexity on the path to success characterized? Some are political, others related to competence at the organizational, team, and individual levels. Some concern leadership capability accompanied by poor communications up, down, or laterally in the organization. Perhaps there are incorrect, ill-defined expectations and a lack of strategic alignment in the project or across the larger organization. Others may reflect significant external market or business change. Regardless, they create a lack of focus and mission, a fragmenting of common purpose into special interests and personal agendas, and ultimately stasis.

A strategic knowledge systems perspective helps to uncover and define project relationships and the risks inherent in project knowledge interfaces. This is critical, since it provides insight into the nature of the realities that others live in. Unless this is analyzed and contingencies are planned for, the risk of failure increases. Fortunately the message is getting through to senior executives. In a conference board (Hackett, 2000) research report on knowledge management (KM), 80% of surveyed organizations had KM activities underway, 60% expected an enterprise-wide KM system within the next 5 years, and 25% had a chief knowledge officer or chief learning officer in place. At the end of the day, capturing and effectively relating the journey to achieve outcomes is a story that each individual and team creates and shares. For NASA, key knowledge imperatives and knowledge tools have been developed over the years to help project teams in their efforts.

NASA KNOWLEDGE SERVICES GOVERNANCE AND STRATEGIC IMPERATIVES

Any NASA knowledge management approach needs to be adaptable and flexible to accommodate the varied requirements and cultural characteristics of each center, mission directorate, and functional office. A federated model was the best fit for the Agency, defining the NASA CKO as a facilitator and champion for agency knowledge services, not to serve as an overseer and direct manager. It struck a balance between autonomy and responsibility, where centers, mission directorates, and functional offices were free to determine the knowledge approach that best fit their particular needs but were responsible to share knowledge that benefited the overall Agency. The governance document for NASA Knowledge, *NPD 7120 NASA Knowledge Policy for Programs and Projects* (National Aeronautics and Space Administration, 2013), was collaboratively rewritten because NASA had greatly expanded its knowledge activities over the past several years to include a wider array of services than simply capturing and retaining lessons learned.

The new policy ensured that NASA manages knowledge resources in a way that enables the Agency to execute programs, projects, and missions with the highest likelihood of mission success, emphasizing a KS-integrated strategic framework. It also defined the roles and responsibilities for CKOs at the centers, mission directorates, and functional offices. The new policy addressed a set of KS priorities that clarified

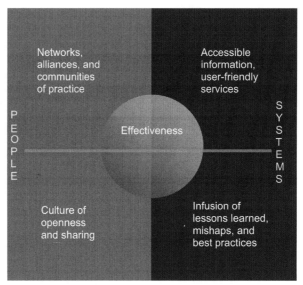

FIGURE 3.1 NASA knowledge services strategic framework

NASA objectives for project knowledge and emphasized the development and implementation of future knowledge initiatives, measures, and metrics (Fig. 3.1):

- In terms of people, sustain and expand the use of the agency's intellectual capital across NASA's enterprises and generations through better networks, alliances, and communities of practice.
- In terms of people, increase collaboration across organizational barriers through promotion of a culture of openness.
- In terms of systems, support the technical workforce in executing NASA's missions efficiently and effectively through lessons learned, mishap reports, and promulgation of best practices.
- In terms of systems, create an integrated infrastructure of knowledge that identifies the value of information and aligns practitioner and organizational imperatives through accessible information and user-friendly services.

One of the most striking things that the Agency's knowledge community discovered at an initial meeting was the sheer depth and breadth of activity underway across the Agency. Some was found through self-service, such as typing a query in a search box and getting answers that point in the right direction, involving one person at a time, and works best with *explicit knowledge* that does not require a lot of context or personal judgment. At the other extreme, *tacit knowledge* that was dependent on context and personal judgment was transmitted through social interaction at meetings and storytelling.

Given this range of knowledge activities, the NASA knowledge community identified an initial set of knowledge categories that addressed most of the activities

FIGURE 3.2 NASA knowledge map and legend

taking place across NASA that could be populated on the first-ever Agency Knowledge Map (Fig. 3.2):

- *Online tools*—include but are not limited to: portals; document repositories; collaboration and sharing sites; video libraries.
- *Search/tag/taxonomy tools*—dedicated search engine for knowledge (eg, Google Search Appliance) and any initiatives related to metatagging or taxonomy.
- *Case studies/publications*—original documents or multimedia case studies that capture project stories and associated lessons learned or best practices.
- *Lessons learned/knowledge processes*—any defined process that an organization uses to identify or capture knowledge, lessons learned, or best practices,

including Lessons Learned Information System vetting process; organization-specific lessons learned processes; benchmarking; cases; knowledge sharing recognition programs; knowledge product validation processes; and communications about expectations related to knowledge sharing.

- *Knowledge networks*—any defined knowledge network, such as a community of practice; expert locator; mass collaboration activity; and workspaces specifically designed to enable exchanges and collaboration.
- *Social exchanges*—any activities that bring people together in person to share knowledge (eg, forums, workshops, Lunch and Learn/Pause and Learn, etc.). The reach of these activities can be multiplied through online tools such as videos and virtual dialogues.

The Agency is now linking all identified products and series to the map and creating active links to the resources. The categories are not a perfect fit for every type of knowledge activity across diverse organizations and multiple disciplines, but the hurdle cleared was the awareness that the perfect is the enemy of the good. The knowledge community used these categories as an initial starting point that could be institutionalized, modified, and clarified during subsequent iterative reviews.

The NASA knowledge community also recognized that there are valuable lessons to be learned from other domestic and international organizations in the federal government, industry, academia, and professional organizations. In extending the community beyond the core NASA footprint, the CKO office is involved with several important communities of practice, two examples of which are the Federal Knowledge Management Community that meets quarterly for sharing best practices and leveraging lessons learned, and the International Project Management Committee (IPMC) and Knowledge Management Technical Committee under the International Astronautical Federation (IAF).

STRATEGIC IMPERATIVES IN THE MODERN PROJECT KNOWLEDGE ENVIRONMENT

What has emerged as driving strategic imperatives that inform the development of KS (knowledge services) at NASA and, through analogy, other organizations?

There are 12 mutually reinforcing strategic imperatives that have emerged from interviews, studies, and experience. These guide the design, implementation, and evaluation of knowledge services for NASA, may resonate with other organizations public and private, and are discussed in no particular order of priority.

One critical strategic imperative is *leadership*. It is ironic that one of the more fragmented disciplines provides valuable answers for the application of KS in organizations. Without effective leadership, KS and its results are at best serendipitous, at worst a failure. The essence of leadership occurs with an insight that things should change, but also a profound realization that the reasons for change may be clear to leaders themselves but not necessarily to others. There exists an external stakeholder community as well as a core internal project team to lead, and both should be understood and managed. Additionally, good leaders align projects with organizational strategy, mission, and goals, admittedly easier said than done in the modern environment of information overload and change. Successful implementation happens with a carefully articulated vision, leadership focus on that vision, and attention to detail on implementation.

It is a *project world*. Varied organizations worldwide require a methodology allowing for rigor in managing temporary, unique initiatives toward the achievement of defined requirements and project goals and outcomes that are aligned to organizational strategy in an era of constrained resources. In this context, PM is uniquely positioned as an adaptable discipline that fits these requirements and can maximize the use of learning to promote efficiency and effectiveness. Again, the alignment of project goals to organizational strategy through good leadership is critical.

Knowledge is the essential element for the creation of successful physical and virtual products and services. It can be viewed as an organized set of content, skills, and capabilities gained through experience as well as through formal and informal learning that organizations and practitioners apply to make sense of new and existing data and information. It can also exist as previously analyzed and formatted lessons and stories that are already adaptable to new situations. The ascendance of leaders that can validate the realities on which projects are able to apply knowledge and base decisions is key.

Talent management addresses the specification, identification, nurturing, transfer, maintenance, and expansion of the competitive advantage of practitioner expertise and competence. It encompasses the broad definition of diversity that goes beyond the classic categories of color, race, religion, and national origin to domestic and international variables important to geographically dispersed multicultural teams, such as multigenerational, crossdiscipline, and crossexperiential variables. This allows diverse groups to bring a diversity of experience, attitudes, knowledge, focus, and interests to the table, strengthening both inductive and deductive problem solving approaches and nurturing innovation. Good leaders link talent management with executive sponsorship, organizational strategy, and the core work of the organization. They also achieve operational efficiencies by learning, working, and collaborating together at a distance independent of time and geography, and leverage smart networks that provide content, access, and connection to project data, information, and knowledge. For NASA, talent management is represented as the variables of abilities, assignments, attitudes, and alliances (Fig. 3.4).

Portfolio management integrates projects with strategy and creates an organizing framework and focus that drives organizational purpose and activities. They provide a centralized function that promulgates a systems view of knowledge, where stove-piped disciplines and activities can transcend boundaries and discover and apply crossdisciplinary knowledge to increase competitive advantage and better achieve results. Organizational expectations can also be tested against reality at this level and adjusted and communicated accordingly to eliminate or mitigate errors and achieve better decisions.

Certification establishes objective, validated standards and functions to benchmark achievement in defined categories of practitioner performance and capability.

It also provides organizations and practitioners a way to establish trust with superiors, peers, team members, customers, and stakeholders, and provides a framework for adapting to change as well as a method to address emerging performance requirements. For practitioners, it provides a roadmap for individual development and serves to link organizational performance and individual capability. Since people are essential in projects, certification allows for objective definitions of the four talent management variables of abilities, assignments, attitudes, and alliances. An example of a discipline standard is the Project Management Body of Knowledge (Project Management Institute, 2013) that specifies the 10 knowledge areas that currently defines the framework of the discipline.

Transparency is an important consideration as the network of organizational portfolio sponsors, project team members, customers, stakeholders, strategic partners, suppliers, and other interested parties tie into organizational strategy and project operations through information and communication technology tools. In this environment, nothing is hidden for long and errors travel at the speed of light. Communications with each interface should be carefully defined across intensity and frequency dimensions, for example, where external stakeholder communities may expect to be informed about progress at a higher level, but not as frequently or in-depth as internal leadership. Transparency that is formally built into the strategic business process encourages innovation, translating economies of scale and a breadth of experiential lessons into innovation and flexibility.

Frugal innovation (The Economist, 2010) is a mindset that views constraints in an era of restricted and diminished resources as opportunities, leveraging sustainability and a focus on organizational core competencies to reduce complexity and increase the probability of better outcomes. Sustainability in particular has gained momentum as the cost to the planet, and availability of resources increasingly impact business decisions. Organizational core competencies for a product or service involves what it must do in-depth rather than what it can do in breadth, ensuring that organizational capacity in areas such as technological, social, political, economic, and learning dimensions are part of the frugal innovation process. In a mutually reinforcing perspective, imperatives such as *transparency* allow the broader team to share knowledge and experience to improve and innovate in terms of products and services, supporting the *frugal innovation* effort.

Accelerated learning is the tactic of employing state-of-the-art digital technologies, traditional knowledge-sharing activities, modern learning strategies, social media processes and tools, and crossdiscipline knowledge into the broadest possible view of learning for an organization. The operational knowledge process is closely linked to key internal and external knowledge sources and serves to clarify organizational expectations to optimize knowledge searchability, findability, and adaptability.

A *problem-centric approach* emphasizes a nonpartisan, nonbiased, nonjudgmental, and pragmatic orientation toward problems and solutions, keeping the focus on achievement, improvement, and innovation. Organizational expectations are kept pragmatic and constructive when a problem-centric approach is encouraged and expected. At the end of the day, it is about problems, communications, power, and building a community of support focused on credible challenges. This orientation serves as the fuel for change while addressing competing agendas and administrative barriers, and directly addresses the issue of bias and heuristics that may introduce errors in decisions.

Governance, business management, and operations provide for pragmatic alignment, oversight, approvals, and implementation of project operations and establishes rigor and processes. In an era of frugal innovation, management of the budget, and clarity of funding requirements that supports the overall effort must be visible and valued by the leadership and the workforce. Nothing brings trouble faster than mismanagement of funds and a lack of focus on funding flow, so the oversight, tracking, and implementation of project activities need definition. Defined governance addresses the issue of siloed implementation and raises executive awareness as well as formalizing successful localized grassroots efforts.

Digital technology makes it possible to examine new frontiers of potential knowledge and access multiple sources of data and information, but simultaneously causes organizations to be increasingly buried in data and information and have less time for focus and reflection. Technology is necessary but not sufficient for KS, but wonderful things can result from the application of technology, such as an open, social network-centric, nonproprietary, adaptable, and flexible framework that accelerates learning processes to deliver the right knowledge at the right time for particular needs while respecting context. The proper application of technology helps achieve learning results and better decisions at a lower cost.

REAL (RAPID ENGAGEMENT THROUGH ACCELERATED LEARNING) KNOWLEDGE MODEL

With the project environment, the strategic knowledge imperatives, and defining events serving as a framework, there was a critical need for a project KS model that describes the interfaces, variables, and components. Alternatively, the last thing needed was a normative model prescribing knowledge methods specific to siloed processes and tools as opposed to broader integrated approaches that are able to accommodate complex organizational strategies. Retaining and learning not only the lesson but also the context allows practitioners the potential to better adapt lessons to diverse project environments.

According to the conference board (Hackett, 2000), executives may not be familiar with or possess experience in the KM discipline, resulting in a lack of specific knowledge objectives and goals that can be integrated, measured, and managed, thus leading to the potential extraction of the wrong lessons. KS suggests a facilitative approach that not only addresses the topic of knowledge, but also emphasizes learning as an organization and ties the importance of knowledge as a resource across operational and strategic imperatives, reinstating the critical context of the information.

The NASA CKO office developed the rapid engagement through accelerated learning (REAL) knowledge model (Fig. 3.3) to promote the capabilities of more

Rapid engagement through accelerated learning (REAL) knowledge flow

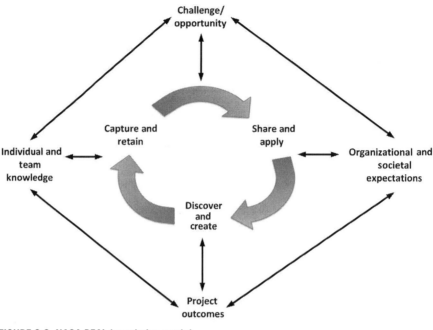

FIGURE 3.3 NASA REAL knowledge model

comprehensively and accurately define a problem; to encourage a pragmatic orienta-tion that informs better decision making; and to help to address the issues of bias, ego, special interests, and personal agendas. At the core of the REAL knowledge model is the operational KM cycle activities of capture, share, and discover, but with an effectiveness measure paired with the knowledge activity. For example, capturing knowledge is the action and retaining is the measure; sharing knowledge is the action and applying is the measure; and discovering is the action and creating outcomes is the measure. Surrounding the REAL knowledge core activities are the individual/team knowledge factors and the organizational/societal expectations that mitigate the journey of the challenge/opportunity from inception through the knowledge cycle to successful project outcomes. Note that the process arrows are bidirectional in terms of influence and input, a guarantee of continuous change, learning, and adaptation.

In describing the REAL knowledge model, the following top-level generic flow serves to illustrate a potential progression of knowledge activity:

1. A *challenge/opportunity* is selected and prioritized (motivated by *leadership, knowledge, project world, portfolio,* and *problem-centric* imperatives).
2. A learning project plan that compliments the project charter and project plan is initiated (motivated by *knowledge, accelerated learning, frugal innovation,* and *governance, business management, and operations* imperative).

3. The functional communities of practice are recruited with points of contact identified (motivated by *leadership*, *project world*, *knowledge*, and *talent management* imperatives).

4. The core operational KM cycle is supported by specific KS learning strategies, methods, models, and technology tools to better define the opportunity; aggregate the data, information, and knowledge; populate the alternatives for project decisions; provide appropriate online and traditional environments to spur and support innovation through discovery and creation; and support implementation through progressive and iterative knowledge support as the project proceeds through the life cycle (motivated by *knowledge*, *technology*, *frugal innovation*, and *accelerated learning* imperatives).

5. *Individual and team knowledge* is leveraged, encouraged, supported, and enhanced through KS activities (motivated by *knowledge*, *talent management*, *accelerated learning*, *transparency*, *frugal innovation*, and *certification* imperatives).

6. External environment *expectations* in terms of the organization and broader society are identified and operationalized into objective definitions of performance over time and space (motivated by *leadership*, *knowledge*, *transparency*, *frugal innovation*, *accelerated learning*, *technology* and *governance, business management, and operations* imperatives).

7. *Project outcomes* are achieved in terms of improvement and innovation, and the activity proceeds through closeout to capture and retain lessons for upcoming projects (motivated by *Knowledge*, *portfolio management*, *transparency*, *accelerated learning*, *governance*, *business management* and *operations*, and *digital technology*.

The REAL knowledge model component definitions are provided along with associated keywords and concepts to aid potential future research in taxonomies and ontologies related to the narrower model and to the broader knowledge and learning disciplines.

- The *challenge/opportunity* is a problem-centered issue in terms of a product or service that presents a potential for action toward defined outcomes. Possible keywords and concepts include: vision and possibilities; requirements; and organizational capacity in technological, social, political, economic, and learning.
- *Individual and team knowledge* are formal and informal individual and collective education, professional development, and lessons from direct and indirect experience applied to a *challenge/opportunity*. Possible keywords and concepts include: assignments; abilities; formal education; professional development; and mentoring.
  - *Attitudes and values* are the predispositions based on learning, experience, and the challenge/opportunity to evaluate the environment in particular ways. Possible keywords and concepts include: personality and inclination; resilience; open-mindedness; curiosity and skepticism; and tempered

optimism. Note that these attitudes and values may also be collectively reflected in organizational and societal expectations.

- *Heuristics and biases* are cognitive shortcuts and simplifications by individuals, teams, and organizations used to reduce complexity. Possible keywords and concepts include: normalization of deviance; problem solving and decision making; fundamental attribution error; and culture of silence. These may be collectively reflected in organizational and societal expectations.

- *Abilities and talent* are learned or natural patterns of action for both individuals and teams that possess potential to achieve goals. Possible keywords and concepts include: critical thinking and creative thinking; problem solving and decision making; creating alliances; and leadership and persuasion. These may be collectively reflected in organizational and societal expectations.

- *Project knowledge* is the sum of the formal and informal individual and team knowledge as previously discussed within the project context that is applied to existing and new data and information to a *challenge/opportunity* to gain efficiency and effectiveness toward project outcomes. Possible keywords and concepts include: success stories and failure stories; learning through analogies; and organizational learning. These may be collectively reflected and applied through organizational and societal expectations.

- *Expectations* are assumptions on the probability of event occurrence for individuals, groups, organizations, and societies based on learning and experience. Possible keywords and concepts include: adaptation to change; reputation; executive communications; and past performance.

  - *Organizational culture* comprises common sets of values and assumptions that guide behavior in organizations that inform problem-solving and decision-making activity. Possible keywords and concepts include: organizational norms and mores; environmental context; and performance management.

- *Knowledge capture and retention* is a core knowledge step involving the identification and storage of relevant content and skills. Possible keywords and concepts include: alliances, communities and networks; cases and publications; risk records, mishap reports, organizational communications; and stories.

- *Knowledge sharing and application* is a core knowledge step involving the representation, promulgation, and utilization of searchable and findable relevant content and skills. Possible keywords and concepts include: digital technology tools; informal learning; and best and emerging practices.

- *Knowledge discovery and creation* is a core knowledge step that covers original content and skills derived and developed from previous relevant content and skills that result in project outcomes. Possible keywords and concepts include: searchability and findability; taxonomies; and innovation.

- *Project outcomes* are the achievement of original or improved products or services as defined by the project charter and validated by organizational expectations. Possible keywords and concepts include: value; improvement; innovation; and learning, knowledge, and growth.

One of the components in the REAL knowledge model, *organizational and societal expectations*, needs to be further discussed due to its importance when addressing the topic of complexity. Human cognition is colored by inherent hardwired preferences in thinking and in shortcuts that accompany decision-making processes, a product of choices, and evolution. *Biases and heuristics* serve to reduce the amount of complexity, but also may introduce error. Additionally, these predispositions may differ across cultures. NASA represents a complex technical organization consisting of several divergent domestic and international cultures with different perceptions. Understanding these perceptions are important for the success of NASA's projects, especially since 80% of NASA programs and projects are international in nature.

Biases and heuristics are not just cognitive distortions that affect decisions, but are also *social biases* that affect individual and organizational behavior as well as learning and memory tendencies that affect perceptions and explanations of the world. In our interview with Nobel Prize–winning scientist Daniel Kahneman (2013) on his recent *New York Times* bestseller *Thinking Fast and Slow*, he clarified how humans address increasing levels of complexity in the project environment through *heuristics* that can introduce errors into decisions, a veritable catalog of fundamental predispositions that characterize human cognition. System 1 thinking is fast, instinctive, and emotional, while system 2 thinking is slower, more deliberative, and more logical. Kahneman delineates cognitive biases associated with each type of thinking, starting with his own research on loss aversion, the unsettling tendency of people and organizations to continue funding a project that has already consumed a tremendous amount of resources but is likely to fail simply to avoid regret. From framing choices to substitution, the book highlights several decades of academic research to suggest that people place too much confidence in human judgment, resulting in different outcomes even given the same information input.

Biases and heuristics should be viewed not exclusively in a negative context, but in one where these distortions and shortcuts can also provide positive outcomes. Many projects would not be started if executives waited until all the data and information were available to make a rational decision. *Biases and heuristics* serve in creating an environment where possibilities and vision can drive an idea toward reality. Busenitz and Barney (1997) found that there is a fundamental difference in the way that entrepreneurs and managers in large organizations make decisions, and that biases and heuristics drive entrepreneurial decisions and are used to reduce complexity in the project environment, simplifying decision making and preventing data and information from overwhelming programs and projects, as well as serving to achieve buy-in and motivating practitioners. This often morphs into a tremendous disadvantage as projects mature from start-up activities to implementation and sustainability requirements. A brief set of examples from a rather extensive catalog are:

- Availability: making judgments on the probability of events by how easy it is to think of examples and their consequences.
- Substitution: substituting a simple question for a more difficult one.
- Optimism and loss aversion: generating the illusion of control over events and fearing losses more than we value gains.

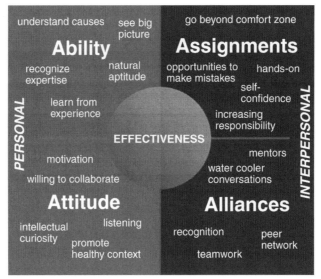

FIGURE 3.4 The 4A Word Cloud

- Framing: choosing the more attractive alternative if the context in which it is presented is more appealing.
- Sunk-cost: throwing additional money at failing projects that have already consumed large amounts of resources in order to avoid regret.
- Mental filter: focusing on one feature of something that influences all subsequent decisions.
- Fundamental attribution error: the tendency to overemphasize personality-based causes of behavior and underemphasize situational-based causes of behavior.
- Egocentric bias: recalling prior events in a favorable light to one's self rather than an accurate objective analysis.

Another important facet of the REAL knowledge model is in what NASA refers to as the four A's: *ability*, *attitude*, *assignments*, and *alliances*. These components of the model are extracted from the interpersonal and team knowledge, attitudes and values, abilities and talent, knowledge capture and retention, and knowledge sharing and application components. They are represented in Fig. 3.4 across a personal and interpersonal dimension of effectiveness.

SUCCESS AND FAILURE COEXIST: THE JAMES WEBB SPACE TELESCOPE

One program that lends itself readily to this need for KS (NASA, 2007) and is also timely in times of tight budgets and other strategic imperatives is the James Webb Space Telescope (JWST), the successor to the Hubble Space Telescope (HST),

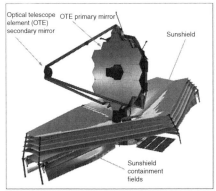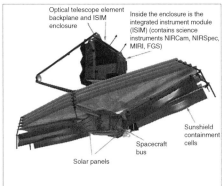

FIGURE 3.5 Artist's concept of the JWST

Front view (a) and back view (b).

(Source: NASA image)

discussed here in terms of the REAL model. Nine years after it was deployed, the HST was producing more stunning images from deep space, generating more data, and drawing more accolades than anyone at NASA had dreamed of. In the year 1999, with the Next-Generation Space Telescope (renamed the James Webb Space Telescope in the year 2002 in honor of NASA's second administrator) on the drawing board, astrophysicists and astronomers were daring to dream even bigger (Fig. 3.5).

At NASA, there were high hopes throughout customers, stakeholders, and the project team (Fig. 3.6) that the JWST would fulfill its science purpose as reflected in the National Academy Decadal Survey in the year 2000 designation as the top-priority recommendation for the new millennium, serving as the premier observatory of the next decade and beyond, studying every phase in the history of the universe from the first luminous glows after the big bang to the formation of solar systems capable of supporting planetary life, requiring a groundbreaking effort by hundreds of engineers and scientists dedicating years to the mission. From its perch a million miles from Earth, protected from solar glare and space radiation by a mammoth sunshield, the JWST would focus its 6.5-m mirror, 7 times the size of the HST main mirror, with a sensitivity 100 times greater to detect light from the earliest stars and to witness the first galaxies forming. The JWST instruments would work mainly in the infrared range of the electromagnetic spectrum. As the universe expands and the earliest stars rapidly recede, the wavelengths of starlight traveling the expanse of space are stretched, elongating into the infrared end of the spectrum and out of the visible range of the HST. The Hubble studied the universe in optical and ultraviolet wavelengths, ranging from 0.1 to 2.5 μm (ultraviolet to the near infrared). The JWST was equipped to have an unfiltered view of a wavelength range from about 0.6 μm (at the red end of the visible spectrum) to 28 μm (visible to the midinfrared light). The risk was the position of the JWST, meaning that once the JWST was deployed, it would be beyond reach, no service and repair missions like those for the HST would be possible. It would either work or not.

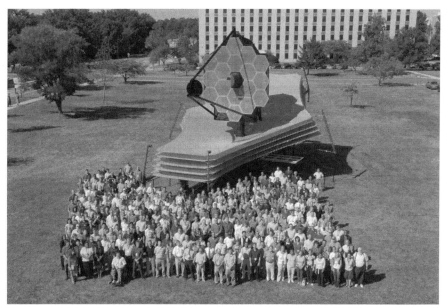

FIGURE 3.6 JWST project team with the observatory model on the Goddard Campus, 2007

To view this part of the spectrum, groundbreaking technology would be required, starting with a much larger mirror than the HST. The main mirror of the new space-based telescope would be 6.5 m (originally conceived as 8 m), or 21.3 ft. in diameter, comprising 18 hexagonal pieces fabricated from the light metal beryllium. The observatory would be shaded by a sunshield the size of a tennis court. Because the mirror and shield could not be fitted fully open onto a launch rocket, both would have to be folded up and opened after JWST's 3-month flight into space. The telescope would be placed in an orbit 940,000 miles from Earth, roughly 4 times the distance of the Moon from Earth, where the gravitational pulls of Earth and the Sun are nearly balanced, optimizing fuel consumption and conditions for infrared observations.

PIONEERING TECHNOLOGY AND INSTRUMENTATION

From the outset, the challenge for the JWST would be how to design innovative technologies in a package 6 times larger but 4 times lighter than the HST. Among the pioneering technologies being developed for *JWST* were:

- Folding primary mirror and ultralightweight beryllium optics for the honeycombed mirror segments.
- Detectors able to record extremely weak signals.
- Microshutters (made up of filaments thinner than human hair) to enable programmable object selection for the spectrograph.
- Cryocooler for the midinfrared detectors because the telescope would have to be cooled to −223°C.

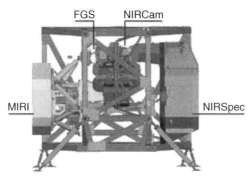

FGS   NIRCam

MIRI   NIRSpec

FIGURE 3.7 Location of instruments

(Source: NASA Image)

Four instruments would be mounted on the telescope (Fig. 3.7):

- The visible/near-infrared camera (NIRCam) dedicated to the detection of light from the first stars, star clusters, or galaxy cores; the study of very distant galaxies seen in the process of formation; detection of light distortion due to dark matter; the discovery of supernovae in remote galaxies; studies of the stellar population in nearby galaxies, young stars in the Milky Way, and the Kuiper Belt objects in our solar system.
- The near-infrared multiobject dispersive spectrograph (NIRSpec), sensitive over a wavelength range that matches the radiation from the most distant galaxies and capable of observing more than 100 objects simultaneously. The key scientific objectives of this instrument are: studying star formation and chemical abundances of young distant galaxies; tracing the creation of chemical elements back in time; and exploring the history of the intergalactic medium (the gaseous material that fills the vast volumes of space between the galaxies).
- The midinfrared camera-spectrograph (MIRI) essential for the study of the old and distant stellar population; regions of obscured star formation; hydrogen emission from previously unthinkable distances; the physics of protostars; and the sizes of Kuiper Belt objects and faint comets.
- The fine guidance sensor (FGS), providing high-precision pointing error signals to the observatory to enable stable pointing at the milliarcsecond level. It will also support star field identification via correlation with a star catalogue as well as spatial and radiometric calibrations.

In addition to the European Space Agency (ESA), the international JWST partnership led by NASA included the Canadian Space Agency (CSA) and prime contractor Northrop Grumman Space Technology (NGST), who would lead the design and development of the telescope. ESA was responsible for the NIRSpec, CSA was developing the FGS, and NASA's Jet Propulsion Laboratory (JPL) would build the MIRI with ESA. Ball Aerospace was chosen to provide the telescope's optical design and mirrors, ITT to integrate and test the telescope, and Alliant Techsystems to supply the telescope's composite structures. Goddard Space Flight Center (GSFC) would manage the project, and the Space Telescope Science Institute would develop and manage the science and mission operations center.

EXPECTATIONS VERSUS PERFORMANCE

In the year 2005, well into the formulation phase of the JWST, the estimated cost had jumped by a billion dollars, putting it at a projected $4.5 billion by the time of the launch. A launch delay of up to 2 years, from 2011 to 2013, seemed imminent. Pressure to demonstrate the readiness of 10 new required technologies was mounting. The program was being scrutinized in a new light, from both inside and outside the space and science communities. No question, there was still plenty of enthusiasm and support, but other opinions were being voiced, including objections to the growing slice of the NASA budget pie being consumed by the giant program.

Two review panels had been convened. The first was a team from the NASA Independent Assessment Office, who would examine the program's new cost/schedule/technical baseline. The second was a Science Assessment Team, an international group of outside experts gathered to evaluate the JWST's scientific capabilities for the year 2015 time frame in light of other astronomical facilities that would be available. The recommendations from these reviews on how to accommodate the cost overrun (assuming the science objectives of JWST were revalidated and no descoping was required that would involve a reduction in the specifications of the mission) could determine the future of the program.

Over the course of the formulation phase, the JWST cost estimate for completion had increased by nearly one-third, from $3.5 billion in year 2004 to $4.5 billion in year 2006. The majority of the increase (around $655 million) was attributed to external factors: a projected 22-month launch delay as JWST waited for approval of the Ariane 5 launch vehicle offered by ESA (estimated $300 million), and fiscal-year funding limitations through 2007. Another estimated $125 million was due to added contingency budget reserves required by NASA. The balance of the additional price (estimated $386 million) was the result of changes in requirements and growth in implementation, including cost increases in getting major suppliers under contract and architecture changes to the cryocooler and electronics components. Integration and test reevaluation also contributed additional costs, including test facility changes and more launcher-related testing, and instrument costs were growing as well.

Previous studies had shown that the risk of overrun at completion declined with the increase in investment in initial lifecycle cost. An analysis of 26 missions demonstrated that the risk of cost growth was less than 5% when more than 25% of development cost was spent during the study phase. It was estimated the JWST would spend 49% of its total cost by the end of phase B in March 2008. Estimated expenditures through fiscal year 2006 would account for 32% of total development cost, a significant indicator of total cost stability. The conclusion was clear: early spending in technologies and architecture definition lowered overall risk. Because of the growing price tag, project leaders began a series of rebaselining efforts to revise their acquisition strategy.

Indecision over the launch vehicle (LV) also hung over the project like a dark cloud. Would engineers ultimately be designing the observatory for launch on the ESA Ariane 5 rocket or for the US Boeing Delta IV heavy booster launcher? In 2005, the issue was tangled in a political thicket. NASA administrator Mike Griffin had signed off on Ariane in June, but the agency was still awaiting US State Department approval of a formal agreement with ESA. The assumption was that approval would be forthcoming, but the issue was complicated domestically. Support for Boeing's launcher came not only from political quarters but also from corporate and institutional interests, as the US rocket industry continued to experience a decline in its number of launches.

In the meantime, while the State Department was reviewing the Memorandum of Understanding (MOU) that would grant NASA authority to negotiate with ESA, the decision delay was driving up the cost of the mission. Making it more confounding to many working on JWST was that it appeared as if the problem could have been pre-empted and a large portion of the cost increase avoided, and if NASA ended up going with a US launch vehicle, there would be an additional cost on top of the delay cost already incurred. Just as exasperating was the fact that the Ariane was a tried-and-true vehicle and would be able to meet the baseline of 14 successful launches prior to JWST, a requirement a US rocket would be unlikely to meet. Many on the project felt that the mission had enough uncertainty without an unproven LV. Others resigned themselves to the fact that this was an issue outside the control of management and even NASA itself.

TECHNOLOGY READINESS

All NASA flights are required to meet technology readiness levels (TRL) throughout the project phases. The JWST had to achieve a specified TRL for its 10 advanced technologies before the technical nonadvocate review (T-NAR) scheduled for Jan. 2007. Achieving this TRL was critical for project funding. Given the range of new technologies and the testing required, meeting the performance standards in time would be challenging. Work on the readiness demonstrations, ranging from the sunshield material to cryocooling systems, was in full swing. The innovative technologies that had to demonstrate readiness were:

1. sunshield membrane: material qualification test report
2. near-infrared detector: focal plane assembly
3. midinfrared detector: focal plane assembly
4. primary mirror: segment assembly
5. NIRSpec: microshutter array
6. sidecar ASIC (application-specific integrated circuit for image digitization)
7. passive cryogenic thermal control: heat switch development
8. WFS&C (wavefront sensing and control subsystem for correcting optics errors)
9. large, precision cryostructure
10. MIRI cryocooler system

The risk level of several of the technologies was quite high, starting with the large primary mirror. This was to be expected, considering that the technologies and subsystems were all new and unique. Each presented its own distinctive engineering challenges. For example, the microshutter subsystem, being built by Goddard, was an intricate system of tens of thousands of minute shutters designed to block out light and enable the telescope to focus on the faintest objects in the distant sky. The opening and closing of the microshutters would be controlled by a computer on Earth. Now, in the midst of phase B of the project, the technology strategy was geared toward achieving the required readiness level, with a preliminary design review on the horizon in 2008. Would the new technologies be on schedule?

WAITING FOR ASSESSMENTS

Even with a cost overrun of 1 billion dollars, an expected 2-year launch delay, and technology readiness issues still hanging in the balance, the larger picture of the JWST seemed bright. The project manager considered the scope of the mission in terms not only of cost and time, but also of technology and potential science. The project was possibly as big and ambitious as anything undertaken at NASA, a first-of-its-kind observatory unburdened by heritage. So many things were novel about the JWST, from its size to the cryogenics to the technology required to fold it all up like a paper airplane inside a rocket. The PM believed that some, if not all, of the cost overrun was simply unavoidable. Certainly, making a decision on the LV would have helped, saving a significant portion of the overrun. But he had informed both Goddard and HQ that there would be considerable costs incurred if the LV decision was not made. He also suspected that ultimately, for financial and reliability reasons, the Ariane would be chosen and that it would be the right choice. As he thought about the imminent reports from the Science Assessment Team and the Independent Assessment Office, the PM also believed that the program would proceed intact. Still, could he do more in terms of risk and cost containment to head off the problems leading to overruns and delays?

JWST IN TERMS OF REAL KNOWLEDGE

The problems that NASA projects seek to solve are often novel in nature, "firsts" or "onlies" that increasingly demand the application of strategic imperatives such as frugal innovation, findable and searchable knowledge, and accelerated learning. REAL knowledge services derived from the model are designed to promote excellence in project management and engineering by building a community of practitioners who understand the knowledge flow framework of the organization and are reflective and geared toward sharing. By facilitating and integrating agency-wide KS through interviews, forums, conferences, publications, research, and digital offerings, the CKO office helps ensure that critical lessons and knowledge remain searchable, findable, and adaptable. The CKO knowledge network extends beyond NASA as well, to include expert practitioners from industry, academia, other government agencies, research and professional organizations, and international space agencies.

For the JWST, the *challenge/opportunity* is certainly initiated in this particular case study in a big way, a problem-centered issue that matters (successor to the HST) in terms of a product or service (the JWST) that presents a potential for action toward defined outcomes (substantial gains in scientific and research capability with significant concomitant advances in new technology). The US National Academy of Sciences had designated the JWST as the nation's highest priority in space science, and expectations were soaring, making KS processes, tools, and techniques absolutely critical in managing knowledge flow on the organizational and societal expectations side of the REAL knowledge model.

For the strategic imperatives and REAL knowledge model components driving the design, implementation, and evaluation of knowledge services for the JWST, the following are particularly salient:

- Exceptional *leadership* employing good *project management* business practice would be required to manage the high expectations, multifaceted communications, and performance requirements at all JWST activity and task levels for the stakeholder community and internal project team and to keep a *problem-centric approach* as the focus for the organizational strategy, mission, goals, and implementation, especially since this project is already under cost scrutiny and facing inevitable changes in an era of constrained resources.
- A corollary of the leadership imperative would be effective and efficient *governance, business management, and operations* that will keep customers and stakeholders as well as the core and extended team informed in a *transparent* project environment, maintaining trust through a free-flow of knowledge across all project boundaries.
- The *knowledge* imperative will need to be effectively and efficiently communicated using *accelerated learning* methods and *digital technology* across the project in light of the new JWST technologies as well as high visibility, defining a JWST-specific organized set of content, skills, and capabilities, perhaps involving *certification* in key technical disciplines, and applied early so that the team can discover, make sense of, and apply new and existing data and information as technological maturity occurs as the project progresses.
- The right people in terms of *talent management* need to be in place for this multiyear effort and linked with executive sponsorship, organizational strategy, and the core work of the organization. Specifications for the variables of abilities, assignments, attitudes, and alliances become objective criteria to maintain the current effort and fill the talent pipeline for future years in the overall multiyear effort, especially critical in light of the new technologies being employed in the JWST.
- Awareness of organizational biases and how they drive expectations would be important for the JWST team due to the international nature of the project; the lack of a heritage baseline in terms of comparing projects; the pressures of time and cost but also of technological advancement and science; and the sheer complexity of the overall effort that might encourage the application of potentially faulty heuristics as well as promulgation of ineffective biases.

- Lastly, effective *portfolio management* would be an increasingly important consideration since the JWST is consuming an increasing percentage of the overall agency budget through cost growth. This focus will better integrate the JWST project with overall strategy and achieve a systems view of knowledge where NASA stove-piped disciplines and activities can apply crossdisciplinary knowledge to increase chances for mission success.

The organizational and societal expectations of the REAL knowledge model should be analyzed in the context of project performance. How far out of line were customer and stakeholder expectations against the realities of the JWST program? Was the ballooning budget being driven by external circumstances driving these expectations, or was it the result of problems within the JWST program, essentially the technical development program for the telescope and other instruments? For example, in today's dollars, the HST total costs including space operations and the servicing missions could ultimately exceed those of the JWST. As with many NASA programs, the mission could be considered as not overbudget but undercosted from the beginning, making overruns inevitable. Would knowledge gained in incremental fashion and shared across the team help in better meeting the technology readiness challenges? Finally, what mechanisms, tools, processes, and procedures would help the JWST PM implement KS with the most efficiency and effectiveness while creating the least administrative burden for the core and extended project team?

CONCLUSIONS

How can organizations and practitioners best leverage project knowledge and knowledge services to achieve success and avoid failures in an unforgiving modern complex project environment?

For NASA, KS was a steady progression of maturity influenced by the requirements of specific missions over time (Hoffman and Kohut, 2012). The agency today is not the same one that went to the Moon. Individual capability driven by internal experts fit the organization at the beginning, but that soon morphed into a team-based approach driven by diverse mission requirements as the purpose of the agency changed over the years.

The complexity of the project environment addressed by this chapter forces KS to adjust to the new realities of knowledge findability, searchability, and adaptability, highlighting the need for accelerated learning within a systems perspective and revealing the synergy between the disciplines of knowledge management and organizational learning. Recent stakeholder messages from 2002 through 2012 have indicated that NASA needs to take advantage of opportunities for greater coordination and collaboration across the organization. The agency formally recognized this need by designating the first NASA CKO to serve at the executive level for the agency.

The strategic imperatives that guide the development of NASA KS are a product of their times, addressing the realities and requirements for planning and action concerning leadership, complexity, limited resources, communication, knowledge, individual and organizational capability, and process. These imperatives can take different forms depending on specific organizational characteristics and needs at the strategic, operational, and tactical levels.

For NASA, the federated approach allowed an effective balance of autonomy and responsibility. With this approach, the knowledge community generated common definitions and purpose and developed reinforcing products and services that addressed both local and agency knowledge considerations to include a new knowledge policy, an agency knowledge map, chairmanships of the federal knowledge community, and the development of the NASA REAL knowledge model. This model allowed the agency to formulate KS activities that addressed the strategic knowledge imperatives, achieve buy-in across diverse communities, and accelerate learning to reduce complexity and ensure risks based on knowledge were identified and mitigated or eliminated.

The REAL knowledge model was presented as a descriptive model of how knowledge flow and knowledge services work at NASA. Future research can advance the understanding of the components of this model to achieve normative assumptions, definitions, and standards that promote effective and efficient knowledge practices that reduce complexity and accelerate learning to achieve successful outcomes. Accordingly, the following future research initiatives should advance understanding and yield practical benefits for project organizations:

1. What are the characteristics of challenges and opportunities that achieve organizational and individual commitment, align individual and organizational agendas, and promote effective project management?
2. How should organizations systematically address talent development in terms of abilities, attitudes, assignments, and alliances?
3. What are the metrics and measures that best capture effectiveness and efficiency in the knowledge processes and outcomes of capturing and retaining, sharing and applying, and discovering and creating?
4. Can biases and heuristics that drive organizational and societal expectations be identified and addressed to inform how organizations can make better decisions and design better measures for the challenge/opportunity, the core knowledge processes, and project outcomes?
5. What are the operational definitions and certification parameters of knowledge behaviors for project practitioners, and how does that address talent development and capability requirements?
6. How can the characteristics that make data and information searchable and findable and result in adaptable knowledge in a systems approach to organizational knowledge and learning be operationalized to effective requirements and behaviors?
7. What is the nature of the relationship between knowledge services, accelerated learning, and reducing complexity, and how is this translated into the agile PM framework?

In conclusion, there is much work and research needed for addressing how organizations and practitioners can best leverage project knowledge and knowledge services to get things done in the modern complex project environment. The potential mitigating and complicating variables that reduce the power of knowledge and learning are too numerous to list, but a descriptive model from a organizational systems perspective can serve as a framework to ensure that the breadth of relevant components are identified and operationalized, as well as serving as a map for future research toward informing a normative project knowledge model.

REFERENCES

Anselmo, J., Hedden, C., 2011. Up & down: a workforce in transition: commercial companies hire as defense and space pare down. Aviat. Week Space Technol., 44–53.

Busenitz, L.W., Barney, J.B., 1997. Differences between entrepreneurs and managers in large organizations: biases and heuristics in strategic decision-making. J. Bus. Venturing 12, 9–30.

Davenport, T., Prusak, L., 1998. Working Knowledge. Harvard Business School Press, Boston, MA.

Hackett, B., 2000. Beyond Knowledge Management: New Ways to Work and Learn (Research Report 1262-00-RR). The Conference Board, New York, NY.

Hoffman, E., Boyle, J., 2013. Tapping agency culture to advance knowledge services at NASA. The Public Manager, Fall, pp. 42–43.

Hoffman, E., Kohut, M., 2012. NASA's journey to project management excellence. Washington, DC. Available from: http://www.pmi.org/~/media/PDF/Knowledge%20 Center/NASA-Journey-to-PM-Excellence.ashx

Kahneman, D., 2013. Thinking, Fast and Slow. Farrar, Straus and Giroux, New York, NY.

National Aeronautics and Space Administration, 2007. James Webb Space Telescope: Large-Program Management on a Long Horizon. NASA, Washington, DC.

National Aeronautics and Space Administration, 2013. NASA Policy Directive 7120.6: Knowledge Policy on Programs and Projects. NASA, Washington, DC.

Neffinger, J., Kohut, M., 2013. Compelling People: The Hidden Qualities That Make Us Influential. Hudson Street Press, New York, NY.

Polanyi, M., 1966. The Tacit Dimension. University of Chicago Press, Chicago, p. 4.

Project Management Institute, 2013. A Guide to the Project Management Body of Knowledge: PMBOK Guide, fifth ed. Project Management Institute, Newtown Square, PA.

Project Management Institute, 2014. Pulse of the profession in-depth report: the high cost of low performance. Project Management Institute, February 2014.

The Economist, 2010. First break all the rules: the charms of frugal innovation. The Economist Newspaper Ltd., April 15, 2010.

Processes: Still the poor relation in the knowledge management family?

4

J.S. Edwards

Aston Business School, Birmingham, United Kingdom

INTRODUCTION

Organizational success in knowledge management (KM) has two central elements: first of all, achieving success with a KM initiative, and second, sustaining it. The state of KM in the organization will only ever be as good as the most recent large-scale initiative. An organization can be good at KM for a time, and then its performance falls off either slightly or completely. There's nothing unusual about this in business. Potentially it applies to any aspect of business, even something as fundamental as competitive advantage. In the long term, the pressures of a changing environment can greatly affect even the most successful organizations, as witness the disappearance of famous names such as airline PanAm and (at least in the United Kingdom, United States, and Canada) retailer Woolworth's, and the struggles of those such as Kodak. Specifically in KM, for example, BP had a tremendous reputation from the late 1990s to the late 2000s (Collison and Parcell, 2004), but has fared badly since then.

As nobody's crystal ball is good enough to foresee long-term changes accurately, we will concentrate in this chapter on KM success and failure in terms of an initiative's initial implementation and its medium-term sustainability.

Defining what is success or failure can also raise issues. Szulanski, who devised the concept of sticky knowledge, gives an example of the answer depending upon whose perspective you take, in an interview with Claus Rerup (Rerup and Szulanski, 2004). His example is one of knowledge sharing as part of a transfer of a business process: a large bank installing its "best practice" process in a smaller bank that it had taken over. At the organizational level, it was a failure from the perspectives of both banks because of the time it took and the disruption it caused to other activities. However, from the perspectives of those transferring the practice and those installing the new computer system, it was a success, because once completed, it did work as planned. This seems to be a banking example of the old British medical saying "the operation was a success, but the patient died." Throughout this chapter we will take the organizational perspective, which will normally be judged on whether or not the KM initiative met its stated objectives.

A KM initiative requires consideration of people, technology, and processes, as we will explain in more detail later; many have argued that the first generation of KM was technology-based while the second was people-based. In the first decade of KM, it was often quoted that 50–70% of KM projects failed, though there seems to be no definite foundation for these figures. Schultze and Boland (2000) credit a figure of 30% implementation success to a report from the Standish Group. It is certainly the case that the Group's annual "Chaos" report typically finds a success rate for IT projects in general that varies by only a few percentage points around that figure. Whatever the precise value, there is no denying that implementing a KM initiative is difficult, and sometimes the technology is not up to the task. For example, Newell et al. (2001) report a KM project that failed because the intranet bandwidth in some locations simply was not sufficient, meaning that each page of a document took 20 s to load. However, most KM failures are not related to the technology (Alsadhan et al., 2008).

A theme of this chapter is that the relative neglect of process aspects is often the cause of the failure of a KM initiative. The following quote, taken from Mathieson (2015), sums this up well: "IT complements any good work you're doing. The IT won't help unless you've got a good process in place" (*Richard Venn, Western Sussex Hospitals NHS Foundation Trust*).

In the rest of the chapter, we will first present a little bit of theory about people, processes, and technology in knowledge management—especially about the processes and how the three elements link together. Then we will use that theory to understand the reasons for various failed KM initiatives and contrast them with more successful ones. Finally, we will speculate on emerging technologies and whether or not they will change the likelihood of successful KM initiatives.

PEOPLE, PROCESSES, AND TECHNOLOGY IN KNOWLEDGE MANAGEMENT

In any KM initiative, we encounter processes on two levels: the business processes and the knowledge processes (which naturally are themselves business processes) that support them. Starting with the knowledge processes, quite early in the history of KM Hendriks (2001) identified that knowledge processes specifically need different consideration from an organization's other business processes, especially where IT support is concerned. We will look at this in more detail when analyzing the examples. In a comprehensive survey of knowledge management frameworks, Heisig (2009) identified considerable consensus about the most common knowledge processes, even if not always about their names. He found the six most common knowledge processes to be:

- share knowledge
- create knowledge
- use knowledge

- store knowledge
- identify knowledge
- acquire knowledge

We can use these as a generic list of the knowledge processes that are most likely to be involved in any KM initiative.

Turning to the business processes, there is no great consensus about what the most common processes are. Indeed, this may not even be a sensible question to ask. Many advocates of a process approach, such as Beer (1985), propose methods for identifying the processes in a specific organization rather than prescribing what they should be in general. There are two noteworthy exceptions. The first is the value chain devised by Michael Porter (1985), which identifies what he calls the primary activities of an organization as inbound logistics, operations, outbound logistics, marketing and sales, and service. These match the top-level business processes well for an "old school" manufacturing organization, but in other sectors the fit becomes less suitable the further the business model diverges from the manufacturing one. The second comes from Wigand et al. (2003), who propose that all businesses can be viewed in terms of four standard processes, which they call offer (or customer-to-order); order (order-to-invoice); product development (idea-to-market); and customer service (failure-to-invoice). While these two contributions are a useful basis for thinking about competitive advantage and information systems design respectively, we have not found either of them to be detailed enough for KM purposes. Any business process is made up of subprocesses, which themselves are made up of further subprocesses. The number of top-level processes in an organization will nearly always be in single figures, perhaps as low as the four of Wigand et al. (2003), but generally we have found that a KM initiative involves working two levels down from the top-level processes, at a level where the whole organization has a few hundred business processes rather than four or five.

Whatever the business process(es) concerned, any KM initiative can be thought of as involving the implementation of some form of knowledge management system (KMS). There are two different views in the literature on what a KMS is, which we will call the narrow and broad views. The narrow view, epitomized by Alavi and Leidner (2001), identifies a KMS solely with information technology. The broad view, which we prefer, sees a KMS as comprising not just the technology, but also people and processes. This is consistent with the wider literature on the effect of technical change on organizations (eg, Leavitt, 1964). Indeed, a KMS may not include any information technology at all. Orzano et al. (2008), looking at family medical practices, found that "Social tools, such as face-to-face-communication for sharing and developing knowledge, were often more effective than were expensive technical tools such as an electronic medical record" (p. 21).

In order to fully understand a KM initiative, whether planning it beforehand or after the event, it is not enough just to think about people, processes, and technology individually. It is even more important to consider the links between them. Fig. 4.1, developed from a graphic we have been using for many years (Edwards, 2005a),

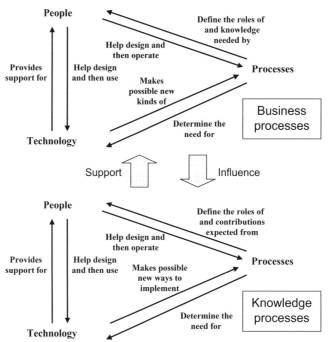

FIGURE 4.1 People, processes, and technology interacting at the business and knowledge levels

Modified from Edwards (2005a, 2015)

shows how these three facets link together for both business processes and knowledge processes.

ANALYZING EXAMPLES OF KM FAILURE AND SUCCESS
CONNECTIONS BETWEEN PEOPLE AND BUSINESS PROCESSES

We will use the structure of Fig. 4.1, especially the links represented by the arrows, to understand examples of successful and failed KM initiatives. Let us begin by describing two contrasting examples from our own experience (Edwards and Kidd, 2003). We disguise the company names for reasons of confidentiality, as will be the case for all the examples of failure in this chapter. The successful example was DeliverThem, a company specializing in magazine distribution to the retail trade; the unsuccessful one was MakeIt, a heavy engineering manufacturing organization.

DeliverThem based their KM initiative around particular business processes. Their first KM project stemmed from an initial interest in making better use of financial information. Initially, the main aim of the project itself was to design a new financial system, but this evolved rapidly into designing a financial systems strategy, and then more slowly into providing a suitable knowledge management infrastructure for not just this project, but further KM projects. The strong link to the business strategy and processes was facilitated by a general recognition within DeliverThem of the importance of knowledge. They were thus able to find knowledge champions and a groundswell of active support for the project. This contributed to them choosing technology for implementing the financial system on the basis of its scalability and additional functionality, and so it was not the technology that would have been chosen for that system in isolation.

MakeIt treated KM as a top-down initiative, with a "one size fits all" approach to the supporting technology. From their strategic perspective, KM was regarded as being solely an information systems issue, to be achieved by the appropriate installation of information technology, in this case a single system for the whole of a very large organization. Such an approach is not likely to produce an effective result for the "people help design and then use technology" link in Fig. 4.1, in contrast to the way that DeliverThem had approached a similar issue. Had MakeIt's top management looked more closely at the business processes, they would have realized that there were also major problems in the associated knowledge processes, especially in knowledge sharing. In one plant, for example, one shift had developed clearly superior operating practices, which the other two shifts working on the same process refused to adopt—an extreme variant of the "not invented here" syndrome. This is a failure of the "people help design and operate processes" link in Fig. 4.1 on both the business and knowledge levels.

A similar failure to that in MakeIt is examined by Scarbrough (2003) in a global bank that he calls Ebank. Ebank's top management decided that technology was the way to produce better knowledge sharing, but rather than involving end users, they simply brought together IT specialists from across the company. Naturally, they returned to their locations and units seeing this as entirely a technology issue, resulting in the development of more than 100 different systems that hardly anyone used even at the local level. Within one of the IT functions, for example, Scarbrough says that the only items shared were the company internal telephone directory and a timetable for the bus service between different company sites. Again, the "people help design and operate processes" link was missing.

Another failure along the same lines is described by Braganza and Mollenkramer (2002) at a pharmaceutical company they call PharmaCorp. In this case, the knowledge management initiative was actually part of a redesign of PharmaCorp's order-handling business process across its entire global operations, moving from country-specific to a focus on individual clients. The knowledge level focus was therefore definitely on the storage and use processes, and this part was executed well. Unfortunately, a key weakness was that PharmaCorp defined their "knowledge communities," their name for communities of practice (Lave and Wenger, 1991), within functions rather than in relation to business processes. Hence, people did not know what knowledge was needed more widely than within their own function. Both the "people help design and operate processes" and "processes define the roles of and knowledge needed by people" links were therefore weak.

A contrasting example of KM success, to show that it is possible to make the links between people and processes work well, is given by Pentland et al. (2014). They intervened in an organization in the health sector, where healthcare professionals were finding it problematic to acquire important new knowledge from published research. The situation was substantially improved by adopting a process-based approach to KM.

CONNECTIONS BETWEEN PEOPLE AND KNOWLEDGE PROCESSES

Our next example of KM failure comes from an oil company in Brazil, reported by Oliveira et al. (2005). The company had processes for sharing knowledge in place, but they were not effective. Knowledge about the drilling equipment acquired from operational activities was not shared with the part of the organization responsible for making strategic decisions about oil extraction, so that their capabilities and their plans did not entirely match. To address this, the company had to change the equipment design business process to include people from a wider range of departments. The fault had been not only in the old "silo" business process, but also in its supporting knowledge processes—the "processes define contributions expected from people" link for knowledge sharing and acquisition particularly.

A more subtle problem, arising from a KM intervention with the best of intentions, was one we found in a nonprofit distributing membership-owned research and development organization that we shall call R&D. R&D had developed an informal induction process in which each new member of staff was assisted by members of senior staff to learn how the organization worked. This was entirely voluntary for both parties and was proving an effective means of knowledge sharing and use. Management decided that it could be even better with some supporting technology and so added dedicated bulletin boards, mailing lists, etc. But this formalization eventually killed the process. Previously, it had been very clear to the new recruits that the senior staff members were doing this voluntarily, and the juniors responded enthusiastically as a result. Now, although it was still voluntary, it seemed to new staff to be just another part of all the company systems that they had to learn about. They became less committed to it, and naturally so did the senior staff, and gradually it died out. This example shows how tightly entwined the three corners of the triangles in Fig. 4.1 are at both levels. In this case, the business processes were acceptable, but for the knowledge processes, the extra technology (which did not involve the people in the design, though that is a small sin in this case as they were all familiar everyday software packages) caused subtle changes via the "processes define the roles of and contributions expected from people" link.

Again, a process-based approach can lead to a more successful KM outcome by helping to make sure that the "processes define the roles of and contributions expected from people" and "processes define the roles of and knowledge needed by people" links work effectively. Capo-Vicedo et al. (2011) give an example from the construction industry in Spain, involving a network of SMEs, and explaining through a network analysis how one "broker" SME ensured that these process definition links were effective.

CONNECTIONS BETWEEN BUSINESS PROCESSES
AND KNOWLEDGE PROCESSES

Sometimes the failures stem from the connections (or rather the lack of them) between the business and knowledge processes. McKinlay (2002) describes two different variations of this in a pharmaceutical company he calls WorldDrug (presumably not the same one as PharmaCorp!). The first was that the company had a well-developed lessons-learned process, called Lessons, which took place after each phase of every new drug development project. However, it was ineffective because there was no real attempt to compile the lessons at the corporate level. McKinlay explains that "for most staff 'Lessons' simply highlighted gaps in standard operating procedures," (p. 79) and that "For its designers and its participants, the objective of 'Lessons' was improved routinisation rather than innovation" (p. 80). This was a failure of the knowledge process to support the business process properly, so that WorldDrug ended up with an inappropriate knowledge process; it was a group-sharing activity, yes, but with the emphasis on identifying knowledge (that WorldDrug already had) rather than on knowledge creation (new ideas for the future).

The second was called Café, an attempt to reproduce the atmosphere of somewhere like Starbucks internally and online. Café worked technically, but was too unstructured and open-ended and restricted to a narrow group of staff who were regarded as innovators, and so delivered little. Here the emphasis was on knowledge creation, definitely, but the current business processes did not influence the knowledge process enough for the outcomes to be useful.

Kalling (2003) gives the example of a European manufacturing organization, anonymized as MNC. One of the unsuccessful KM projects was intended to share and improve knowledge about the performance of MNC's products. It was conceived as working in two phases. First, acquire knowledge from the downstream supply chain partners (direct customers, delivery warehouses, transport companies, end-consumers) for MNC's sales staff and designers. Then, on the basis of this, one of the overall objectives was "teaching customers how to use and transport the company's products" (p. 74). The first phase, not surprisingly, took a software-based codification approach, the knowledge processes being storage and use. However, the system was little used. Sales staff said that it merely supplied information that they already knew, and so they only used it effectively as a presentation tool the first time they saw a new customer. Interestingly, this lack of use was partly because of MNC's direct customers' reluctance to take notice of any end-consumer input into the system. The cause of failure here, then, was MNC's lack of understanding of its own cross-organizational order fulfillment business process. In the minds of the direct customers, the end-consumers had no connection to MNC except through them. It would of course be possible to change this, but that would be by negotiation with the direct customers, not by the implementation of a knowledge management system.

Another example of "getting the wrong knowledge process" comes from Storey and Barnett (2000). It concerns a "large, European-headquartered company" they call International Resources. Senior management wished to improve the company's capability in "learning to learn." Note that learning is not a specific knowledge process by itself; we will come back to this in a moment. This was to be achieved by the company-wide implementation of a number of communities of practice, each with a knowledge champion, supported by appropriate IT. Responsibility for delivering the KMS was "inexplicably," as Storey and Barnett highlight, split between two departments, IT and media affairs. Each had very different views on what the initiative was about. IT not surprisingly thought it was about codification, ie, knowledge storage and use. Media affairs thought it was about knowledge creation. During the delays in system development caused by the "tug of war" between these two departments, it also emerged that many parts of International Resources did not have a knowledge-sharing culture anyway. The final death-knell for the system was sounded by a turn-down in the company's business cycle, which led top management to concentrate on other projects rather than on clarifying this one. The key learning point for us here is that it is not enough to identify a business process as needing a knowledge management system. There also has to be agreement about the nature of the knowledge process support that is needed.

Fortunately, there are many published examples that show it is possible to connect the business processes and knowledge processes effectively: among them, Baloh et al. (2012) discuss effective and ineffective connections at Parsons Brinckerhoff, a US engineering company, and Samsung Electronics, headquartered in South Korea; while Oluikpe (2012) explains how KM was successfully embedded in the business processes at the Central Bank of Nigeria.

YOU CAN'T WIN THEM ALL!

We close this section with a cautionary tale from Hsiao et al. (2006) that demonstrates that for a KM initiative, even getting the process aspects right may not be enough. Hsiao et al. (2006) investigate an unsuccessful adoption of a knowledge-sharing system in a complex international supply chain. The names they used were SPEED Technologies for the US-based customer driving the supply chain KM project, and QUICKLY for one of its first tier suppliers. QUICKLY had its design engineers in Taiwan and a manufacturing plant in China. One of the reasons for the project was "inept" sharing of knowledge from Taiwan to China resulting in product quality problems at the manufacturing plant—a lack of absorptive capacity (Cohen and Levinthal, 1990). The proposed KMS was, sensibly, to be very much people-rather than technology-based, but the analysis by Hsiao et al. identified four issues that would be almost insuperable barriers to any KM initiative. All four are related to suspicion between the Taiwanese and Chinese parts of the workforce. First, with ineffective protection of intellectual property in China, the Taiwanese design engineers felt that sharing knowledge with the Chinese workforce greatly increased the risk of QUICKLY's knowledge leaking away to its competitors by "job-hopping": a Chinese worker who acquired the Taiwanese design-to-manufacturing knowledge could move to a competitor and achieve at least a 50% increase in salary. Second, if something went wrong when a modification was introduced, neither group wished to take responsibility for the problem and each blamed the other. Third, both groups actually perceived the lack of absorptive capacity of their counterparts. The design engineers thought the manufacturing staff had no framework to absorb their suggestions, while the manufacturing workers thought the knowledge of the design engineers was often impractical. Fourth, when the Taiwanese design engineers travelled to China, they were socially segregated, enjoying better conditions than the local Chinese workers. These four problems were so acute that the explicit incentives to share knowledge, which formed part of the KM initiative, were actually found to reinforce counterproductive behavior. It would clearly be a long haul just to create the conditions within QUICKLY in which a KM initiative might have any chance of success.

As for other barriers to implementing a KM initiative, a study we carried out some years ago (Edwards, 2005b) found that the two most common barriers were lack of time to spare from daily operations and the absence of a knowledge champion—someone to make sure that implementation happens at a local level. We also found that the knowledge process that was hardest to improve was, rather to our surprise, storing knowledge. This was because of the challenge of retaining the knowledge that staff who are leaving have in their heads. Our more recent experience is that these are still the three most problematic aspects of implementation, especially with the "baby boomer" generation in many Western countries reaching retirement age.

CONCLUSIONS: REFLECTIONS ON THE FUTURE

As we have seen, many failures in KM initiatives have resulted from insufficient or ineffective consideration of process aspects, involving either or both of the organization's business processes and the knowledge processes that support them. Nevertheless, some failures have resulted from failures of the technology in the KMS, and some organizations are simply not in a suitable state for any KM initiative to succeed.

In general terms, we think that the future will not be very different from the past. The main lesson is that *all* the elements and links in Fig. 4.1 are important to a KM initiative. New technologies such as intelligent agents and wearable devices offer new possibilities for both business processes and the supporting knowledge processes, but as the inexorable advance of smart phones and social media has shown, these present as many challenges as opportunities. The blurring of boundaries between the formal and informal that personal devices enable makes it especially important to think very carefully about all the business processes in an organization, not just the formal parts of them. Beer (1985) was perhaps the first to point this out.

As for knowledge processes, big data and analytics offer the prospect of better knowledge process support, especially for identifying knowledge and creating knowledge. Developments in visualization of data may prove to be the most significant here, but that may require a great deal of user education. After all, many people, especially in marketing, seem to love pie charts with a three-dimensional effect added, even though they have been shown to be misleading, since segments in the foreground of such a chart are perceived as larger than equally sized sectors in the background.

In summary, to make a KM initiative succeed, the people, process, and technology elements all need to go hand in hand, and then its effectiveness needs to be regularly reviewed in the light of the constantly changing business environment.

REFERENCES

Alavi, M., Leidner, D., 2001. Review: knowledge management and knowledge management systems: conceptual foundations and research issues. MIS Quarterly 25 (1), 107–136.

Alsadhan, A.O., Zairi, M., Keoy, K.H.A., 2008. From p economy to k economy: an empirical study on knowledge-based quality factors. Total Qual. Manag. Bus. 19 (7–8), 807–825.

Baloh, P., Desouza, K.C., Hackney, R., 2012. Contextualizing organizational interventions of knowledge management systems: a design science perspective. J. Am. Soc. Inf. Sci. Technol. 63 (5), 948–966.

Beer, S., 1985. Diagnosing the System for Organisations. Wiley, Chichester.

Braganza, A., Mollenkramer, G.J., 2002. Anatomy of a failed knowledge management initiative: lessons from PharmaCorp's experiences. Knowl. Process Manage. 9 (1), 23–33.

Capo-Vicedo, J., Mula, J., Capo, J., 2011. A social network-based organizational model for improving knowledge management in supply chains. Supply Chain Manag. 16 (5), 379–388.

Cohen, W.M., Levinthal, D.A., 1990. Absorptive capacity: a new perspective on learning and innovation. Adm. Sci. Q. 35 (1), 128–152.

Collison, C., Parcell, G., 2004. Learning to Fly: Practical Knowledge Management from Some of the World's Leading Organizations, second ed. Capstone, Chichester.

Edwards, J.S., 2005a. Business processes and knowledge management. Khosrow-Pour, M. (Ed.), Encyclopedia of information science and technology, vol. I, Idea Group, Hershey, PA, pp. 350–355.

Edwards, J.S., 2005b. Knowledge management strategy—what happened next? Paper presented at the 6th European Conference on Knowledge Management, Limerick, Ireland, September 8–9, 2005.

Edwards, J.S., 2015. Business processes and knowledge management. In: Khosrow-Pour, M. (Ed.), Encyclopedia of Information Science and Technology. third ed. Information Science Reference, Hershey, PA, pp. 4491–4498.

Edwards, J.S., Kidd, J.B., 2003. Knowledge management sans frontières. J. Oper. Res. Soc. 54 (2), 130–139.

Heisig, P., 2009. Harmonisation of knowledge management. J. Knowl. Manage. 13 (4), 4–31.

Hendriks, P.H.J., 2001. Many rivers to cross: from ICT to knowledge management systems. J. Inform. Technol. 16 (2), 57–72.

Hsiao, R.-L., Ho, A., Liu, C., 2006. To share or not to share: hidden agendas in knowledge sharing. Pacific Asia Conference on Information Systems 2006, Sections 1–8 (896–913). Available from: http://www.pacis-net.org/file/2006/1150.pdf.

Kalling, T., 2003. Knowledge management and the occasional links with performance. J. Knowl. Manage. 7 (3), 67–81.

Lave, J., Wenger, E.C., 1991. Situated Learning: Legitimate Peripheral Participation. Cambridge University Press, New York.

Leavitt, H.J., 1964. Applied organization change in industry: structural, technical and human approaches. In: Cooper, W.W., Leavitt, H.J., Shelly, M.W.I. (Eds.), New Perspectives in Organization Research. John Wiley, New York, pp. 55–71.

Mathieson, S.A., 2015. How can IT contribute to NHS efficiency? Computer Weekly. http://www.computerweekly.com/feature/How-can-IT-contribute-to-NHS-efficiency?utm_medium=EM&asrc=EM_MDN_48114930&utm_campaign=20150930_Spark%20user%20survey%20suggests%20growth%20beyond%20Hadoop_&utm_source=MDN

McKinlay, A., 2002. The limits of knowledge management. New Technology, Work and Employment 17 (2), 76–88.

Newell, S., Scarbrough, H., Swan, J., 2001. From global knowledge management to internal electronic fences: contradictory outcomes of intranet development. Brit. J. Manage. 12 (2), 97–111.

Oliveira, J., de Souza, J.M., Lima, M., Farias, R., 2005. GCE: knowledge management applied in a design reengineering process. In: Luo, Y. (Ed.), Cooperative Design, Visualization, and Engineering, Proceedings, vol. 3675. Springer-Verlag, Berlin, pp. 94–102, Lecture Notes in Computer Science.

Oluikpe, P., 2012. Developing a corporate knowledge management strategy. J. Knowl. Manage. 16 (6), 862–878.

Orzano, A.J., McInerney, C.R., Tallia, A.F., Scharf, D., Crabtree, B.F., 2008. Family medicine practice performance and knowledge management. Health Care Manage. Rev. 33 (1), 21–28.

Pentland, D., Forsyth, K., Maciver, D., Walsh, M., Murray, R., Irvine, L., 2014. Enabling integrated knowledge acquisition and management in health care teams. Knowl. Manage. Res. Pract. 12 (4), 362–374.

Porter, M., 1985. Competitive Advantage: Creating and Sustaining Superior Performance. Collier Macmillan, New York, London.

Rerup, C., Szulanski, G., 2004. Imperfection, transfer failure, and the replication of knowledge. J. Manage. Inq. 13 (2), 141–150.

Scarbrough, H., 2003. Knowledge management, HRM and the innovation process. Int. J. Manpow. 24 (5), 501–516.

Schultze, U., Boland, R.J., 2000. Knowledge management technology and the reproduction of knowledge work practices. J. Strategic Inf. Syst. 9 (2–3), 193–212.

Storey, J., Barnett, E., 2000. Knowledge management initiatives: learning from failure. J. Knowl. Manage. 4 (2), 145–156.

Wigand, R.T., Mertens, P., Bodendorf, F., König, W., Picot, A., Schumann, M., 2003. Introduction to Business Information Systems. Springer-Verlag, Berlin, Heidelberg, New York.

KM successes and failures: some personal reflections on major challenges

A.K.P. Wensley
University of Toronto-Mississauga, Mississauga, ON, Canada

INTRODUCTION

Rather than provide detailed case studies or more general analytic insights, this chapter provides me with the opportunity to look back over several decades and pull together insights about debates within knowledge management (KM). As both a KM researcher and an editor of a KM journal, I have had the opportunity to see many aspects of the theoretical and practical approaches to explore the varied terrain that is encompassed by the term knowledge management. In my opinion, this provides the opportunity to highlight potential challenges that may lead to success or failure of knowledge management initiatives. In general, we are really very much at the beginning of research into the domain of knowledge management.

In the context of this chapter, I would argue that careful consideration of issues that we have raised in the following pages leads one to identify sources of potential success or failure in the development and implementation of knowledge management initiatives. One overarching concern that we have relates to what might be considered to be knowledge management hubris. As many have argued (and amply demonstrated), knowledge management can and has been applied with success in many organizations. However, it is not a universal nostrum capable of curing all management ailments, and it may also not be generally applicable throughout the organization. In a related domain, that of information systems, although some grand, integrated systems have been successfully developed, many have failed spectacularly. For example, the expansive NHS information integration project in the United Kingdom failed at a cost of billions of pounds. Likely, there are similar cases of knowledge management initiatives (though perhaps not resulting in quite such extensive losses). It is my belief that those developing knowledge management applications should keep in mind the richness of knowledge present in many organizations and judiciously apply knowledge management initiatives.

Again, taking a leaf from insights derived from information systems research, there are numerous examples of failures that have resulted from a lack of attention to the need to demonstrate (and deliver) benefits to all potential users of systems.

As I have noted, the field of knowledge management has been around for some time. In the next section, I will review the evolution of the field and associated challenges.

EVOLUTION OF KNOWLEDGE MANAGEMENT

In some real sense, humans have been involved with knowledge management for millennia. In another sense, we may roughly date the current interest in knowledge management to the work of such researchers, culturally sensitive commentators, and authors such as Nonaka and Takeuchi (1995).

I tend to find somewhat tedious the endless discussions at the beginning of many knowledge management papers concerning the nature of knowledge. This is not simply because such discussions rarely add any value to the subsequent content of the paper, but more problematic is the fact that they often fail to adequately take into account a vast sea of prior research and thinking. Although an extensive review and understanding of this prior research is hardly necessary for providing an adequate foundation for knowledge management research and practice, it does provide a key to a variety of both theoretical and pragmatic challenges. In the following section, I would like to provide my own idiosyncratic review of some of these challenges. My own background spans an extensive education in philosophy and science, and a lifelong interest in the history and philosophy of science, which explains, to some extent, the range of challenges we explore.

PROBLEMS WITH THE NATURE OF KNOWLEDGE

I remember chuckling when one of the leaders of knowledge management–thinking attributed the characterization of knowledge as "justified, true belief" to Nonaka rather than its true author Plato. Although later acknowledged to be an error, it does point to some of the problems faced by researchers in knowledge management. The very "stuff" of their discipline has been researched from a wide variety of different perspectives for many centuries. Early research was distinctly abstract and philosophical. More recently, philosophy of science and philosophy has engaged in an instrumental turn, seeing knowledge, in part, as that which leads to appropriate action.

There is a need to link knowledge management research to a more grounded scientific tradition, though with care, because the management of enterprises is not essentially a scientific exercise. It is, at best, a pragmatic activity. Knowledge needs to be appropriately actionable. However, there are no grand theories, no central paradigms. We often seem to talk as if there are, but such talk is not to be taken at face value. I would suggest that, at the very least, a review of the seminal works of Popper (2002).

A failure to adequately grasp the nature of knowledge reverberates through subsequent challenges in developing and implementing knowledge management processes and systems. For example, considering knowledge as relatively invariant may lead to systems and processes that are insufficiently flexible to change. In addition, systems that fail to take into account the status of knowledge—tentative, well grounded, uncertain, etc., will likely be both incomplete and unreliable.

Let me highlight a related issue at this point. Without memory, there is no mechanism to bring knowledge to the point of decision or action. However, if memory is not dynamic then there is a danger that decisions or actions become inappropriate, as memory is not modified to reflect the changing status of knowledge. One of the areas where this is a potentially serious problem is in large, comprehensive, enterprise resource planning (ERP) systems that are designed to represent initially firms and increasingly supply networks in all their richness. Once knowledge is embedded in such systems it is extremely difficult to locate and even more difficult to modify (Wensley and van Stijn, 2006). Essentially, a significant component of organizational memory is fixed. Furthermore, in an echo of problems that are likely to arise with big data (discussed later), the sheer magnitude of available memories (data) may make action difficult to specify.

A further aspect of knowledge is the extent to which it is both distributed and social. One interesting feature of this distribution of knowledge is the importance of group knowledge and transactive memory (Lewis and Herndon, 2011) as a way of binding groups together. Integral to the notion of the social dimension of knowledge are such issues as the context of knowledge—this issue reverberates throughout this chapter.

FAMILIAR CHALLENGES IN KNOWLEDGE ELICITATION

Many disciplines provide tools for knowledge elicitation, though they may not use this terminology. Clearly failures in knowledge management may arise because the approach to knowledge elicitation results in incorrect, incoherent, or incomplete knowledge. It is also worth noting that there is a tendency of individuals to "fit" their knowledge to the representation tools available. Again, such a mismatch is likely to result in significant challenges and potential knowledge management process and systems failures. There may be a variety of causes of incompleteness of a knowledge base once elicitation has taken place. Knowledge may be incomplete because an inappropriate representation has been chosen. In my own research into accounting knowledge, the user of a representation based on first order predicate logic (FOPL) was inappropriate due to the fact that much of the knowledge, although temptingly expressed in logical form, required considerable contextual knowledge to be captured along with the "logical" knowledge (Boritz and Wensley, 1995). Furthermore, the knowledge may be incomplete because some knowledge may be unrepresentable for a number of reasons, most commonly because some knowledge is not available to conscious inquiry. The term "tacit" knowledge has been used in this context, though rarely has sufficient diligence been applied to its correct use (see, for a thoughtful consideration of many aspects of knowledge and organizational knowledge, Tsoukas, 2005).

Much work was done in the 1980s and 1990s with respect to knowledge elicitation through the development of various approaches. Some of this work has been essentially replaced by machine learning though there is still considerable scope for further research. An interesting set of questions arise with the work relating to situations where we either believe that we know something (or the structure of something) when we actually do not know it or are not able to articulate the basis for judgments that we make.

STUDIES IN THE NATURE OF EXPERTISE AND JUDGMENT

Beginning with the work of Newell and Simon, there is a long history of research into human decision making and the nature of expertise. Although expertise may generally be considered to be knowledge-based, it is not necessarily the case that all knowledge-based performance is in the area of expertise. Indeed, we may consider that one of the great advances of the last 20 years has been to create very competent behavior based on the gathering and processing of appropriate knowledge.

CHALLENGES IN KNOWLEDGE REPRESENTATION

As we have begun to note, much work has been done with respect to knowledge representation, most particularly in the field of artificial intelligence. However, many knowledge-based disciplines have developed knowledge representation tools. Likely, we have been too restricted in the types of knowledge representation that we have utilized. One interesting aspect of knowledge representation is the representation of uncertainty. Although an area of active research in artificial intelligence, this is an area that has been scarcely touched by researchers in knowledge management. I particularly invite readers to explore approaches such as fuzzy set/belief theory (Zadeh, 1986). Furthermore, the representation of causal relations has also received a considerable boost as a result of the widespread application of QCA analysis (Ragin, 1998).

WHAT WE KNOW AND DO NOT KNOW

One of the problems that I have addressed in my research relates to the need to constantly review what we know and the status of that knowledge within the organization. This is critical for a number of reasons. In the first place, as we have noted previously, knowledge is likely to be of a variety of different "statuses." It will have characteristics relating to its provenance, reliability, and warrant that will influence how it may be used, modified, and so on. Failure to appreciate these characteristics is likely to cause significant challenges with respect to organizational decision-making, and the design, implementation, and maintenance of processes. Such challenges likely will result in reduced efficiency, effectiveness, and even impact such organizational characteristics as reputation, cohesiveness, and stability/adaptability.

I have already touched on the importance of creating a dynamic memory within an organization and the problems associated with increasingly embedding knowledge in complex information systems. It is interesting to speculate how new theories from cognitive science might inform us concerning the creation of knowledge-intensive organizations. Of particular interest is the work of Clark (2016). If Clark's cognitive theories are correct, how can we use them to design/redesign organizations to be appropriately adaptive?

PROBLEM OF BIG DATA AND MACHINE LEARNING

One of the interesting challenges going forward is how to integrate the outcomes of machine learning and human learning into an overall knowledge management process. In the past, as indicated earlier, we have been primarily concerned with finding ways of identifying human knowledge, representing it in some appropriate manner, and sharing and utilizing it. This has involved developing techniques for helping individuals articulate their knowledge. This, in itself, has been challenging and often frustrating. As I have noted, it has also involved important issues with respect to the context within which knowledge is used, combining different items of knowledge that, while not in conflict, are somewhat incoherent, and, perhaps most challenging of all, establishing the status of knowledge.

One of the key issues that rears its head when we study the manner in which human beings "learn" is the importance of what has become known as "tacit" knowledge in some domains. Over the history of research into knowledge management, the distinction between tacit and explicit knowledge has probably caused more confusion than any other. It is also relevant to a discussion relating to big data and machine learning in that these approaches lead to systems acting on what may be termed structural or embedded knowledge.

Machine-learning research became popular in the 1970s and early 1980s but fell somewhat into a relatively fallow period until Moore's Law saw dramatic expansions on raw computing power, allowing vastly superior computing power to become available at drastically reduced cost. In parallel (literally), new approaches to programming bring new vigor to machine-learning research (Domingos, 2015; LeCun et al., 2015).

To the extent that machine learning bootstraps itself, human beings may well, in principle, not be able to comprehend the nature of the knowledge that has been identified and embedded by the machine learning algorithm. In this context, knowledge management becomes essentially an automatic procedure. It is interesting to review recent cognitive science research in this area (again, Clark, 2016, is a useful source).

KNOWLEDGE, KNOWLEDGE MANAGEMENT, AND CULTURE

It is by no means original to suggest that it is important to be aware of the larger context within which knowledge is elicited and managed. One aspect of this larger environment relates to the culture of the organization. To what extent are there conditions within the organization that favor the creation and sharing of knowledge? For example, it is clearly critical for organizations to have a firm hold on the relevant levers of knowledge creation particularly if they are in knowledge-intensive domains. It is likely that the levers will be somewhat contingent on particular aspects of the knowledge culture and the organization. What is intriguing are the organizations that are comprised of what we might call "mixed epistemic cultures." It would be worthwhile to review the work of Knorr Cetina (1999) in this context, as she provides various studies of different "epistemic cultures" that are both rich and nuanced.

It would seem to be the case that there are many organizations in which different parts of the organization essentially view knowledge in different ways (perhaps all organizations are actually like this?). Obvious examples of these types of organization are scientifically intensive organizations, such as pharmaceutical companies, where knowledge creation primarily involves the scientific domain. This will tend to mean that the dominant "model" of knowledge is scientific, and the approach to knowledge management is a scientific one.

However, this does not mean that such a science-based approach to knowledge and knowledge management is appropriate throughout the organization. The challenges involve how to integrate the different approaches to knowledge within the organization and how to provide for the translation of one form of knowledge into another. It is no surprise that, particularly in the medical field, the teaching and the study of "knowledge translation" has become increasingly important. One interesting aspect relating to the management of knowledge in this context relates to the adoption of open innovation models. For example, a number of major pharmaceutical firms have made major portions of their compound databases "open source" (with a variety of restrictions). It is likely that this policy would not be applicable to much of the other knowledge created and managed by these corporations and, in order to preserve the value of these other types of knowledge, employees will have to be able to negotiate and manage a variety of different knowledge cultures. It would also be interesting to explore the implications of the interactions between fundamentally different knowledge management policies in these organizations on the development and implementation (and subsequent success or failure) of knowledge management initiatives.

If we then look to the broader environment within which an organization operates, we will again find richness in terms of knowledge cultures. For example, as in the case of the pharmaceutical companies, employees may engage in knowledge cultures that recognize other boundaries than strictly organizational boundaries. In addition, regulatory agencies may play a significant role in establishing the nature and value of the knowledge possessed by the organization. For example, one only needs to be aware of insider trading laws in various countries and the importance of privacy with respect to personal information to recognize that organizations may possess knowledge that is potentially very valuable if used in inappropriate ways. Certainly there are instances where it is vitally important to review existing procedures relating to the use and combination of knowledge within the organization to determine whether appropriate policies are being adopted and constantly monitor changes in regulation and performance.

In an even broader context, any organization exists within what we might term a "dominant culture." We might consider this to be a national culture, as many studies have investigated. There are significant concerns as to the importance and salience of studies relating aspects of national culture to knowledge and knowledge management practices and the success or failure of such practices. On the surface, it would seem that there would be correlations between, say, the extent of trust within a culture and, for example, knowledge-sharing behaviors. However, one of the concerns is with respect to the level of generality and vagueness that exists with these broad cultural factors and, additionally, the extent to which they may or may not have any influence at the organizational level. There is ample opportunity for meticulous empirical research in this area to tease out the fine strands of influence. Much of the existing research has been too coarse-grained. It has tried to establish broad propositions with respect to the dominance of some national cultures with respect to the success or otherwise of knowledge management initiatives.

I have mentioned in the previously the notion of trust and related it to knowledge sharing *en passant*. In the following section, I would like to investigate some more specific reflections on the relationship between trust and knowledge sharing.

IMPORTANCE OF TRUST AND THE SHARING OF KNOWLEDGE

There have been a wide variety of investigations into the impact of trust on the various stages of knowledge management, most particularly knowledge sharing and utilization. These studies offer interesting insights into the nature of these knowledge management processes and also the organizational structures that are necessary to support both the individual knowledge processes and the overall knowledge management initiatives. I would particularly direct readers to Evans's work in a legal context (reported in Evans and Wensley, 2009). Evans's work is a careful, nuanced example of fine-detail empirical work that seeks to understand knowledge sharing at a project-based level.

As we increasingly construct fragmented and virtual organizations, issues concerning the fragmentation of business rear their head. This is even more so in the case of outsourcing. Trust is clearly one aspect of these challenges. Other challenges relate to the ownership of knowledge, the maintenance of knowledge, and, generally, all aspects relating to knowledge management. Referring back to an earlier discussion, clearly the pharmaceutical industry has developed trust-based relationships with academic researchers (and others) that would be interesting to investigate in detail to determine how generally applicable they may be and to what extent they rely on an underlying legal structure.

Another related perspective is that a great deal of knowledge within an organization is in digital form, and thus research and practice relating to the management of digital assets may be relevant.

DIGITAL ASSET MANAGEMENT

There is considerable scope for applying digital asset management (DAM) techniques in the context of knowledge management and knowledge processes. For example, knowledge assets can be provided with a "best before" date; the system will flag the need to review and potentially update them. There will also be a need to identify where new knowledge impacts existing knowledge and, for example, where the deletion of existing knowledge requires the modification of other knowledge. Likely the adoption of a life cycle approach to the management of knowledge assets would be beneficial and reduce subsequent knowledge management process failures.

Much that has been written and researched about digital asset management has focused on graphical and software objects. There is clearly a significant opportunity to expand this research into the knowledge management field. It is further interesting to observe that the management of digital archives may provide insights that are relevant to knowledge management as well.

We have noted previously that there may sometimes be too much emphasis on eliciting and representing knowledge and too little on the need to forget in an organizational setting. We return to this issue later.

IMPORTANCE OF FORGETTING

There has been considerable recent research into how organizations can create an environment that is supportive of forgetting (Cegarra-Navarro and Sanchez-Polo, 2007). What are the indicators of an organizations failure to forget? One such indicator is likely to be engaging in inappropriate actions. Of course, there may be many reasons for such failures. Knowledge obsolescence failures may be difficult to tease out of complex interactions between processes and routines. When processes fail is it because of the inappropriate design of processes, or because of the knowledge embedded in the process or the knowledge necessary for interacting with the process? These are fertile areas to study.

Even when we have identified items that need to be forgotten it is important to observe that it is both difficult to forget as an individual and also as an organization. Failure to respond to this challenge may lead to inappropriate actions or decisions when new routines/processes are implemented, but the employees do not "forget" earlier processes and knowledge. Often this failure to forget is not appreciated by the organization. Training may involve essentially rote learning of new processes and ignore "work-arounds" that employees use to ensure actions or decisions that are consistent with old, obsolete knowledge. Thus, we need to engage in significantly more research into organizational learning AND unlearning. As we have noted previously, the creation of a dynamic, responsive approach to knowledge management and organizations becomes paramount. Failure to do so may result in the creation of knowledge management initiatives that appear to be successful in the short term but end up as being disastrously opaque and inflexible.

This area is very challenging and in need of considerable research. Clearly most organizations limit their approach to knowledge revision out of necessity. As we have noted, typically revisions will take place when some failure has occurred—some process has failed or, perhaps, it is obvious that knowledge is missing. However, in some cases this may be inappropriate; there is a need to make every effort to be preemptive. The increasing use of simulation may help here as we have the opportunity to investigate possible futures and ask questions about seemingly counter-intuitive results. We would also note that some interesting ties may be established between ways of creating organizational cultures that support innovation and those that encourage unlearning. There are tantalizing links between the view that innovation involves breaking rules and going against established procedures and the need to actively unlearn.

I have noted earlier that much of the embedded knowledge in organizations is represented by organizational routines. It is important to recognize the nature of these routines and understand the ways they may dynamically change and may be actively changed. Of particular relevance in this case is the extensive research literature on organizational routines (Becker, 2003).

SUPPORT AND CHANGING OF ROUTINES

A fundamental infrastructure component of organizations are organizational routines. These routines are developed in a particular organizational context and allow the efficient response of organizations to their environment. Essentially such routines are the "normal operating procedures" that gather and respond to information available from the external and internal environments. These routines often embed significant knowledge of an organization, its products, stakeholders, customers, and associated institutions. One of the problems associated with these routines is that the embedded knowledge is deeply embedded. It may be difficult to identify this embedded knowledge. In a discrete sense, it is like the knowledge embedded in software; typically the comments embedded with the software only tell part of the story. This is particularly likely in situations where the software team is more focused on the software rather than providing appropriate explanations for the design and structure of the software in the comments.

Consider, for example, a situation where a different organizational routine is invoked when the volume of a product exceeds a certain level. Why has a particular level been considered? It may be that the production technology results in a step change with respect to the costs of production, that the associated financing costs experience a step change at this level, or many other explanations relating to the broader characteristics of the environment within which the organization operates. It is clearly important that some attempt is made to articulate this embedded knowledge. Furthermore, when a routine is changed it is necessary to explore in detail changes in the knowledge that is required to perform the routine and ensure that individuals interacting with the routine have this knowledge. An interesting example occurred in my own research when a relatively simple change to a routine led to problems as a result of the accuracy of the data being entered and NOT any change in the data itself. The employees needed to be provided with an explanation about why improved accuracy was important and about the implications of failure to provide appropriate accuracy. To presage a later topic, the value of relatively inaccurate data had dropped to zero (if not a negative value) on the implementation of the new routine!

Another reason why knowledge management initiatives may fail is that knowledge may be lost, either, as we have noted, in the creation or modification of the existing system or because of a component of the system—often a human component has left the organization. In these instances, it may be necessary to actively recapture knowledge to ensure future knowledge management success.

RECAPTURING KNOWLEDGE

How does one relearn once one has forgotten? There is a need to put in place structures and processes for such relearning. However, we also need to think about the nature of such structures and processes. Clearly they will be integrated with processes related to knowledge revision in general and processes related to establishing knowledge inventories as well. As we have already noted earlier, one interesting insight is the familiar adage that knowledge exists in context. For example, much of the knowledge associated with the creation and maintenance of atomic weapons has been lost and is difficult to recreate. This is of particular concern when one thinks of the thousands of nuclear warheads that are desperately in need of maintenance. How does one recreate such knowledge when the original processes on which such knowledge was built are no longer implementable since the weapons concerned may no longer be manufactured?

The study of approaches to recapturing knowledge are potentially fascinating as they allow us to explore such phenomena as "path dependency." How did we initially learn to incorporate knowledge into our actions and decisions? As the context changes, technology changes and likely the tools for knowledge representation and access change. How does it change the way we learn and what we learn? These changes, in turn, will likely alter the way in which we interact with knowledge-intensive processes. As a tantalizing indicator of what may be going on in these situations there is considerable interest as to why children's IQ scores have consistently risen over the decades. One simple explanation is that children are simply better at taking IQ tests, but why? Well it may be that they now have at their fingertips more extensive embedded knowledge. Again, there is a need to focus on the dynamic nature of knowledge when we design and implement knowledge management initiatives and policies.

We have noted previously that changes in the context within which knowledge management systems (or knowledge management policies) operate may well alter the value of the system and the value of the knowledge represented by the system. It is clearly important to grasp some of the parameters that determine these values.

In addition, when we are trying to justify investments in knowledge management initiatives, some attempt must be made to identify the benefits of the system. In the next section we consider, briefly, the value of knowledge.

VALUE OF KNOWLEDGE

There is a distinct set of problems with respect to knowledge valuation. This is a vital point with respect to assessing investment in knowledge and knowledge processes. It is very challenging to make these assessments as it may well be difficult to identify the precise cash flows that may be associated with specific knowledge. Indeed, in many cases the valuation of specific items of knowledge is simply not possible for a number of reasons. In the first place, a specific item of knowledge may have completely undetermined value by itself. In its simplest sense, knowledge has value in terms of outcomes that may be associated with that knowledge. Given that knowledge derives much of its value in context it may be difficult to determine value without considering all the other knowledge that is necessary to possess such that some outcome is achievable. Furthermore, as we have noted in other cases, changes in context may lead to radical changes in value. For example, prior to the much heralded Year 2000 problem, knowledge of such obsolete computer languages as FORTRAN and COBOL became very valuable for a short period of time. Following the rewriting of many core information systems such knowledge again lost its value. Furthermore the value of the knowledge embedded in the core systems no longer depended on the possession of FORTRAN or COBOL knowledge. It is interesting to note that although knowledge plays an increasingly central role in current economic thinking, there is a relative paucity of research as to the nature of this value and its determinants.

In specific cases, some knowledge may lead to a variety of options. In this case, valuation of such knowledge likely will require the application of option theory. In other cases, it may be relatively easy to quantify the instrumental value of knowledge.

One other interesting avenue for future research involves attempts to address some of the legal aspects of knowledge and its protection. In the last two decades, there has been increasing focus by companies on the various legal strategies that may be adopted to protect some knowledge assets.

KNOWLEDGE PROCESSES

Rarely do we design knowledge processes from the ground up. Typically some processes (both knowledge processes and otherwise) are redesigned and others left in place. This is likely a recipe for at worst failure and at best likely inefficiency. There is a need, as indicated previously, to design and implement knowledge processes to ensure that they are integrated with existing organizational processes. This requires ensuring that appropriate knowledge is provided to support decisions and actions within the organization and that participants in the processes possess appropriate knowledge to act accordingly.

CONCLUSIONS

At the beginning of this chapter, I promised a more conceptual discussion of potential success and failure of knowledge management initiatives. The focus has been on areas that involve significant challenges to the development and implementation of knowledge management initiatives. Failure to address these challenges is likely to lead to an increased risk of failure. However, some of the challenges we have identified are just that, challenges. There is a need to conduct research to identify appropriate approaches to address them and hence, hopefully, eliminate or at least reduce other potential sources of failure.

REFERENCES

Becker, M.C., 2003. The Concept of Routines Twenty Years after Nelson and Winter (1982): A Review of the Literature. DRUID Working Paper No 03-06. Available from: http://www3.druid.dk/wp/20030006.pdf

Boritz, J.E., Wensley, A.K.P., 1995. CAPEX: A Knowledge-Based Expert System for Substantative Audit Planning. Sage Publishing, London.

Cegarra-Navarro, J.G., Sanchez-Polo, M.T., 2007. Linking unlearning and relational capital through organisational relearning. Int. J. Hum. Res. Dev. Manage. 7 (1), 37–52.

Clark, A., 2016. Surfing Uncertainty: Prediction, Action, and the Embodied Mind. Oxford University Press, Oxford.

Domingos, P., 2015. The Master Algorithm. Basic Books, New York.

Evans, M.M., Wensley, A.K.P., 2009. Predicting the influence of network structure on trust in knowledge communities: addressing the interconnectedness of four network principles and trust. Electron. J. Knowl. Manage. 7 (1), 41–54.

Knorr Cetina, K., 1999. Epistemic Cultures: How the Sciences Make Knowledge. Harvard University Press, Cambridge, MA.

LeCun, Y., Bengio, Y., Hinton, G.E., 2015. Deep learning. Nature 521, 436–444.

Lewis, K., Herndon, B., 2011. Transactive memory systems: current issues and future research directions. Org. Sci. 22 (5), 1254–1265.

Nonaka, I., Takeuchi, H., 1995. The Knowledge Creating Company: How Japanese Companies Create the Dynamics of Innovation. Oxford University Press, New York.

Popper, K.R., 2002. Conjectures and Refutations, second ed. Routledge, London.

Ragin, C.C., 1998. The logic of quantitative comparative analysis. Int. Rev. Soc. Hist. 43 (6), 105–124.

Tsoukas, H., 2005. Complex Knowledge. Oxford University Press, Oxford.

Wensley, A., van Stijn, E., 2006. Enterprise information systems and the preservation of agility. In: Desouza, K. (Ed.), Agile Information Systems: Conceptualization, Construction, and Management. Butterworth-Heinemann, London, pp. 178–187.

Zadeh, L., 1986. A simple view of the Dempster–Shafer theory of evidence and its implication for the rule of combination. AI Mag. 7 (2), 85–90.

Lessons learned from nearly 200 cases of KM journeys by Hong Kong and Asian Enterprises

E. Tsui

Knowledge Management and Innovation Research Centre (KMIRC),
The Hong Kong Polytechnic University, Hong Kong, China

INTRODUCTION TO THE NATURE OF THE KNOWLEDGE MANAGEMENT INITIATIVE AND ITS SPECIFIC OBJECTIVES

The Knowledge Management and Innovation Research Centre (KMIRC) of The Hong Kong Polytechnic University has firmly established itself as one of the principal knowledge management (KM) and intellectual capital (IC) consultancy and training service providers in Hong Kong and in Asia. Responding to an insatiable demand over the last decade for KM training and consultancy services, KMIRC has played a pivotal role in many KM projects (of which many have evolved into fully-fledged programs) in the private sector, nonprofit social services organizations, and government departments. Through expert advisory and in many cases direct involvement, KMIRC has helped numerous organizations/companies to launch various KM projects, many of which have also taken on our students as interns or even taken on our graduates to become members of their KM team. Over the years, close to 200 company-based senior undergraduate, research, and consultancy projects have been carried out. The objectives of the Centre's work are to

1. Raise the awareness and the importance of managing knowledge at the individual, organizational, and societal levels.
2. Assist government departments, private organizations, and nongovernment organizations (NGOs) to introduce and permeate various KM tactics/tools in daily operations to support knowledge-intensive business activities.
3. Perform benchmarking among comparable organizations and industries to gauge the adoption, maturity, and effectiveness of KM; identify good practices; and derive lessons learned to enhance continuous improvement.
4. Provide platforms for effective and regular dissemination of KM trends, good practices, lessons learned, and newly developed tools and techniques among

KM researchers and practitioners. Typically, this is being done via seminars, conferences, workshops, webinars, and site visits, supplemented by an online repository and various social media channels.

On the type of project, they range from KM readiness assessment, knowledge audit, strategy formulation, taxonomy design and maintenance, cultural assessment and organizational change, knowledge retention from near-retirees, knowledge-enabled business process management, requirement elicitation and selection of collaboration tools including portals, search engine assessment, configuration and continuous improvement, intellectual capital (IC) reporting, and many more. Through implementing custom-developed solutions recommended by the KMIRC, the involved organizations have harnessed and benefited from sharing of good practices; minimized reinventing the wheel; cultivated new forms of collaborations; enhanced enterprise-wide awareness of information and knowledge; expedited the timely and proactive delivery of relevant information to staff, customers, and consumers; and realized process and productivity enhancements.

THE INFRASTRUCTURE—PEOPLE, SYSTEMS, HARDWARE, SOFTWARE, ETC.—REQUIRED TO LAUNCH THE INITIATIVE

As mentioned previously, KM initiatives and projects that have been introduced by KMIRC for organizations are wide-ranging. For example, common people and process-oriented KM initiatives include:

- cultural and readiness assessment
- formulation of a KM strategy, framework, & strategic planning
- knowledge audit and knowledge management audit
- change management
- KM assessment including the definition of metrics and reporting of intellectual capital (IC)
- community of practices/special interest groups (SIG)

On the other hand, examples of technology-oriented KM projects include:

- search engine configuration, testing, and deployment
- taxonomy development, maintenance, and governance
- collaboration system(s)
- enterprise portal
- electronic document management system (EDMS)
- knowledge/information repositories
- content management system (CMS) and applications (CMA)
- E-learning
- intelligent system(s)
- blogging/weblogs/RSS readers/wikis

Through our work, the involved organizations learned that rarely a KM project is entirely technical or entirely people/process-oriented. In fact, more likely than not, it is an appropriate combination of the aforementioned two categories of KM initiatives/systems plus good content management, which together form the basis of a KM foundation for an organization. Second, KMIRC has also, through a series of carefully devised deployments, demonstrated to organizations that it is highly preferable to commence a KM initiative on a small scale involving business input (eg, a pilot), then reflect, modify, and scale up and/or expand gradually. During the course of the journey, there is often the need for organizations to assess and reformulate the knowledge strategy, to review progress and identify knowledge gaps, to reassess critical knowledge and flow via knowledge audit and social network analysis, respectively, for example. Through these efforts and more, participating organizations truly realize that KM as a journey needs to start with a solid foundation/base and evolve from there with ongoing nurture and support; it should never be viewed/treated as a project (see Fig. 6.1).

We are proud to report that all of our client organizations are continuing with their KM journey ever since the KMIRC introduced and helped them to kick start their journey. Some organizations regularly seek advice from KMIRC at different stages of their KM journey. A third point to note is that KMIRC has also helped to correct many myths about KM, including the idea that "KM often needs big investments;" indeed it is possible to start with a "0 budget KM" journey. Many organizations asked if they need to set aside a large sum of investments (primarily for IT systems/tools) in

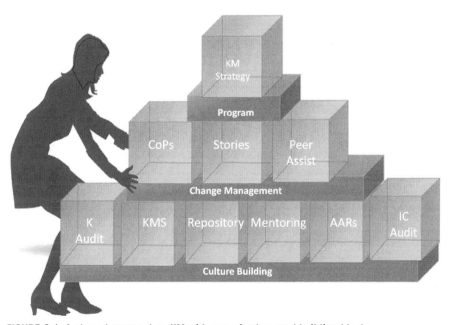

FIGURE 6.1 A phased approach to KM with some fundamental building blocks

FIGURE 6.2 Storytelling team at the Hong Kong police

order to start their KM journey. KMIRC has demonstrated convincingly that there is no need to do so. For example, at the Hong Kong police where KMIRC staff trained the force with the technique of storytelling (Fig. 6.2), storytelling sessions are being held regularly among police officers to share knowledge and experience. At the Department of Health, another client of the KMIRC, a standard template for documenting meeting minutes incorporating a section to record any lessons learned since the date of the last meeting is routinely being used. Both of the aforementioned demonstrated KM techniques/processes can be permeated into existing daily operations and no separate/additional investments on IT is needed.

On resourcing, KMIRC only has one full-time KM specialist in the team. In all of our projects, we always stress and routinize knowledge transfer with the client. We demand the client to assign resources to work and colearn together with us; we codevelop and practice the techniques with them; and operate with an aim that the organization can plot its own KM course in the medium to long term.

THE CHALLENGES THAT WERE ENCOUNTERED, HOW THEY DEVELOPED, AND HOW THEY WERE OVERCOME

Many challenges had been encountered and overcome among our 200 or so projects. Many of them are common difficulties that have been reported by Western organizations adopting KM. For example, they include difficulty in measuring return on investments, lack of skills and resources to carry out KM projects, how to validate and ensure the quality of the harnessed knowledge, fear of not being able to sustain the

KM journey, etc., but some (eg, power-distance culture, groupthink, bias on reliance on people/process over technology, etc.) tend to be more specific challenges rooted in the Asian culture.

Obviously it is impossible to list all the challenges that we have confronted after 200 or so projects, but nevertheless I have singled out some in the following table for further discussion.

Challenge	Solution(s)
The business–IT divide leads to insufficient end-users and subject matter experts' (SMEs) input	Create joint teams, group together stakeholders from different departments in a KM project, avoid any single department to be the sole "owner" of a project. Rotate members and expand teams when opportunity exists
Technology is adopted before a strategy has been created, eg, a KM system is installed but it was later found out to be misaligned with user's needs	Insist on the formulation of a KM strategy at the early part of the journey. While not always necessary, a knowledge audit may be carried out to identify the critical knowledge, the knowledge gap, type of knowledge, and the people who create and use this knowledge. Having such information greatly enhances the alignment of any KM tools with user needs. Manage the client's expectation that the strategy and the audit may need to be carried out routinely; they are not a one-off activity
Over-emphasis on KM systems (ie, the containers), insufficient focus on the knowledge content	Conduct knowledge audit; some knowledge may not be migrated to the new system. Identify critical knowledge assets and develop taxonomies to help categorize the assets in the KM systems
KM is treated/viewed as a project	Demonstrate and convince senior management that recurrent funding is important to support the KM journey as there are on-going needs (eg, change in external/internal environment) to maintain the taxonomy, content, systems, user learning of new techniques, etc.
Poor configuration of the search engine and lack of user training leads to the under-exploitation of a high-power enterprise search engine that has been deployed	This is a common problem across many projects. Insist on having regular business input in the configuration, tuning, and testing of the search engine; review search engine log to identify improvement areas and set up a governance model to gather feedback, identify, and act on improvements on a regular basis. Publishing of usage tips and conduct of user training can also help to raise awareness and usage of high-power search engine
Doing KM for the sake of KM	Some clients rush into a KM journey because they were somehow "told" to do KM. This is wrong. In these cases, we performed readiness assessment and if there is a strong resentment to adopt KM (for whatever reason), we actually recommended them NOT to proceed with a KM project/journey but to first focus on raising awareness and a change program. It is important to cultivate and gain grassroots support, among other things, to enhance the chance of success of a KM journey

Challenge	Solution(s)
Skepticism about how to monitor and govern the use of Web 2.0 tools for bottom-up knowledge sharing	Advised organizations to adopt wiki and RSS (rather than blogs) for trials inside the organization. Wikis are used to foster interdepartmental collaboration on compiling complex, decentralized documents, for example. RSS is adopted to keep up information awareness on specific topics; feeds are calibrated to deliver new and relevant information to individuals, teams, groups, and the entire organization, usually via the Enterprise Knowledge Portal. As these two types of Web 2.0 tools can be easily aligned to support collaborative work and learning (and information awareness), they are seen as easy entry points for introducing Web 2.0 into the workplace. Once knowledge and confidence are gained, other Web 2.0 tools can be explored for adoption
Capture and share tacit knowledge in processes	With input from the business and IT departments, KMIRC has helped organizations to customize their electronic document management system (EDMS) or business process management system (BPMS) thereby requiring users to codify and record the tacit knowledge behind their decisions into the system so that other users can better ascertain the chain of reasoning throughout the execution of a business process.

Learning has no boundaries. KMIRC has adopted the principle of treating the real world as an "open KM laboratory"; the learning from the consultancy and research projects in the KMIRC often become highly regarded teaching materials and industry case studies that are used throughout the Master of Science in Knowledge Management program. Doing so substantially enhances the sharing of practice knowledge gained from the trenches.

HOW THE INITIATIVE WAS RECEIVED BY THE USERS OR PARTICIPANTS

As mentioned previously, once started, all of the clients of KMIRC continue with their KM journey. This is strong evidence that KM is yielding good value/return in these organizations. For some organizations, such as the Hong Kong police and CLP Power, they have been adopting KM for nearly a decade and are often seen as role models in the public and private sector respectively in the region. MTR, the local train company, has been operating their KM and Innovation program for more than 6 years and has the largest (with around 10 full-time staff) KM team in Hong Kong. These companies have great commitments in their KM efforts. Over the last decade, we can further derive the following observations on organizations in Hong Kong that have adopted KM.

For organizations that are *new* to KM, their focus is on:

- awareness raising/readiness assessment
- strategy formulation/strategic planning
- identify, rank, and pilot of KM initiatives
- knowledge audit, social network analysis
- EDMS, search engine, portal deployment
- taxonomy creation and maintenance

For organizations that have *already started* KM, their focus is principally on:

- sustainability of KM programs, culture building
- strategy revisit, gap analysis
- embodiment of knowledge in business processes
- knowledge distillation and harnessing
- soft KM tools/skills
- health checks and benchmarking

Additional independent evidences of user adoption, KM advancements, and successes among organizations that KMIRC have helped include the following:

- In the last 5 years, many Hong Kong organizations are recipients of the MAKE award, a de facto industry award in KM at the city, regional, and global levels. These organizations include Hong Kong police, MTR Corporations, CLP Power, Towngas, Efficiency Unit of the HKSARG, Arup Ove, and others. Clearly, their achievements are being recognized and endorsed worldwide by independent and vigorous assessments.
- Leaders of the KM journey in the aforementioned organizations and more are highly sought speakers in the Asia Pacific KM circuits for their sharing of success, good practices, and lessons learned from their KM program; many other organizations in the region are looking to these HK organizations as role models to follow.
- A considerable number of staff from the aforementioned organizations and more come to KMIRC and PolyU for further training and learning in KM, either supported by the organization or at their own expenses. These people have shown genuine interest and passion in KM.
- KMIRC has trained over 2000 professionals in industry and government sectors on KM in the past decade.
- Over the years, various commissioners and assistant commissioners of police have publicly thanked the KMIRC for helping the Hong Kong police in its KM pursuit.
- The writer (Eric Tsui) has been appointed a KM advisor to the Hong Kong Police College by the commissioner of police since May 2011 as well as a community of practice advisor to the Efficiency Unit (another HK government department) since May 2015.

- More than a dozen of the KM officers/managers/directors in Hong Kong are current students and graduates of PolyU's Master of Science in Knowledge Management program.
- Many KM luminaries noticed and asked "KM is always active and thriving in Hong Kong. What is the magic formula?" Of course, full credit goes to the organizations that have committed resources and are patient about returns from KM. We like to think KMIRC also has a role in this, however. Patrick Lambe, two-time past president of iKMS (Singapore), summarized it nicely in one of his blog articles.

"Even more interesting was the turnout at KMAP (a KMIRC-hosted event) last week. At its peak, there were close to 700 delegates in the conference hall during the keynotes day – this is a number unmatched in Asia for a straight KM conference as far as I know – and though it's got a steady and growing range of KM initiatives in both public and private sectors, Hong Kong is not generally noted for its KM enthusiasm. Previous KM conferences in Hong Kong have drifted around the 100 participants mark.

Of this number perhaps a quarter were from public sector organizations in Hong Kong, demonstrating a growing interest there. But there were also delegates from private sector companies and delegates from mainland China, Malaysia, New Zealand, Iran, UK, USA, Finland, Sweden, Germany, and Australia. Some of this diversity is what you'd expect from an academic conference, it's what universities can contribute to the conference scene.

But the particular strategy and role of the HKPolyU also played a significant role, I believe. HKPolyU (more precisely the Dept of Industrial and Systems Engineering) is unusual among universities with KM on their agendas. They do research, and they have a <u>Master's in KM</u> course, to be sure, as do other universities. More than that, however, their KM group has been aggressively building a strong KM consulting practice in both private and public sectors – not as sidelines for their professors and teachers, but as a kind of action research learning experience for both the clients and the KM group itself.

This is interesting. Most KM consulting work is done, to be frank, in secret. Organisations are frequently uncertain about their KM pathways, and often reluctant to share until they have some results. Similarly, private sector consultants tend not to want to share until their assignments are complete and they are confident of keeping competitors at bay. This means that in novice KM markets, KM activity is opaque, and it's hard for beginners to see many visible examples of KM in action. This multiplies the initial uncertainties and hesitancies. In an action research kind of context with a university, the picture – at least in Hong Kong – seems to have shifted. KM work becomes more visible, so onlookers are encouraged to explore and experiment. This is a major factor, I believe, behind the strong turnout at KMAP – there are now sufficient visible projects associated with HKPU to become, in themselves, attractors for attention and networking."
(Source: http://www.greenchameleon.com/gc/blog_detail/universities_and_km_practice/)

THE EFFICIENCY, EFFECTIVENESS, OR COMPETITIVE ADVANTAGE OUTCOMES THAT WERE ACHIEVED AND HOW THEY WERE MEASURED AND EVALUATED

Overall speaking, KM initiatives help to accomplish some/all of the following. In terms of enhancements and improvements, good KM leads to increases in:

- sales
- customers
- quality of decision making
- consistency in process executions
- organizational memory
- social and professional networks
- response time
- flexibility in time and delivery channel
- knowledge about customers, partners, market

and reductions in:

- time to search for information
- time/effort needed to locate/connect with knowledge experts
- time to carry out "knowledge-intensive" tasks
- time/effort needed to resolve a problem
- printing and mailing costs
- travel cost and time
- costs of providing training and learning programs

As the number of projects/journeys is close to 200, it is impossible to list out all the details. Nevertheless, the following table provides a subset of the various KM initiatives that have been introduced in organizations, together with its outcomes, measurements, and evaluations.

Initiative/ Technique/ Tool/System	Outcomes	Method of Measurement/Evaluation
Taxonomy creation and search engine customization	Improved schema for storing information; common consensus among staff on where to save/ find information; enabled faceted search and enhanced the ranking of search results in the display	Complexity of the taxonomy in terms of levels, no. of branches, levels and size of the controlled vocabularies Reduced time to search for information, both for the navigation method and keyword searching More intelligent search engine that identifies synonyms, recovers from incorrectly typed words Monitor and analyze search engine log for entered keywords with no matches; reviewing this on a regular basis can provide valuable information to fine tune the taxonomy as well as the search engine configurations

Initiative/ Technique/ Tool/System	Outcomes	Method of Measurement/Evaluation
Near-miss reporting database	Overcome people's reluctance to report nearly occurred accidents in hospitals. Culture change. Design and development of a database capturing near-miss cases reported from and shared among 10 hospitals	The steadily growing size of the database Frequency of access and download of these cases from the site Survey on the rise in awareness and usefulness of the database for accident preventions A culture among staff to willingly report near-miss cases with fear of reprisals
Revamp of a knowledge portal	Redesign of the user interface, the layout and content of the portal, introduction of Web 2.0 tools (wiki and RSS) to enhance collaboration and information awareness, change management to help users adopt the portal	User-adoption statistics Reduced time on the retrieval of information and documents from the portal Refined and more accurate search results from the search engine Monitoring and review of the search engine log to identify abnormal search queries and common keywords encountered but not adopted in the taxonomy Governance model established to review, discuss feedback on a regular basis, and act on improvements
Scenario-based e-learning tool	Developed a platform for rapid authoring of scenarios to support learning using open source tools	Successful adoption of this tool by MTR Corporation and the Langham Place Hotel for internal training purposes Both organizations continue to develop and update the learning content over the years. This is evidence of sustained usage of the tool MTR Corporation also uses this tool to provide videos to help drive change in their KM journey. More specifically, the tool is used to produce videos showcasing why new joiners and junior staff should actively ask questions and share in the Community of Practice forums
Knowledge audit	Identified a ranked list of important explicit assets. Knowledge flow in the audited processes showing the creator/owner/originator/user of a knowledge asset. Social networks revealing connections among people involved in the audited processes and any major knowledge centers (people and repositories, where others approach for information) in the network	Verified list of critical knowledge revealed by the knowledge audit by subject matter experts in the organization Follow-up interviews with stakeholders especially to validate some unusual findings in the knowledge audit Adopted different methodologies for knowledge audit to benchmark findings and identify variations Carry out knowledge audit periodically to obtain updated information to support decision making on KM strategies, systems, and processes

Initiative/ Technique/ Tool/System	Outcomes	Method of Measurement/Evaluation
Formulation of a KM Strategy	SWOT analysis from a knowledge perspective	Organizations proceeded with the pilot projects; start small to embark on their KM journey
	The balance between the use of codification and personalization approach	Depending on the KM initiative, for community of practice, measurements are based on the number of members, rate of membership growth, no. of assets uploaded/downloaded. For discussions, measurements are often based on threads posted, no. of replies and time lag for the reply, the nature of the reply, etc.
	Identification of appropriate soft and technical KM tools to support the set KM objectives	
	Recommendation of pilot projects with timeframes and as part of a multiphased approach to KM	Revisit the strategy to determine its on-going appropriateness and effectiveness; gap analysis to determine if the strategy and its implementation need to be realigned
Stories database	Elicited stories about a given theme/topic are transcribed into a database. Indices and keywords are created to tag these stories for easy and fast retrieval	Stories are verified by the tellers before they are being finalized
		Measurements include the number of stories elicited, the percentage of stories deemed to be admissible to the story database (for its completeness, integrity, and perceived usefulness), the organization continuing efforts to adopt storytelling and stories as knowledge-harnessing and knowledge-sharing methods
		Anecdotal feedback on the usefulness of the collected stories, comparison of the revealed knowledge with existing training materials, monitoring the access/retrieval of the stories for training and learning purposes

GAP BETWEEN KM IN THE BOOKS AND IN PRACTICE

Having done close to 200 KM projects, one can clearly identify several major areas where KM theories (as covered in most KM books) and practice differ, as well as those practical issues that are not commonly addressed but nevertheless important. We have again summarized the discussions into the following areas.

KNOWLEDGE AUDIT AND KNOWLEDGE STRATEGY: WHICH ONE COMES FIRST?

It does sound like a "chicken–egg" situation. Our experience is that either one can come first, depending on the situation. For example, a century old engineering organization wants to harness and better retain and share their critical knowledge. In that case, almost certainly the team of experienced engineers would know about their core area(s) of expertise and how these are related to the achievement of corporate objectives. However, a knowledge audit may not only reinforce what the engineers believe but also provide evidence-based support for specific additional critical knowledge areas/assets that should also be harnessed, retained, and shared. The knowledge strategy can come second after the identification of critical knowledge assets. On the other hand, for an organization that is entirely new to KM, it is sensible to first derive a KM strategy then proceed to carry out pilot projects so identified in the strategy. There is no definitive right or wrong decision on choosing which one should proceed first; it is determined on the needs and priority of the client organization.

KM JOURNEYS ARE RARELY STARTED FROM SCRATCH

Organizations and societies evolve all the time. Therefore, there is rarely the case that an organization truly begins its KM journey from a "clean sheet of paper." This starting point is often ignored in books as KM strategies and operational steps outlined in books tend to assume the journey starts from scratch. The reality is the organization may be already doing something related to managing knowledge but does not call it KM. Worse, an organization may have introduced KM before but, due to whatever reason, the journey failed and had poor ramifications among staff. Whatever the case, an organization's past efforts on KM need to be understood and factored into the strategy for implementation. Our experience is that, more likely than not, there are knowledge assets to filter out and migrate, methods and/or processes to fine tune, culture building among staff, sceptics to deal with, among others, before a journey can move forward. In other words, all organizations have "baggage" that needs to be dealt with and cannot be ignored when enacting change.

NATURAL KM "ENTRY POINTS" IN ORGANIZATIONS

Although it is never easy to convince someone to adopt KM let alone embark on a KM journey, we found that there are natural "entry points" for organizations to take up KM. These entry points are completely natural and almost need no further substantiation. One entry point is when organizations realize their staff is wasting substantial time every day in finding/searching things but to no avail; a taxonomy project can help here. Another one is the global phenomenon of the baby boomers retirement syndrome, which refers to the over-proportion of retirees from organizations beginning 10 years ago and continuing into the next 5 years. No organization is immune from this exodus of staff, and no doubt leaders would be receptive to adopting any KM method that can help to reduce some of the lost knowledge by retaining it in knowledge repositories as well as in the heads of the remaining staff.

KM STRATEGIES VARY AMONG MULTINATIONAL CORPORATIONS, LOCAL COMPANIES, AND SMALL TO MEDIUM-SIZED BUSINESSES

We also found that there are substantial differences among the adoption of KM in MNC (multinational corporations), local companies, and SMBs (small to medium-sized businesses). Especially for those MNCs where their headquarters are in the United States or Europe, deployment of KM in local region/offices is typically a rollout or extension of a KM program (including strategy, system, blueprint, operational groups, communities, etc.) that is being handed down from their headquarters; the local team's responsibility is basically to operationalize the program with some minor fine tuning or variations. For local (large) organizations, their adoption of KM has, in most cases, a good alignment with the typical KM journey as prescribed in books and literature. For SMBs, due to a lack of budget, multiskilling of staff, and the proprietor's dominance in decision making, their KM journeys need the most vigorous return on investment (ROI), and the course of the KM journey can change radically due to, among others, staff departure, change of decision by the proprietor, market volatility, business performance, skills and competencies of staff, and their ability to learn new things.

FACTORS FOR SUSTAINING THE USE OF KNOWLEDGE MANAGEMENT SYSTEMS THAT DIFFER FROM FACTORS THAT AFFECT ADOPTION

KM books and research papers cover extensively the topic of knowledge management systems (KMS) adoption and the factors that influence users to take up and start using a KM system. While knowing these factors are no doubt very useful for planning and the deployment of a KM system, it is even more important to know the factors that lead users to continue their use of the KM system in a sustained way. Our own research, as well as the knowledge gained from working with these 200 projects, leads us to believe that the two sets of factors (ie, for preadoption and postadoption) are different; for example, peer influence, demonstrated usefulness, personal experience, and personalization are among factors that make users continue their use of KM systems in a sustained way.

IC IS MUCH HARDER THAN KM TO SELL

Among the 200 or so projects conducted, a small number of these projects are intellectual capital (IC)–related projects. Speaking overall, we found that compared to KM, it is more difficult to convince directors to adopt IC projects, possibly because IC is very new (as many organizations are only just starting to use the balanced scorecard for reporting and tracking performance) and the benefits of IC are not immediately realizable. There are, however, a few major organizations leveraging IC for value creation, reporting, and business planning. More time is needed to determine whether IC is a liftoff in Hong Kong or not.

(An earlier version of the author's presentation on this topic is available for replay at http://158.132.103.175/temp/eric/KM%20developments%20in%20HK%20-%20over%20100%20projects/)

Knowledge loss and retention: the paradoxical role of IT

N. Levallet*, Y.E. Chan**

*Ohio University, Athens, OH, USA; **Queen's University, Kingston, ON, Canada

INTRODUCTION

In today's global and fast-changing environments, knowledge represents a critical resource that organizations must leverage to enhance their competitive positions. Effective knowledge management is essential to develop superior business innovation abilities, which allows organizations to differentiate themselves from their competitors (Grant, 1996; Spender, 1996). Knowledge management (KM) broadly refers to the processes used by an organization to manage its intellectual capital. KM comprises three main phases: creation, retention, and reuse. Knowledge creation aims at developing an organizational knowledge base, while knowledge retention focuses on the acquisition, storage, and retrieval of knowledge, with the ultimate objective of increasing knowledge reuse (De Long, 2004).

Information systems (IS) are pervasive in all organizational functions and complement other resources and competences, such as knowledge management, that contribute to overall performance (Bharadwaj et al., 2007). As a component of KM, knowledge retention combines strategies that use both non-IS and IS-based mechanisms (Alavi and Leidner, 2001; Nevo and Chan, 2007). An example of a non-IS-based mechanism includes the transfer of knowledge between a knowledge contributor (an individual generating knowledge) and a knowledge seeker (an individual searching for knowledge) during one-on-one discussions. Similarly, different information systems can help retain knowledge by "connecting people, accelerating learning, capturing knowledge and mapping human knowledge" (De Long, 2004, p. 119). A large body of research suggests that IS serves as an effective mechanism to retain knowledge, especially knowledge that can be easily codified and stored in knowledge management systems (KMS), such as repositories, expertise sharing systems, and directories (Alavi and Leidner, 2001; Nevo and Chan, 2007; Sambamurthy and Subramani, 2005).

While research has shown the benefits of KMS for knowledge retention, little is known about the potential downsides of these IS on knowledge retention. Some studies point to the potential negative impact of knowledge management systems on knowledge reuse (Garud and Kumaraswamy, 2005). It is possible that in some cases, a system that has some positive KM effects (eg, providing increased access to knowledge) might also have negative effects (eg, hindering knowledge retention or increasing knowledge loss, therefore reducing knowledge reuse). Knowledge loss refers to knowledge attrition following the creation of knowledge, that is, knowledge that is not retained by the organization and can result from employee departure, poor documentation, poor archiving, etc. (De Long, 2004). Knowledge loss can occur at the time of knowledge acquisition but also when stored knowledge is forgotten and is not reused (Martin de Holan and Phillips, 2004).

Studies on knowledge retention examine specific aspects of retention, for instance acquisition or retrieval, usually associating the presence of knowledge loss with a lack of knowledge acquisition (Levy, 2011). However, knowledge loss may occur as a result of the interaction between different knowledge retention phases. Studying the different phases of knowledge retention is important to understand how retention and loss may coexist, especially when using IS-enabled KMS.

In a recent study, using the knowledge-based view (KBV) of the firm as our theoretical lens, we explored both facets of KMS—their benefits and their potential downsides—and how this may affect knowledge retention and reuse. We studied four sectors in a large, public service organization, all using the same document repository. Findings from the case study confirm previous anecdotal evidence and demonstrate that the same system can both enhance knowledge retention and increase knowledge loss. This apparent paradox is revealed using rich case data.

REVIEW OF THE LITERATURE
KNOWLEDGE AND THE KNOWLEDGE-BASED VIEW

The KBV perspective has emerged from the strategic research field, as an extension of the resource-based view (RBV) of the firm (Grant, 1996). The RBV posits that an organization that possesses valuable resources and competencies not easily copied and implemented by competitors will develop a competitive advantage (Barney, 1991). Within the KBV perspective, knowledge constitutes the most critical resource for organizations as, without knowledge, organizations are not able to develop other resources or competences such as products or services (Grant, 1996; Spender, 1996). In particular, with the KBV, an organization's primary purpose is to integrate knowledge. Organizational members are expected to be able to reuse knowledge and adapt it to their tasks at hand (Grant, 1996).

We define knowledge as an object or an asset that employees and organizations use to serve specific objectives (Alavi and Leidner, 2001). We recognize that knowledge can be interpreted in other ways than the aforementioned definition, for instance as a state of mind or as practice (Cook and Brown, 1999; Orlikowski, 2002). However, under the KBV perspective, knowledge is frequently considered as an asset that can be aggregated and transferred at the organization level (Denford and Chan, 2011; Grant, 1996).

Knowledge varies in the degree to which it can be codified (Kogut and Zander, 1992). Some knowledge is largely explicit, meaning that it can be articulated, codified, and transmitted through the use of symbols or language (Alavi and Leidner, 2001; Nonaka, 1994). Explicit knowledge can vary in complexity, ranging for instance from organizational charts to standard operating procedures (SOP). While organizational charts give an overview of an organization's structure, SOPs provide specific and articulated written details of approved processes to perform tasks or procedures. As such, SOPs seek to codify and simplify complex knowledge about how to perform a specific task (Kogut and Zander, 1992). Knowledge that is largely based on personal experience, practice, and beliefs is usually referred to as tacit knowledge (Nonaka and Takeuchi, 1995). Because of the inherent personalized, context-sensitive nature of tacit knowledge, it is much harder to simplify and codify to facilitate its reuse by other individuals (Ford and Chan, 2003).

KNOWLEDGE RETENTION AND LOSS

The ability to successfully manage explicit and tacit knowledge in organizations involves different phases: knowledge creation, knowledge retention, followed by knowledge reuse within the organization and/or with other organizations (Argote et al., 2003; Khodakarami and Chan, 2014). Knowledge retention processes, as essential components of knowledge management, relate to actions taken to develop and maintain the organization's knowledge base, also called organizational memory (De Long, 2004). The objective of knowledge retention is to ensure that organizational members can reuse knowledge. Three main phases compose knowledge retention: knowledge acquisition, knowledge storage, and knowledge retrieval. Throughout the process, knowledge loss can also occur.

Knowledge acquisition focuses on modifying knowledge to make it more potentially reusable. For instance, implicit procedures can be formalized and entered into a repository. Knowledge storage refers to the processes and practices used to hold knowledge until it is needed. Last, knowledge retrieval activities aim at accessing knowledge for reuse, for instance, by searching through a document repository (De Long, 2004).

The use of IS has been shown to facilitate knowledge retention and reuse within organizations (Alavi and Leidner, 2001; Grover and Davenport, 2001; Iyengar and Sweeney, 2015; Nevo and Chan, 2007; Sambamurthy and Subramani, 2005). IS-enabled KMS facilitates the transformation of individual knowledge into collective knowledge held by the organization. Specifically, knowledge management systems like knowledge repositories represent a low-cost and fast way to acquire, store, retrieve, and reuse collective knowledge throughout the organization (Von Krogh, 2009). Repositories are especially helpful for the retention of explicit knowledge, which can be used for replication purposes (Jasimuddin et al., 2012) and lead to improved individual, group, and organizational performance (Choi et al., 2010; Ko and Dennis, 2011; Wu and Hu, 2012).

Much research attention has been devoted to identifying individual, group, and organizational factors that facilitate knowledge retention. Individual factors impacting knowledge contribution to or retrieval from repositories include individual motivation, efforts required, benefits derived, preference toward personalized approaches to knowledge sharing, trust in the system, and perception of the quality of the system (Dulipovici and Robey, 2013; Durcikova and Gray, 2009; Gray and Chan, 2000; Gray and Durcikova, 2005; Kankanhalli et al., 2005; Wang et al., 2013). Group or social factors include social network ties and social interactions that influence the use of repositories (Dulipovici and Robey, 2013; Hansen, 1999; Parise et al., 2006). Provided an organization closely monitors its incentives toward knowledge contributions and retrieval to avoid unintended negative consequences (Garud and Kumaraswamy, 2005), knowledge acquisition strategies should yield positive effects in terms of productivity and overall organizational performance (Denford and Chan, 2011). Similarly, repositories should be designed to facilitate storage and retrieval, for instance, through proper knowledge categorization and links to other related knowledge resources (Butler and Murphy, 2007).

Knowledge retention is a critical KM process, but it is also closely linked to knowledge loss. As outlined earlier, knowledge loss refers to knowledge attrition when part of the created knowledge base is not retained by the organization (De Long, 2004). While knowledge may be created by individuals or groups within the organization, this knowledge may be lost if it is not acquired by a knowledge retention entity (eg, a work process or knowledge management system; De Long, 2004). Knowledge loss can be further defined by two characteristics: level of intentionality and level of knowledge newness (Martin de Holan et al., 2004; Martin de Holan and Phillips, 2004).

Some new or existing knowledge may be intentionally forgotten, for instance, to change bad habits, with the objective of increasing overall productivity. Knowledge can also be lost unintentionally. For this study, our interest is in accidental knowledge loss or forgetting. Two types of accidental knowledge loss have been discussed: failure to consolidate new knowledge and failure to maintain established knowledge (Martin de Holan et al., 2004; Martin de Holan and Phillips, 2004). Failure to consolidate new knowledge occurs when the organization neglects to go through the knowledge acquisition phase. In this case, knowledge is lost before it can be captured. Second, failure to maintain established knowledge occurs when stored knowledge is forgotten over time and stops being retrieved. Often, individuals forget the type of available knowledge that could help them with their tasks (Von Krogh, 2009). Knowledge loss can also occur when codified knowledge is not contextualized, for instance, by codifying knowledge about the expert contributors themselves (Kotlarsky et al., 2014), or when knowledge is not refined or reshaped over time (Majchrzak et al., 2013). Following accidental knowledge loss, the organization has to recreate the knowledge before it can be reused, which has negative impacts on organizational performance (Martin de Holan et al., 2004; Martin de Holan and Phillips, 2004).

Past research often implicitly assumes that improving knowledge retention means reducing knowledge loss (Levy, 2011). However, accidental knowledge loss does not represent the other end of the knowledge retention spectrum, since actions taken to increase knowledge retention do not necessarily translate into less knowledge loss. A document may be captured by a KMS, but never retrieved and reused. This example shows that paradoxically knowledge can be both retained knowledge and lost over time.

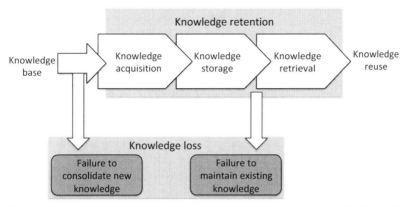

FIGURE 7.1 Research model (based on De Long, 2004; Martin de Holan and Phillips, 2004)

RESEARCH MODEL

The previous discussion is summarized in the research model in Fig. 7.1. It combines the knowledge retention framework proposed by De Long (2004), and the organizational knowledge forgetting or loss taxonomy proposed by Martin de Holan and Phillips (2004).

To explore this research model, we chose to keep the knowledge storage tool constant by studying in depth a single knowledge repository of significant importance. With one type of knowledge storage tool, we can focus on understanding the acquisition and retrieval activities that may lead to both knowledge retention and knowledge loss. The following research methodology provides details about our approach.

RESEARCH METHODOLOGY

It was important to study organizations in a context that would allow us to better understand and assess the model presented in Fig. 7.1. Specifically, we wanted to empirically examine the extent to which the use of a single system could both benefit from knowledge retention and increase knowledge loss. Our ideal organization was an organization that considers knowledge as a core aspect of its activities. We also wanted to be able to compare different groups or divisions that use the same type of system. With this objective in mind, we conducted our study in a large Canadian public service organization. Public service organizations are knowledge organizations with a mandate to share their expertise with other governmental institutions, private sector organizations, and citizens. Knowledge represents a core asset for this type of organization. Public service organizations also tend to be large, with multiple entities within one organization, each with a specific mandate. The implementation of information systems is often decided for the whole public service. We were therefore likely to study separate teams or departments using the same technology.

For these reasons, we examined our model in the context of an organization within the Federal Government of Canada that we call GovHR.[a] GovHR supports the public service in terms of human resources management. It has full decision authority within a larger central agency. The organization has approximately 550 employees, including about 450 indeterminate positions and 100 temporary positions (term, casual, student, secondment, and agency/contract).

We received access to the four organizational sectors comprising GovHR, notably labour-management relations and compensation operations (Labour and Compensation), governance and policy development (Governance and Policy), Executive Workforce Management, as well as Pension and Benefits. All sectors had access to and were encouraged to use GovSystem, a government-wide repository that records and tracks official government documents.

We received full support from and were in close contact with GovHR senior executives on a number of occasions over the course of a year. We met with senior officials, organized and participated in general information and discussion sessions, and gathered several internal documents. In total, we conducted 26 interviews focusing on knowledge retention between knowledge contributors and knowledge seekers. The knowledge contributors (16 interviewees) and knowledge seekers (10 interviewees) we interviewed held various positions ranging from senior analyst, manager, and senior executive to administrative assistant. Two of the knowledge contributors we interviewed were also key informants with deep corporate and background knowledge on the organization. Table 7.1 provides details on the position of interviewees within their sector.

The semistructured interviews for both knowledge contributors and seekers were developed based on the academic literature and in collaboration with the organization. Before conducting the interviews, we tested the interview protocol with IS-related university employees, PhD students, and professors to assess question validity. Some questions were refined following comments received from the pretest participants.

We used a positivist perspective when conducting the case study. We analyzed the findings, using a provisional coding approach (Saldaña, 2009). Provisional coding is based on a list of predetermined codes that are developed prior to data analysis. As data analysis progresses, it is possible to revise the codes and to add new codes. The lead

Table 7.1 Interviewees by Sector, Group, and Knowledge Position

Government Sector	Knowledge Contributor	Knowledge Seeker
Labour and Compensation	6	2
Governance and Policy	5	1
Pension and Benefits	2	4
Executive Workforce Management	1	2
GovHR's Head Office	2	1
Total	16	10

[a]All names are pseudonyms.

author coded all manuscripts. The second author and a third researcher independently coded a subset of the manuscripts. We discussed and resolved all coding differences.

FINDINGS
GOVSYSTEM OVERVIEW

GovSystem is defined by the government of Canada as "an electronic enterprise records and document management solution that increases efficiency in organizing, structuring and sharing information in a corporate repository" (Treasury Board of Canada Secretariat, 2015). GovSystem records and tracks official and final documentation, such as decision letters, briefing notes, and policies, for most government agencies. The system captures descriptive information on each document, which is meant to facilitate future knowledge retrieval using the search functions (Office of the Information Commissioner of Canada, 2010).

No strict guidelines have been developed to formalize and standardize the use of GovSystem. For instance, managers should simply encourage employees to set access rights "as widely as possible to promote the sharing of information" when capturing a document within GovSystem (Treasury Board of Canada Secretariat, 2015). GovHR has not developed an organization-wide approach to the use of GovSystem. Instead, each sector is left to decide how to encourage employees to contribute to and seek information from GovSystem. Some sectors, like Executive Workforce Management, developed contribution guidelines, while others, like Labour and Compensation, did not. The following sections describe the varying approaches to the use of the KMS, and depict the impacts these variations have had on knowledge retention and loss. We demonstrate that paradoxically the same system can facilitate knowledge acquisition and result in loss.

BRIGHT SIDE OF GOVSYSTEM: EFFECTIVE KNOWLEDGE ACQUISITION AND RETRIEVAL

Knowledge acquisition through GovSystem is encouraged and mostly successful in three sectors, Executive Workforce Management, Governance and Policy, and Pension and Benefits. Both the Governance and Policy and the Executive Workforce Management sectors have developed a naming protocol that facilitates acquisition and retrieval.

Executive Workforce Management has also implemented an effective process that ensures that all employees appropriately capture knowledge in GovSystem. Executives created a working group to develop a naming protocol for GovSystem, as well as a procedure to ensure versions of the same document are created within GovSystem. While a document is assigned a unique identification number by GovSystem when it is first created, it is possible to specify a document version. The use of document versions allows knowledge seekers to know they are retrieving the most recent version of a document. Interviewees from Executive Workforce Management indicated that all relevant documents are properly captured in GovSystem. All employees are also automatically granted access to documents created in GovSystem by Executive Workforce Management employees. By developing specific procedures to work around the system's access limitations, they do not face any of the access restrictions that we will describe next.

The pension and benefit sector has developed a tracking system, which allows the sector to know what new knowledge has been captured in GovSystem. The tracking system is maintained outside of GovSystem. It facilitates knowledge retrieval because knowledge seekers use it to identify the documents that they need to retrieve from GovSystem.

DARK SIDE OF GOVSYSTEM: KNOWLEDGE LOSS DURING ACQUISITION AND RETRIEVAL

Despite the efforts made by some sectors to facilitate knowledge contributions, other sectors have difficulties with knowledge acquisition. Many employees in all of GovHR's sectors also indicate that even if the system may facilitate knowledge contribution, knowledge retrieval is inefficient and complex. This is summarized by a senior executive working for GovHR's Head Office:

> "I can put documents into GovSystem, our records management system. But it's one thing for the information to be there; it's another thing for other people to know that the information is there." (Senior Executive, GovHR's Head Office)

Many employees have a negative opinion of GovSystem, especially within Labour and Compensation. This affects their willingness to contribute to it. According to interviewees, three system shortcomings limit knowledge acquisition from contributors: the system is not stable; saving a document in GovSystem is too time consuming; and the system cannot be trusted for secure documents.

First, GovSystem is integrated within the Windows operating system. Users are automatically prompted to save all created files in GovSystem. However, many of our respondents indicated that often their computer "crashes" when they save a file in GovSystem. In many instances, users lose important information during the saving process that they then have to recreate. Second, many interviewees indicated that saving a document in GovSystem is time consuming and cumbersome. Mandatory fields to fill out include access control (ie, who can see, read, or edit the document), author, creation date, document name, and security level (Office of the Information Commissioner of Canada, 2010). In addition, knowledge contributors are encouraged to fill out as much information as possible to facilitate document retrieval, for instance keywords. A manager summarizes this:

> "GovSystem is annoying because it takes forever to load up, it crashes all of your other programs and it's not intuitive. It takes a long time to select people, it's just not easy. And because it takes so much time and it's complicated for people, people don't want to use it." (Manager, Pension and Benefits)

Third, in areas dealing with highly sensitive information like Labour and Compensation, employees feel they cannot control the level of security on GovSystem. Due to the sensitivity and importance of the files available on GovSystem, access to files is granted on a per-document basis, at the discretion of the document author (access control). Default access can also be granted, for instance, to all members of a team. However, respondents are concerned that employee turnover is not well reflected in GovSystem, and that some individuals receive access to some files that were not intended for them, while others lose access to important files. Files are saved under folders created for each sector. This perceived lack of access transparency prompts knowledge contributors to distrust GovSystem and to use alternative systems to save their documents, for instance, shared drives. This is outlined by a knowledge contributor in Labour and Compensation for highly sensitive documents:

> *"I don't trust it [GovSystem]. The area we work in is classified, and that system is nothing if not porous. There are things you don't share broadly because of the nature of the beast, especially if you are working in legislation and those kinds of negotiations. Discretion is the better part of valour in these things. And so I don't put anything in GovSystem if I can help it." (Senior Policy Analyst Advisor, Labour and Compensation)*

Retrieving documents from GovSystem is also difficult, as many interviewees report. Some difficulties are directly related to the knowledge acquisition process. For instance, because it is time consuming to save a document in GovSystem, users do not fill out information that would be useful for retrieval, such as keywords. In addition, the absence of a naming protocol in most sectors makes it more challenging to identify and retrieve documents. A knowledge contributor summarizes retrieval issues derived from knowledge acquisition:

> *"There's no real protocol or business process for naming your files. So often it's hard to find files that are there. It's not like going to a shared drive, we can click on a folder and you can see everything that's there. So we have challenges with GovSystem." (Manager, GovHR)*

Two additional factors make knowledge retrieval especially challenging: a lack of filing structure and access control within GovSystem. First, the lack of filing structure, combined with the absence of a naming protocol within GovSystem, further complicates searches. This knowledge contributor from Labour and Compensation explains how retrieving his documents can prove to be difficult for knowledge seekers:

> *"GovSystem has a file structure, it's in my view somewhat limited. GovSystem, at the high level for our division, has eight, perhaps even ten sort of broad files, categories that you can put things in. But the vast majority of the work that I do from a policy perspective, it all gets dumped into one area." (Manager, Labour and Compensation)*

The importance of filing structure and naming protocol is echoed by a knowledge seeker in the Pension and Benefits sector:

> *"There's so many times in which I've tried to find things, but it's never what you really want and just because it's never clearly identified what the file is." (Analyst, Pension and Benefits)*

Access control is initially set during knowledge acquisition, when a knowledge contributor saves a document in GovSystem. The knowledge contributor can

Table 7.2 Summary of Findings at GovHR

Sector \ Knowledge Activity	Acquisition	New Knowledge Loss	Retrieval	Existing Knowledge Loss
Labour and Compensation	Limited	Extensive	Limited	Extensive
Pension and Benefits	Limited	Extensive	Limited	Extensive
Governance and Policy	Facilitated	Occurring	Limited	Extensive
Executive Workforce Management	Facilitated and systematic	Limited	Facilitated	Occurring

determine who has access to the document, and the type of access (eg, reading only, editing rights). Access control not only limits who can read or edit a retrieved document, it also limits whether the knowledge seeker is able to see a document in search results. Indeed, GovSystem search results do not show documents to which a knowledge seeker does not have access. As a Governance and Policy manager working on a special project and recently assigned to her position, this interviewee expressed her frustration with document retrieval in GovSystem:

> "I'm a new person. I haven't been given access rights to any of the old documents. If I do a search for a document, the documents that I haven't been given access to don't come up." (Manager, Governance and Policy)

As a result of these shortcomings, simple "browsing" through accessible files cannot be achieved. If knowledge seekers successfully conduct a search and find the document, they do not have access to related documents that may be helpful to their work.

FINDINGS SUMMARY

Table 7.2 depicts a summary of our findings by organizational sector, based on knowledge acquisition, retrieval, and loss of new and acquired knowledge.

Even in sectors where knowledge contribution to and retrieval from GovSystem is facilitated and encouraged, like Executive Workforce Management, knowledge loss occurs. This is discussed as follows.

DISCUSSION AND IMPLICATIONS
DISCUSSION

The objective of this research was to determine empirically the extent to which knowledge management systems could both paradoxically facilitate knowledge retention while also simultaneously increasing knowledge loss. We studied four sectors of the same public organization, all of them using the same repository, GovSystem. Our findings show that indeed, GovSystem simultaneously facilitates knowledge retention and knowledge loss.

Prior literature suggests that when organizations develop and implement strategies to increase knowledge retention, they should also experience an associated decrease in knowledge loss (Levy, 2011). For instance, knowledge retention strategies mitigate potential knowledge loss from departing employees (Liebowitz, 2009; Parise et al., 2006). Knowledge management systems are routinely used to support knowledge retention and reduce knowledge loss (De Long, 2004). In our study, when the right acquisition processes are in place, like in the Executive Workforce Management sector, new knowledge is effectively acquired by GovSystem in the form of documentation. At the same time, limited knowledge loss is noted. Similarly, sectors that are reluctant to use GovSystem experience more loss of new knowledge. With the right knowledge retention processes in place, GovSystem both enables knowledge retention and mitigates knowledge loss. This finding is in line with past research that lays out the various factors facilitating knowledge retention using IS (Dulipovici and Robey, 2013; Durcikova and Gray, 2009; Gray and Durcikova, 2005; Kankanhalli et al., 2005; Wang et al., 2013).

However, our study also indicates that knowledge loss should not always be conceptualized as the simple opposite of knowledge retention, and can occur even as knowledge retention occurs. Past research findings suggest that existing knowledge is lost when it is forgotten over time and not reused (Martin de Holan et al., 2004; Martin de Holan and Phillips, 2004; Parise et al., 2006). We extend this research by showing that KMS may not only increase knowledge retention, as suggested previously, but also knowledge loss. Knowledge captured within a repository such as GovSystem is available for retrieval. On the one hand, system shortcomings, especially access control, make most of the retained knowledge difficult to retrieve, which increases the amount of knowledge that is not reused. This is the case in the Pension and Benefits sector. Despite entering as many keywords and information as possible in their document searches in GovSystem, knowledge seekers are often unable to locate, retrieve, and reuse critical documents. In addition, although other sectors like Executive Workforce Management have developed processes to facilitate knowledge retrieval, including tracking systems, naming protocols, and broad access rights, knowledge loss is also present in the Executive Workforce Management sector in the form of failure to reuse existing knowledge.

GovSystem was implemented as the government level. Organizational sectors have no control over the system's functionality and cannot make system modifications. Within the repository, most documents are captured and stored in isolation, with no link to similar documents. Even when knowledge seekers can retrieve a specific document, they cannot see related documents the same way they would within a folder in a shared drive. This lack of document visibility is compounded by access limitations that do not allow knowledge seekers to see documents for which they have not been granted access.

IMPLICATIONS

These findings have research and practical implications for knowledge retention. Research on knowledge retention has mainly focused on the study of specific retention phases such as knowledge acquisition, storage, or retrieval processes and tools. While these studies' findings have greatly enhanced our knowledge of how to manage each component of knowledge retention independently, we still need to better understand how these knowledge retention phases interact. Based on our findings at GovHR, we believe that IS-enabled knowledge retention phases should not be studied in isolation. By focusing on the relationship between knowledge acquisition and retrieval at GovHR, we were able to identify paradoxical issues surrounding knowledge management systems, which can both enhance knowledge retention and loss at the same time.

In this study, we focused on accidental knowledge loss as an unexpected result of using an IS-based knowledge retention tool. Future research should investigate knowledge loss with other types of KMS. More generally, by taking a more systemic or holistic approach to study knowledge retention, researchers can better understand the complex role that IS plays in knowledge management. This has implications for how knowledge retention studies should be designed. For this research, we followed a case study approach. While this method is well suited to understanding complex phenomena such as knowledge retention, other methods may also be appropriate to study the interactions among knowledge retention phases. For instance, set-theoretic configurational approaches such as qualitative comparative analysis (Ragin, 1994, 2000) have been recently introduced to the IS field for research on the complex relationships among IS strategy, organizational strategy, and performance (El Sawy et al., 2010). This method could be applied to the study of knowledge retention. With configurational approaches, it is possible to identify groups of factors that interact to produce an outcome of interest. Configurational methods would be especially useful to understand how specific aspects of knowledge retention might interact to increase both reuse and loss.

For managers, our findings indicate the need to revisit the ways in which knowledge retention strategies are designed and implemented. Organizations should design strategies that go beyond simple knowledge acquisition and specifically target ways to improve knowledge retrieval and reuse. Knowledge loss can occur both during the acquisition and the retrieval phases. While most strategies implicitly aim at reducing knowledge loss during the acquisition phase, they also need to target other types of knowledge loss, such as the failure to maintain existing knowledge. The inability for an organization to prevent such knowledge loss during the retrieval phase can have negative consequences on knowledge reuse, and eventually on the organization's ability to innovate. To counter these potential downsides, knowledge retention strategies should explicitly include ways to manage all types of knowledge loss, whether intentional or accidental, and in all phases of the knowledge life cycle—acquisition, storage, and retrieval. These strategies should also include explicit targets and metrics to evaluate reuse and loss prevention.

CONCLUSIONS

The purpose of this study was to understand the relationship between knowledge retention and knowledge loss. We build on previous literature suggesting that knowledge retention is facilitated and knowledge loss mitigated when knowledge acquisition and knowledge retrieval are done using information systems, like knowledge management systems. Using a case study of four sectors within a large public service organization, all using the same repository, we demonstrate that, contrary to previous beliefs, knowledge loss cannot always be equated with the opposite of knowledge retention. Rather, in some cases, paradoxically a KMS can facilitate both knowledge retention and loss.

REFERENCES

Alavi, M., Leidner, D.E., 2001. Review: knowledge management and knowledge management systems: conceptual foundations and research issues. MIS Q., 107–136.

Argote, L., McEvily, B., Reagans, R., 2003. Introduction to the special issue on managing knowledge in organizations: creating, retaining, and transferring knowledge. Manage. Sci. 49 (4), v–vii.

Barney, J., 1991. Firm resources and sustained competitive advantage. J. Manage. 17 (1), 99–120.

Bharadwaj, S., Bharadwaj, A., Bendoly, E., 2007. The performance effects of complementarities between information systems, marketing, manufacturing, and supply chain processes. Inform. Syst. Res. 18 (4), 437–471.

Butler, T., Murphy, C., 2007. Understanding the design of information technologies for knowledge management in organizations: a pragmatic perspective. Inform. Syst. J. 17 (2), 143–163.

Choi, S.Y., Lee, H., Yoo, Y., 2010. The impact of information technology and transactive memory systems on knowledge sharing, application, and team performance: a field study. MIS Q. 34 (4), 855–870.

Cook, S.D., Brown, J.S., 1999. Bridging epistemologies: the generative dance between organizational knowledge and organizational knowing. Org. Sci. 10 (4), 381–400.

De Long, D.W., 2004. Lost Knowledge: Confronting the Threat of an Aging Workforce. Oxford University Press, New York.

Denford, J.S., Chan, Y.E., 2011. Knowledge strategy typologies: defining dimensions and relationships. Knowl. Manage. Res. Pract. 9 (2), 102–119.

Dulipovici, A., Robey, D., 2013. Strategic alignment and misalignment of knowledge management systems: a social representation perspective. J. Manage. Inform. Syst. 29 (4), 103–126.

Durcikova, A., Gray, P., 2009. How knowledge validation processes affect knowledge contribution. J. Manage. Inform. Syst. 25 (4), 81–108.

El Sawy, O.A., Malhotra, A., Park, Y., Pavlou, P.A., 2010. Research commentary—seeking the configurations of digital ecodynamics: it takes three to tango. Inform. Syst. Res. 21 (4), 835–848.

Ford, D.P., Chan, Y.E., 2003. Knowledge sharing in a multi-cultural setting: a case study. Knowl. Manage. Res. Pract. 1 (1), 11–17.

Garud, R., Kumaraswamy, A., 2005. Vicious and virtuous circles in the management of knowledge—the case of infosys technologies. MIS Q. 29 (1), 9–33.

Grant, R.M., 1996. Toward a knowledge-based theory of the firm. Strateg. Manage. J. 17, 109–122, (winter special issue).

Gray, P.H., Chan, Y.E., 2000. Integrating knowledge management practices through a problem-solving framework. Commun. Assoc. Inform. Syst. 4 (12), 1–22.

Gray, P.H., Durcikova, A., 2005. The role of knowledge repositories in technical support environments: speed versus learning in user performance. J. Manage. Inform. Syst. 22 (3), 159–190.

Grover, V., Davenport, T.H., 2001. General perspectives on knowledge management—fostering a research agenda. J. Manage. Inform. Syst. 18 (1), 5–21.

Hansen, M.T., 1999. The search-transfer problem: the role of weak ties in sharing knowledge across organizational subunits. Admin. Sci. Q. 44 (1), 82–111.

Iyengar, K., Sweeney, J.R., 2015. Information technology use as a learning mechanism—the impact of IT use on knowledge transfer effectiveness, absorptive capacity, and franchisee performance. MIS Q. 39 (3), 615–641.

Jasimuddin, S.M., Connell, N., Klein, J.H., 2012. Knowledge transfer frameworks: an extension incorporating knowledge repositories and knowledge administration: knowledge transfer frameworks. Inform. Syst. J. 22 (3), 195–209.

Kankanhalli, A., Tan, B.C., Wei, K.-K., 2005. Contributing knowledge to electronic knowledge repositories: an empirical investigation. MIS Q. 29, 113–143.

Khodakarami, F., Chan, Y.E., 2014. Exploring the role of customer relationship management (CRM) systems in customer knowledge creation. Inform. Manage. 51 (1), 27–42.

Ko, D.-G., Dennis, A.R., 2011. Profiting from knowledge management: the impact of time and experience. Inform. Syst. Res. 22 (1), 134–152.

Kogut, B., Zander, U., 1992. Knowledge of the firm, combinative capabilities, and the replication of technology. Org. Sci. 3 (3), 383–397.

Kotlarsky, J., Scarbrough, H., Oshri, I., 2014. Coordinating expertise across knowledge boundaries in offshore-outsourcing projects: the role of codification. MIS Q. 38 (2), 607–627.

Levy, M., 2011. Knowledge retention: minimizing organizational business loss. J. Knowl. Manage. 15 (4), 582–600.

Liebowitz, J., 2009. Knowledge Retention: Strategies and Solutions. CRC Press, Boca Raton, FL.

Majchrzak, A., Wagner, C., Yates, D., 2013. The impact of shaping on knowledge reuse for organizational improvement with wikis. MIS Q. 37 (2), 455–469.

Martin de Holan, P., Phillips, N., 2004. Remembrance of things past? the dynamics of organizational forgetting. Manage. Sci. 50 (11), 1603–1613.

Martin de Holan, P., Phillips, N., Lawrence, T.B., 2004. Managing organizational forgetting. MIT Sloan Manage. Rev. Winter, 45–51.

Nevo, D., Chan, Y.E., 2007. A Delphi study of knowledge management systems: scope and requirements. Inform. Manage. 44 (6), 583–597.

Nonaka, I., 1994. A dynamic theory of organizational knowledge creation. Org. Sci. 5 (1), 14–37.

Nonaka, I., Takeuchi, H., 1995. The Knowledge Creating Company. Oxford University Press, New York, NY.

Office of the Information Commissioner of Canada, 2010. Information Management Manual, Office of the Information Commissioner of Canada.

Orlikowski, W.J., 2002. Knowing in practice: enacting a collective capability in distributed organizing. Org. Sci. 13 (3), 249–273.

Parise, S., Cross, R., Davenport, T.H., 2006. Knowledge-loss crisis. MIT Sloan Manage. Rev. Summer, 31–38.

Ragin, C.C., 1994. Constructing Social Research—The Unity and Diversity of Method. Pine Forge Press, Thousand Oaks, CA.

Ragin, C.C., 2000. Fuzzy-Set Social Science. University of Chicago Press, Chicago, IL.

Saldaña, J., 2009. The Coding Manual for Qualitative Researchers. SAGE Publications, Thousand Oaks, CA.

Sambamurthy, V., Subramani, M., 2005. Special issue on information technologies and knowledge management. MIS Q. 29 (1), 1–7.

Spender, J.C., 1996. Making knowledge the basis of a dynamic theory of the firm. Strateg. Manage. J. 17 (Winter), 45–62.

Treasury Board of Canada Secretariat, 2015. Guideline for Employees of the Government of Canada: Information Management (IM) Basics, Treasury Board of Canada Secretariat. Available from: http://www.tbs-sct.gc.ca/pol/doc-eng.aspx?id=16557.

Von Krogh, G., 2009. Individualist and collectivist perspectives on knowledge in organizations: implications for information systems research. J. Strateg. Inform. Syst. 18 (3), 119–129.

Wang, Y., Meister, D.B., Gray, P.H., 2013. Social influence and knowledge management systems use: evidence from panel data. MIS Q. 37 (1), 299–313.

Wu, I.-L., Hu, Y.-P., 2012. Examining knowledge management enabled performance for hospital professionals: a dynamic capability view and the mediating role of process capability. J. Assoc. Inform. Syst. 13 (12), 976–999.

Knowledge and knowledge-related assets: design for optimal application and impact

G.S. Erickson*, H.N. Rothberg**

*Ithaca College, Ithaca, New York, USA; **Marist College, Poughkeepsie, New York, USA

INTRODUCTION

As this chapter was being written an interesting piece appeared in *The Wall Street Journal* (Naik, 2015) concerning theory development around black holes. In particular, there has been much serious thought about what happens to information when it enters a black hole. Einstein posited that its gravitational pull was so strong that once in, nothing, not even light, could escape it. Stephen Hawking added that black holes emit enough radiation that eventually they evaporate, intimating that all that has succumbed to the black hole was gone forever.

And then Hawking changed his mind, calling this assumption, that information could be lost forever, the "biggest blunder" of his career. Instead, working very recently with other physicists on the "information paradox," Hawking has articulated a new view: if information can't be destroyed, then it lives on the black hole's event horizon, waiting to be set free.

And so it goes with organizations over the past three decades trying to capture information, data, and knowledge. Through knowledge management (KM) structures and practices, firms have sought to collect, codify, and redistribute knowledge. But other knowledge-related assets disappeared into the black hole, collected but never released. With the advent of big data and business analytics, we have new potential for releasing and applying these other intangible assets. But will KM systems be a part of the equation or will the potential of a wider purview for knowledge and knowledge-related assets slip through our hands, as it did with competitive intelligence systems?

BACKGROUND: KNOWLEDGE MANAGEMENT

The roots of knowledge management (KM) are often traced back to the innovation literature, with key scholars such as Schumpeter (1934) and Nelson and Winter (1982) emphasizing the role of intangible assets such as knowledge in creating new products and economic growth. As it is discussed in strategy circles, knowledge is seen as the key to competitive advantage. In reference to the resource-based view of the firm (Wernerfelt, 1984), scholars suggested knowledge as the key differentiating resource available to organizations. The knowledge-based view of the firm is predicated on the idea that people are the unique, sustainable source of competitive advantage—that is, identifying, harvesting, and better applying what they know (Zack, 1999a; Teece, 1998; Grant, 1996).

In moving from creativity and innovation to the knowledge-based perspective, however, a subtle shift occurred in how we think about knowledge and related intangibles. The emphasis is less on creating new knowledge but rather on better using existing knowledge assets. This tendency was never absolute and countless counterexamples can be identified. But in large part, creativity and insight were left to be more fully explored in other disciplines (eg, innovation, new product planning & development) while KM increasingly focused on the mechanics of knowledge sharing. This can be seen by taking a deeper look at some of the key themes of KM.

From the beginnings of the discipline, leading scholars specifically identified an interest in knowledge only (Zack, 1999b), with other intangibles labeled precursors of knowledge but unimportant in and of themselves. Ackoff's (1989) DIKW hierarchy (data, information, knowledge, wisdom), in particular, was referenced for what value knowledge provided and for what lower levels such as data and information did not. Within the knowledge category, heavy attention was focused on the difference between tacit knowledge (highly personal, less structured) and explicit knowledge (more structured/codifiable, more easily shared) (Nonaka and Takeuchi, 1995; Polanyi, 1967). In particular, Nonaka and Takeuchi's SECI framework designated the nature of the knowledge exchange (tacit to tacit, tacit to explicit, etc.), leading to the heavy attention on the mechanisms to better share and exploit knowledge in organizations.

On the explicit side, these mechanisms tended toward information technology (IT) solutions (Matson et al., 2003; Thomas et al., 2001). On the tacit side, use of person-to-person interchanges such as communities of practice (CoP) or mentoring (Brown and Duguid, 1991) tended to steer practice and scholarship into organizational behavior topics. In both cases, the willingness of individuals to engage with the KM program was a key topic. Whether individuals will contribute their knowledge to the IT system (or use knowledge stored in it) was an important question. So was willingness to participate in communities of practice (CoPs) or contribute to storytelling. As a consequence, core individual and organizational behavior concepts such as motivation/incentives, trust, power, social capital/social networks, and others were increasingly emphasized by both scholars and practitioners (Nahapiet and Ghoshal, 1998; Gupta and Govindarajan, 2000).

These are all important topics and central to our discipline. But they are also clearly focused on the exchange of knowledge, the better exploitation of existing knowledge as opposed to the creation of new knowledge. With an emphasis on collecting individual knowledge and turning it into an organizational asset, initiatives have tended to center on maximizing the opportunities for capture and redistribution. In a number of ways, KM systems became something of a library function, collecting, cataloguing, and then sharing out identified knowledge assets.

New knowledge must come from somewhere, but Nonaka and Takeuchi (1995) also planted the seed early on that knowledge creation was individual, so knowledge management systems exploited existing individual knowledge but did not focus on creating new knowledge. New knowledge was often referred to as learning, know-how, or in similar terms, indicating the tendency of applications to focus on process improvement or procedures. Many of the illustrative examples that became well-known in the field (Xerox technicians, Buckman Laboratories, Nucor, Intel's Copy Exactly, etc.) leaned heavily to operations applications and efficiency. In the vernacular of innovation studies, we are talking about incremental improvements as opposed to pioneering insights.

Part of the reason for this is the lack of analysis of knowledge once captured or cataloged by the organization. If individuals learn things, then their knowledge is shared with the organization or individuals within the organization, per the KM process. But once distributed back to individuals, the knowledge is usefully applied but not exploited further. Rarely is there analysis for trends, similarities, differences, or any of the other practices that might lead to additional insights. The role of the individual is application, not analysis. Even those KM processes that do include some additional individual intervention are somewhat limited. Knowledge markets, for example, will sometimes utilize a knowledge broker to identify, feature, and reward the most used or most valuable inputs (Matson et al., 2003). But that function is more about tracking use and popularity than insight or creativity, so the individual's role post-KM processing remains limited. The importance of this perspective will become clearer as we contrast KM systems with those employed for other types of intangibles.

RETHINKING THE DIKW HIERARCHY

When doing this contrast of standard KM systems with other alternatives, we have found it helpful to think about the entire range of intangible assets, not just knowledge. As mentioned earlier, the foundation for this discussion is the DIKW, data–information–knowledge–wisdom, hierarchy (Ackoff, 1989). But more recent thinking on the nature of knowledge-related assets provides additional perspective.

Kurtz and Snowden (2003) constructed the Cynefin domains, a fairly wide-ranging reassessment of knowledge exchange and strategic decision-making in different contexts. In particular, the different contexts or domains were more or less ordered and more or less centralized. By understanding the domains, practitioners could more easily navigate their specific context, be it "known," "knowable," "complex," or "chaos," with tools ranging from process reengineering to uncanny action.

This framework is rich in thought and supporting details, but for our purposes, Simard's (2014) recasting is most helpful. Here, the domains are defined according to some more familiar concepts, specifically:

- Common (known), fixed relationships, data/information
- Complicated (knowable), linear, explicit knowledge
- Complex (partially knowable), nonlinear, tacit knowledge
- Chaos (unknowable), disorganized, intuition

We have systems for managing data and information (including enterprise systems and big data), explicit knowledge (often IT-based), tacit knowledge (person-to-person), and intuition (creativity, insight), with greater or lesser success as the domains become more difficult to organize and understand. As noted, however, the KM approaches in the middle tend to stick to knowledge assets and exchange. If additional potential can be found in bringing similar intangible, knowledge-related assets into the discussion, perhaps knowledge can be applied in more strategic, value-added applications. If not, KM may fail to sustain the level of interest and investment being garnered by newer fields such as big data and business analytics.

COMPETITIVE INTELLIGENCE SYSTEMS

Consider the case of competitive intelligence (CI). CI grew up at much the same time KM did, receiving increasing amounts of attention from both practitioners and scholars throughout the 1990s. Focused on understanding competitors and identifying and even anticipating their strategies, tactics, and activities, CI has a number of similarities with KM (Rothberg and Erickson, 2005). In much the same manner as knowledge systems, CI will look to identify and catalog knowledge-related assets. Typically, these are specific to a particular competitor or technology, but parts of the process are much the same as KM.

But several differences are also seen. CI operations are interested in all sorts of inputs (data, information, knowledge) from all sorts of sources, both inside and outside the firm (Prescott and Miller, 2001; Gilad and Herring, 1996; Fuld, 1994). In collecting publicly available information, CI does have something of a library function similar to KM collections. And human intelligence harvests inputs largely considered person-to-person tacit knowledge in the realm we have been discussing. But CI also targets and actively seeks out additional information and knowledge sources (McGonagle and Vella, 2002), a gap-filling exercise less prominent in KM circles.

CI also tends to do more with the inputs once collected. A wide variety of analytical techniques are available to individuals or teams looking to further process the information and knowledge for deeper insights (Fleisher and Bensoussan, 2002), including scenario planning, war games, and others. CI analysts are a recognized

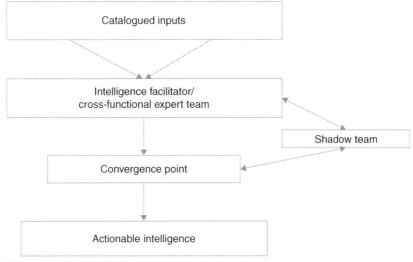

FIGURE 8.1 Competitive intelligence system

feature of the process, bringing an individual element back into the mix once the organization has collected the inputs. Their effectiveness tends to increase as their network of contacts and level of experience grow (Wright et al., 2002; Rouach and Santi, 2001). CI operations, at their most effective, will also have direct access to top decision-makers, so the results of analysis will tend to come forward in a manner leading to actionable recommendations at all levels (strategic, tactical, operational). The point is not just process improvement, though that may happen, but potentially game-changing moves in competitive environments (Bernhardt, 1993).

The system is illustrated in Fig. 8.1, from Gilad (1994) and Gilad and Gilad (1988), as modified by Rothberg and Erickson (2005).

As just described, an array of knowledge and knowledge-related inputs are gathered and cataloged by the organization. These inputs are then subjected to analysis by a CI facilitator, either on her own or with a designated cross-functional expert team. The facilitator and/or team may make use of their additional web of contacts to enhance the analysis, perhaps including a shadow team (Rothberg, 1997) tasked with continuous monitoring and analysis of a specific competitor firm or technology. The insights are delivered to an individual or team with authority to act, often at the highest levels of the organization (the convergence point). And the result is actionable strategic, tactical, or operational intelligence.

One would expect the two disciplines, KM and CI, to have some cross-fertilization given the similar environments in which they operate (harvesting and processing knowledge and knowledge-related assets). And there have been attempts to make sense of the whole knowledge/intelligence world (Andreou et al., 2007) and/or bring KM/CI together directly (Rothberg and Erickson, 2002; Liebowitz, 2006). But there has never been a broad meeting of the minds, something of a loss for both disciplines, but a missed opportunity for KM, in particular, to expand its domain of study and potential for contribution to practice.

THE KNOWLEDGE-RELATED HIERARCHY AND THE DISCIPLINES

The missed opportunity in the KM discipline is both epitomized by and repeated in current trends in big data and business analytics. For a number of reasons, the structure of business analytics platforms much more resembles CI practice than KM. The explanation would be in the nature of the process and how it creates value for decision-makers. Some of the reasons behind the difference can be foreshadowed by another look at the modified knowledge-related hierarchy and how it relates to the different disciplines, as illustrated in Table 8.1.

Starting with the bottom rows, the hierarchy moves in a direction from more structured to less structured form, from data/information easily codified and widely shared through systems through individual insight, almost impossible to teach or share (Kurtz and Snowden's "uncanny" intuition). These distinctions simply extend what we in the KM field have always discussed about explicit vs tacit knowledge. But data/information is even more structured and sharable than explicit knowledge while intuition or insight is even less structured and more personal than tacit knowledge. Further, big data from extended enterprise systems, for example, is easily distributed throughout a network, including all parts of a business and even its collaborators. At the other end of the spectrum, however, intuition/insight is highly personal, even more than tacit knowledge, and may be nonsharable. Explaining the insight process to another individual could be a huge challenge. The results (new investment strategy, new product application) may be a different matter, but the process itself could be impossible to teach.

In terms of the disciplines and as discussed earlier, knowledge management can effectively capture and share explicit and tacit knowledge. But data/information is typically overlooked and not incorporated into the system. And insight/intuition doesn't really come into play as the system is designed to distribute organizational

Table 8.1 Knowledge-Related Hierarchy and Disciplines

Discipline	Data/ Information	Explicit Knowledge	Tacit Knowledge	Intuition/ Insight
Knowledge management		XXX	XXX	
Competitive intelligence	XX	XX	XX	XXX
Big data/business analytics	XXX	X	X	XXX
Characteristics	Structured--Unstructured			
	Systems/mass----------------------------Human/individual			
Range	Network	Company	Group	Individual

knowledge, not subject it to further scrutiny by analysts. Exceptions always exist, but in large part KM practice starts and stops with knowledge proper.

Competitive intelligence, on the other hand, incorporates all manner of inputs, from data/information to explicit knowledge (including publicly available sources) to tacit knowledge (including human intelligence). After the organization accumulates the knowledge, the analyst and/or team further studies it. In the most effective organizations, talented analysts have the ability to discern competitive strategies, intentions, and other insights based on the amassed information, knowledge, and personal insights. High-performance CI operations use all the knowledge-related intangibles to generate actionable intelligence, including that based on "uncanny" insights.

BIG DATA AND BUSINESS ANALYTICS

This brings us to big data and business analytics (BD/BA) (aka business intelligence). As indicated in Table 8.1, we see some similarities in BD/BA to the systems associated with CI. Fewer similarities are apparent with KM systems, perhaps an indication of a missed opportunity for input by KM scholars and practitioners.

BD/BA, as implied by the name, is really a combination of two different types of initiatives in contemporary businesses. They are often discussed together because both use huge databases as an input, but it's also important to recognize the differences in this discussion. Big data systems have been with us for a time, as the massive amounts of data generated by enterprise systems, including supply chain and customer relationship management applications (Vance, 2011a), were becoming apparent almost two decades ago. More recent advances in transaction tracking, internet analytics, and social media metrics have only added to the pile of data available to organizations. What has changed recently is the drop in data processing and storage prices, enabled by the growth of cloud computing, allowing firms to maintain and study these databases (Bussey, 2011; Vance, 2011b). Big data is often characterized by three V's: velocity, volume, and variety (some say a fourth "V" for veracity) (McAfee and Brynjolfsson, 2012; Laney, 2001). The advances in storage and processing have enabled the first two. Data is available in huge quantities (volume) and can be acted upon in real time (velocity) given modern information technology (IT) capabilities.

The third V, variety, is also important and becoming more so with advances in technology. Big data has always been able to move data and information around but current software, such as Hadoop architectures, not only handles simultaneous processing from numerous clusters but can also handle unstructured data. Bringing unstructured data into the mix opens up all sorts of new capabilities, as inputs such as text, visuals, and other such varied sources can be added to the mix. So variety is also rapidly increasing and allowing the sharing and analysis of an ever fully range of inputs.

Big data has had the capability to collect and catalog such inputs, especially data and information, for some time now. What has changed is the capacity, speed, and variety, as just noted. But systems for exchange have been available, with managers determining key performance indicators that they would like continuously monitored, often on dashboards (Watson and Marjanovic, 2013; Chen et al., 2012). The data are increasingly in real time and can provide important input on operational, marketing, or other conditions. But they are not necessarily altered in any way, just exchanged. Nor are they necessarily analyzed, chiefly just monitored. In many ways, these types of big data systems do resemble KM systems, effectively sharing knowledge-related assets and increasing operational efficiencies.

Business analytics, on the other hand, takes a different approach. The data are not just gathered and monitored but analyzed for deeper insights (Watson and Marjanovic, 2013; Chen et al., 2012). Again, advanced technology lends a hand as contemporary data analytics software can apply powerful techniques to the massive datasets in short order. Predictive analytics, clustering studies, text analyses, and similar treatments are behind the ubiquitous stories about analysts discerning unexpected patterns in the databases. In terms of our previous discussion, the inputs come into the organization from a range of individuals/teams and are then analyzed by teams of IT scientists, data scientists, and business analysts. In this way, BD/BA, as fully formed, actually resembles the structure of CI systems more than KM systems. Indeed, high-performance BD/BA organizations may have cross-functional "centers of excellence" combining IT, data analysis, and discipline-specific experts (Davenport, 2013; Brown et al., 2013) while sourcing inputs and distributing outputs throughout the organization (LaValle et al., 2011). And that is not where the similarities end, as illustrated in Table 8.2.

Table 8.2 Knowledge-Related Systems

Characteristics	KM	CI	Big Data/BI
Inputs			
Variety	Knowledge (tacit/explicit)	Data, information, knowledge (tacit/explicit), intuition	Data, information, knowledge (tacit/explicit), intuition
Internal/external	Internal (network)	Internal/external	Internal/external
Actors	Individuals/teams	Individuals/teams	Individuals/teams
Process			
Collection	Yes	Yes	Yes
Variety of models	No, chiefly exchange	Yes (scenario planning, war games, etc.)	Yes (predictive modeling, clustering, etc.)
Analysis	No, chiefly exchange	Yes	Yes
Actors	Organization (but silos)	Organization/teams/individuals	Organization/teams/individuals
Outputs			
Format	Applied knowledge	Insight	Process information, insight
Actionable	Yes, operational	Yes, all levels	Yes, all levels
Level/actors	Operational	Strategic/tactical/operational	Strategic/tactical/operational

In the terms we've discussed, the BD/BA have grown to resemble CI systems much more than KM systems, at least in terms of the business analytics side of the equation. As already noted, the inputs come from a variety of sources. Yes, big data is heavily dependent on data and information, by definition, but it also requires skilled teams of analysts providing insights based on their knowledge and/or even more personalized intuition. The "rock stars" in financial services, for example, who find investment insights in big data have individual, uncanny capabilities, allowing them to see things others do not. So the full range of knowledge-related resources can be put to use. When internal, these can include the full network of business partners (from the enterprise, transactional, and customer relationship management systems noted earlier) as well as the organization itself. Data/information on activities of individuals and teams as well as individual knowledge is fed into the big data system.

All of the systems in question have to do with collecting knowledge-related assets and, to some extent, all catalog and share them. But, again, BD/BA systems more closely resemble CI systems in some other aspects. Most importantly, the intangible catalogs are analyzed in some manner, using a variety of techniques, depending on the purpose. CI teams will employ different methodologies depending on whether analysts are looking to understand a competitor's strategic intent, anticipate an acquisition, or predict the path of a new technology. Similarly, BD/BA analysts will look to predict the best customers for a new product introduction, market baskets of products that sell together more profitably, or when social media activity indicates a brand is heading for trouble. Different tools for different applications. Further, as already noted, both CI and BD/BA are decentralized, collecting knowledge-related assets across the organization and its extended network while also dispersing insight wherever it can be applied. Knowledge management applications are often exclusive to a purpose, hence the popularity of tools such as communities of practice (individuals sharing common concerns, interacting regularly to learn better practices) that are more job-specific.

The outputs of the processes are all of value and can lead to immediate applications. As just noted, however, both CI and BD/BA systems can generate analytical insights that can inform strategic and tactical decisions, in addition to immediate operational actions. Big data and monitored dashboards are particularly useful in the operational context while also informing the higher-level decisions. KM is often limited to operational opportunities. Exceptions exist, but, again, KM IT systems are often pointed to identifying and cataloging best practices and optimizing processes. Similarly, communities of practice, mentoring, and more person-to-person techniques are focused on job performance. The objective is reactive, improving the present, but not proactive, looking to own the future. There are possibilities of higher-level insight but most KM systems are not geared to such purposes.

DISCUSSION: WHAT IS KM MISSING?

So what's the point? This is a book about the missteps that may have occurred in the development and practice of knowledge management, so what is the payoff concerning KM in this context?

What KM does, it is capable of doing very well. Identifying knowledge assets that may be valuable to the organization, cataloguing these assets when possible, and installing appropriate explicit (IT system) and tacit (person-to-person) knowledge management frameworks are all part of the success stories we tell concerning KM. KM theory and practice has also been effective in giving us deeper insights into human behavior concepts such as how to motivate and incentivize individuals to participate in KM systems, whatever the type. A better understanding of social networks, exchanges, trust, and numerous other such topics are enhanced by our better understanding of how individuals exchange and use knowledge.

But we also see a sequence of missed opportunities for the KM discipline, opportunities to broaden its remit, influence theory and practice to an even greater extent, learn from related disciplines, and help develop a broader theory applicable to all knowledge-related assets. This opportunity was missed as KM and CI developed side-by-side but is not irretrievable. And it's certainly not too late to participate in the maturation of big data and business analytics.

Even beyond the different structures, KM and IC have intersected infrequently. The divergence between KM and CI has been clear anecdotally for over a decade (Rothberg and Erickson, 2005) and especially so since metrics were first attached a few years ago, at the industry level, to KM development and CI activity (Erickson and Rothberg, 2012). There are industries in which knowledge needs are very high and competitive intelligence activity is also very high (pharmaceuticals, software), a scenario that is not particularly surprising. Knowledge-related assets are valued by both the generating institution and its competitors. Similarly, there are industries in which knowledge needs are apparently few and competitive intelligence is muted as well (regulated utilities, mature manufacturing). Again, not surprising.

What is interesting are the industries in which the intangibles are valuable to one party but not the other. Industries high in knowledge development but low in competitive intelligence (branded consumer goods, retail) suggest the two disciplines diverge. Similarly, low knowledge development but high competitive intelligence activity (financial services) also show a lack of congruence. An environment in which knowledge is considered unambiguously valuable and in which KM investment is viewed as something to be pursued in all circumstances has a hard time explaining these circumstances. A broader view might not.

One professional at a global business services firm, for example, reported in an interview that the KM and CI functions were managed with a single mind in his organization. Both KM and CI fed data, information, and knowledge into the system from industry-oriented "pockets," and there is an IT system to collect it all and serve as a convergence point. While 140,000 users participate worldwide, there is also a core of 400 knowledge services specialists focusing on 35 core areas of interest. The KM function contributes typical operational improvements, but the collection is further examined for strategic and tactical insights by the specialists. Indeed, CI contributions include specifics on competitors' KM efforts. The systems are complementary, allowing KM to contribute at a higher level, across multiple disciplines, and in a more insightful manner.

At the other end of the spectrum, interviews with two informants from a major international energy firm noted the difficulties of managing KM and CI. While KM was initiated, it never received the same top-level support as the CI function did (even though the latter depended on knowledge contributions for input). CI was viewed as facilitating strategy, so people engaged. KM was viewed as a repository, so people didn't. The KM system never got its incentives right, and so individuals throughout the world did not participate at the level sought. CI had to operate more on its own and had, in fact, lived and died repeatedly; it had "nine lives." The disconnect between strategic-level CI and operations-level KM made it hard for both systems to function effectively and was further complicated by a very "leaky" culture that allowed important knowledge to flow to competitors. Even with the best intentions, failure to integrate the two systems led to major difficulties with both.

A wider view, encompassing not only competitive intelligence and knowledge management initiatives but also big data/business analytics, has the potential to enlarge the role of KM and better explain the dynamics between all the different types of knowledge-related assets. In financial services, for example, big data stocks are enormous and heavily mined, competitive intelligence activity is rampant, but knowledge management activities do not show up in the metrics (Erickson and Rothberg, 2016). A broader yet more in-depth view of the circumstances suggests that data/information are important assets and become particularly valuable when subjected to analysis. Indeed, financial services is a prime example of the "star" system in which hard-to-replace employees are hired and retained with an outsize reward system (Crocker, 2014; Groysberg et al., 2010). So insights coming from highly personal tacit knowledge or even uncanny intuition are the differentiator— and they are extremely hard to manage with KM techniques, if not impossible.

On the other hand, in industries with big consumer brands, big data/business analytics are less but still substantial, knowledge assets are highly valued, but competitive intelligence effort is minimal. A deeper look suggests that part of the difference is considerable explicit knowledge, not only of production processes and logistics, but also customer relationships (relational capital in the intellectual capital vernacular). Big data can contribute directly to this explicit knowledge, tuning it in operational ways. There may be select opportunities for new insights from tacit knowledge and/or uncanny intuition, but these do not show up in the KM metrics in the same manner as explicit knowledge does. Tacit efforts are hard to scale to the extent they show up in financial statements. Competitive intelligence is not highly valued because much of what the high-performing firms do is readily apparent and because powerful brands and established logistical systems are extremely hard for competitors to duplicate. Nothing the high-performing firms are doing is a mystery but duplicating the strategies, tactics, and operations can be quite difficult.

What do we recommend for the knowledge management community? Much should be obvious by now and the case examples certainly provide some guidance. But bringing in the more attractive elements of the more open CI and BD/BA systems would be a start. In particular, a wider perspective on which inputs are of value, cross-functional integration, and a more analytical approach, leading to actionable intelligence at the strategic and tactical levels would all hold promise.

Looking more widely at inputs provides a nice start. Not only can data and information be important precursors to knowledge (particularly explicit), but they can be the gateway to deeper insights through analysis by individuals or teams with applicable tacit knowledge and/or intuition. If a more complete catalog of knowledge-related assets is collected, the potential for impact is increased. KM as a discipline can provide guidance on how to encourage participation in collection, distribution, and analysis systems. And KM as a discipline can learn from the impact gained from deeper analysis (and deeper understanding) of the different types of inputs. Understanding the differences between a highly developed explicit knowledge system, tacit knowledge exchanges, and the needs of industries with star employees can provide new and impactful opportunities for competitive advantage.

Cross-functionality can help get KM applications out of their silos. As previously discussed, knowledge initiatives are often about operational improvements, whether in the supply chain, in operations per se, or in transactional relationships. But they do not necessarily reach beyond these initiatives. KM tends to be institutionally focused, not really allowing for the insights coming from the "eureka" moments an outside perspective, external (to the organization) inputs, or critical analysis can generate. By sharing knowledge-related inputs of all types across functions, the potential for tacit knowledge creation or intuitive insights can be increased. The whole of broadly sourced knowledge-related assets, analyzed effectively, can be considerably more than the sum of the parts.

Finally, moving out of the silos can allow KM and the related intangibles systems to contribute at a higher level. As previously noted, KM can often get stuck in a pattern of incremental improvements to processes, whether supply chain, operations, customer relationships, or other day-to-day activities. CI, on the other hand, works most effectively when it has the ear of those at all levels, particularly top-level strategists who can benefit from the big insights. BD/BA is mixed, but if the emphasis is overly heavy on immediate, day-to-day improvements, the potential exists that both it and KM systems will continue to contribute only on the limited operational level. And as important as those improvements can be, there is no reason for them to be the only contribution. With concerted attention paid to appropriate analysis of all inputs, at all levels, across all functions (and including external contributions), the potential exists to find helpful operational knowledge and new insights at the strategic and tactical levels as well.

CONCLUSIONS

KM systems need not be black holes. They can be event horizons where their contents serve as fuel for other integrating and investigative systems such as CI and BD/BA. Working in unison, these different yet related information and knowledge processes can generate both tactical and strategic support to organization decision making. They can harness the full complement of an organization's information and not only help to release knowing but insightful intelligence as well.

But only if the KM discipline abandons some of its limiting and parochial views. A full range of knowledge-related assets exists, not only tacit and explicit knowledge but also data, information, and intuition/insight. Rather than focusing solely on the capture, cataloguing, and exchange of knowledge-related assets, opportunities exist to subject such inputs to more careful analysis, looking for deeper insights. And the findings of such analysis can be used not only to improve operational processes but can go beyond, using highly personal (and rare) tacit knowledge or uncanny intuition to find new strategies, tactics, and approaches that will be hard for competitors to duplicate—much harder than easily captured and shared explicit knowledge applications. In a number of ways, we feel the future of KM lies in taking on this broader set of responsibilities and grasping the higher sense of contribution that comes from interacting at higher levels of the organization.

REFERENCES

Ackoff, R., 1989. From data to wisdom. J. Appl. Syst. Anal. 16, 3–9.

Andreou, A.N., Green, A., Stankosky, M., 2007. A framework of intangible valuation areas and antecedents. J. Intell. Capital 8 (1), 52–75.

Bernhardt, D., 1993. Perfectly Legal Competitive Intelligence—How to Get It, Use It and Profit From It. Pitman Publishing, London.

Brown, J.S., Duguid, P., 1991. Organizational learning and communities-of-practice: toward a unified view of working, learning, and innovation. Organ. Sci. 2 (1), 40–57.

Brown, B., Court, D., Wilmott, P., 2013. Mobilizing your C-suite for big-data analytics. McKinsey Q. November, 1–11.

Bussey, J., 2011. Seeking safety in clouds. Wall St. J. September, B8.

Chen, H., Chiang, R.H., Storey, V.C., 2012. Business intelligence and analytics: from big data to big impact. MIS Q. 36 (4), 1165–1188.

Crocker, A., 2014. Combining strategic human capital resources: the case of star knowledge workers and firm specificity. Acad. Manage. Proc. January, 10705.

Davenport, T.H., 2013. Analytics 3.0. Harv. Bus. Rev. 91 (12), 64–72.

Erickson, G.S., Rothberg, H.N., 2012. Intelligence in Action: Strategically Managing Knowledge Assets. Palgrave Macmillan, London.

Erickson, G.S., Rothberg, H.N., 2016. Intangible dynamics in financial services. J. Service Theory Pract., forthcoming.

Fleisher, C.S., Bensoussan, B., 2002. Strategic and Competitive Analysis: Methods and Techniques for Analysing Business Competition. Prentice Hall, Upper Saddle River, NJ.

Fuld, L.M., 1994. The New Competitor Intelligence: The Complete Resource for Finding Analyzing, and Using Information About Your Competitors. John Wiley, New York.

Gilad, B., 1994. Business Blindspots. Probus Publishing, Chicago.

Gilad, B., Gilad, T., 1988. Business Intelligence Systems: A New Tool for Competitive Advantage. AMACOM, Chicago.

Gilad, B., Herring, J. (Eds.), 1996. The Art and Science of Business Intelligence. JAI Press, Greenwich, CT.

Grant, R.M., 1996. Toward a knowledge-based theory of the firm. Strategic Manage. J. 17 (Winter), 109–122.

Groysberg, B., Lee, L.-E., Abrahams, R., 2010. What it takes to make 'star' hires pay off. Sloan Manage. Rev. 51 (2), 57–61.

Gupta, A.K., Govindarajan, V., 2000. Knowledge management's social dimension: lessons from Nucor Steel. MIT Sloan Manage. Rev. 42 (1), 71–80.

Kurtz, C.F., Snowden, D.J., 2003. The new dynamics of strategy: sensemaking in a complex-complicated world. IBM Syst. J. 42 (3), 462–483.

Laney, D., 2001. 3D data management: controlling data volume, velocity and variety. Available from: http://blogs.gartner.com/doug-laney/files/2012/01/ad949-3D-Data-Management-Controlling-Data-Volume-Velocity-and-Variety.pdf.

LaValle, S., Lesser, E., Shockley, R., Hopkins, M.S., Kruschwitz, N., 2011. Big data, analytics and the path from insights to value. MIT Sloan Manage. Rev. 52 (2), 21–31.

Liebowitz, J., 2006. Strategic Intelligence: Business Intelligence, Competitive Intelligence, and Knowledge Management. Auerbach Publications, Boca Raton, FL.

Matson, E., Patiath, P., Shavers, T., 2003. Stimulating knowledge sharing: strengthening your organizations' internal knowledge market. Organ. Dyn. 32 (3), 275–285.

McAfee, A., Brynjolfsson, E., 2012. Big data: the management revolution. Harv. Bus. Rev. 90 (10), 60–66.

McGonagle, J., Vella, C., 2002. Bottom Line Competitive Intelligence. Quorum Books, Inc, Westport, CT.

Nahapiet, J., Ghoshal, S., 1998. Social capital, intellectual capital, and the organizational advantage. Acad. Manage. Rev. 23 (2), 242–266.

Naik, G., 2015. Steven Hawking's black hole challenge. Wall St. J. November, C3.

Nelson, R.R., Winter, S.G., 1982. An Evolutionary Theory of Economic Change. Harvard University Press, Cambridge, MA.

Nonaka, I., Takeuchi, H., 1995. The Knowledge-Creating Company: How Japanese Companies Create the Dynamics of Innovation. Oxford University Press, New York.

Polanyi, M., 1967. The Tacit Dimension. Doubleday, New York.

Prescott, J.E., Miller, S.H., 2001. Proven Strategies in Competitive Intelligence: Lessons from the Trenches. John Wiley and Sons, New York.

Rothberg, H.N., 1997. Fortifying competitive intelligence systems with shadow teams. Compet. Intell. Rev. 8 (2), 3–11.

Rothberg, H.N., Erickson, G.S., 2002. Competitive Capital: A Fourth Pillar of Intellectual Capital? In: Bontis, N. (Ed.), World Congress on Intellectual Capital Readings. Elsevier Butterworth-Heinemann, Woburn, MA, pp. 94–103.

Rothberg, H.N., Erickson, G.S., 2005. From Knowledge to Intelligence: Creating Competitive Advantage in the Next Economy. Elsevier Butterworth-Heinemann, Woburn, MA.

Rouach, D., Santi, P., 2001. Competitive intelligence adds value: five intelligence attitudes. Eur. Manage. J. 19 (5), 552–559.

Schumpeter, J.A., 1934. The Theory of Economic Development. Harvard University Press, Cambridge, MA.

Simard, A., 2014. Analytics in context: modeling in a regulatory environment. In: Rodriguez, E., Richards, G. (Eds.), Proceedings of the International Conference on Analytics Driven Solutions, pp. 82–92.

Teece, D.J., 1998. Capturing value from knowledge assets: the new economy, markets for know-how, and intangible assets. Calif. Manage. Rev. 40 (3), 55–79.

Thomas, J.C., Kellogg, W.A., Erickson, T., 2001. The knowledge management puzzle: human and social factors in knowledge management. IBM Syst. J. 40 (4), 863–884.

Vance, A., 2011a. The data knows. Bloomberg Businessweek September, 70–74.

Vance, A., 2011b. The power of the cloud. Bloomberg Businessweek March, 52–59.

Watson, H.J., Marjanovic, O., 2013. Big data: the fourth data management generation. Bus. Intell. J. 18 (3), 4–8.

Wernerfelt, B., 1984. The resource-based view of the firm. Strategic Manage. J. 5 (2), 171–180.

Wright, S., Picton, D., Callow, J., 2002. Competitive intelligence in UK firms, a typology. Market. Intell. Plan. 20 (6), 349–360.

Zack, M.H., 1999a. Developing a knowledge strategy. Calif. Manage. Rev. 41 (3), 125–145.

Zack, M.H., 1999b. Managing Codified Knowledge. Sloan Manage. Rev. 40 (4), 45–58.

Knowledge management success and failure: the tale of two cases

S. Larson

School of Business, Slippery Rock University, Slippery Rock, PA, USA

INTRODUCTION

Knowledge management (KM) refers to the practices and strategies that a company uses in an attempt to create, distribute, and enable adoption of strategic insights and specific experiences (O'Leary, 2002). In service organizations, collaboration and sharing of knowledge have clear benefits for internal and external stakeholders, enhance business performance (Wong et al., 2014), and build customer loyalty.

Service companies know that good knowledge management of their customers is the main successful factor of current corporations (Hall, 2001). Many service companies are brokers of knowledge to their stakeholders (Jarvenpaa and Staples, 2001); the two companies in this chapter fall specifically into this category.

Porter (1979) discusses differentiation as one of the three strategies for competing in the marketplace. Implementing a knowledge management system is a way to decrease costs and differentiate your company from competitors. This sentiment is shared by Riege (2005), who found that "in a knowledge-driven economy, organizations' intangible assets are increasingly becoming a differentiating competitive factor, particularly in services industries."

As such, service industries must instill in their employees a desire and enthusiasm to share their knowledge with coworkers and customers. "For an organization to achieve the desired level of collaboration and knowledge sharing, it needs to communicate to its employees how the generation, sharing, and then application of knowledge is valued at the individual level, while also recognizing group or team-based performances and collective accomplishments" (Riege, 2005).

Zetie (2003) argues that one barrier to adoption and integration of a knowledge management system into our daily work lives will probably be human reluctance to potentially become redundant or be replaced by a machine. This is particularly true for service and knowledge companies—the employees fear that sharing their knowledge that can then be easily accessed by customers will render them unnecessary and irrelevant. The barriers to knowledge sharing and the implementation of knowledge management systems are as numerous as the companies who strive to implement knowledge management systems.

The literature is replete with studies showing the relationship between commitment to the organization and sharing knowledge. Hall (2001) argued that people are more willing to share their knowledge if they are convinced that doing so is useful and that sharing their knowledge will be appreciated, and the shared knowledge will actually be used. Additionally, van den Hooff and de Ridder (2004) concluded that an individual who is more committed to an organization is more likely to be willing to share their knowledge, a conclusion shared by Jarvenpaa and Staples (2001).

CASE STUDY 1: LANGUAGE, CULTURE, AND LEADERS: A CASE STUDY OF THE CHALLENGES OF INSTALLING A KNOWLEDGE MANAGEMENT SYSTEM IN A TAX FIRM
BUSINESS SETTING

The organization in this study is a tax division in the Tokyo, Japan, branch of a multinational tax firm. Their business depends on making time sensitive, informed tax decisions for their customers. The company and its tax analysts rely heavily on extensive internal research and external data sources for the latest tax rules and compiling this information to make actionable decisions, which are then recommended to customers.

As a way to improve their service and better compete, the company, like others, agreed with Shen et al. (2009) that it "needed to continually develop and improve its working practices, culture and environment, systems, and tools by implementing knowledge management initiatives and developing a knowledge management strategy to more formally identify, manage, and apply its knowledge assets."

The tax division for expatriate taxes consists of several tax managers, an English editorial manager, a few partners, and one managing partner. When the tax manager receives a request from a client about a tax issue, the team follows a process to research the issue, find a solution, and then write an opinion letter to the client. Specifically, the process steps are:

1. Customer contacts tax manager with problem/issue.
2. Tax manager and his/her team researches issue and potential solutions.
3. Tax manager writes up an opinion letter and sends to the tax partner in charge of the customer.
4. Tax partner reviews for correctness. Returns to tax manager for revisions.
5. Tax manager revises and sends to English editor, who reviews for correct English, then returns it to tax manager.
6. Tax manager resends opinion letter to partner.
7. Partner reviews and approves (if not, restart at appropriate step) and sends to managing partner.
8. Managing partner gives final review and approval.
9. Letter sent to customer on company letterhead.

BUSINESS PROBLEM

While this process works, it is not as efficient as the firm would like it to be. The senior partners have "always done it this way" and did not see a need to change. As they moved up through the ranks, they worked the same way and felt that the current method was sufficient. However, the managers would like to see changes to the process and technologies used, both to decrease costs and to speed up the process. Specifically, the managers see the following problems with the current process:

- The "print, review, correct, and repeat" cycle is too lengthy.
- Two tax managers may be researching similar customer problems/issues. This can result in redundant research and/or the managers may reach dissimilar solutions.
- There is no collaboration among the managers; hence, future customers with similar issues do not benefit from previous research by managers on a different team.
- With each problem/issue and solution, the opinion letter is printed multiple times, increasing the cost.
- There is no index or catalogue of the issues. This makes it difficult to keep track of issues and their solutions.

It was clear that a new process was needed, and technology would facilitate the change.

GOALS OF THE KM SYSTEM

The goals of the new KM system were threefold:

1. Cut costs of researching and publishing an opinion letter.
2. Take less time to research an issue and publish each opinion letter.
3. Take advantage of previous research efforts by sharing.

PROPOSED SOLUTION

To rectify the problems with the current process, we recommended a knowledge management system set up as follows:

1. All tax research done and all opinion letters can be added to the KM system.
2. All documents in the KM system will be indexed, and the text of each document fully searchable.
3. The documents and opinion letters should only be printed once, just before sending to the customer. All reviews should be made electronically and changes tracked. All versions should be kept in the system.
4. Metadata should be added to the final version of each opinion letter to facilitate indexing and searching.

The tax partners at the firm were enthusiastic about the new KM system, as it appeared it would enable them to cut costs and increase revenue. The costs of researching an issue would be lowered as much redundant research could be saved. Additionally, the research could be shared among many clients, but the partners believed they could charge the same fee for the research to each client that required it. The senior partners were enthusiastic that the entire tax department could work as one team; indeed, the Japanese culture emphasizes cooperation and teamwork (Morris and Empson, 1998). The hope was that by working as one team instead of several independent teams, the research could be shared and overall costs would decrease.

IMPLEMENTING THE KM SYSTEM

The easiest part of the new KM system was the hardware and software. For this system, a commercial off-the-shelf server with Windows Server OS was purchased. The documents placed in the file share were indexed and searchable with a search engine installed on the server, with a web interface.

Users were trained in the KM system's use; topics included preparing documents for inclusion, adding metadata, saving documents to the system, searching the repository, saving a search for later use, downloading a document to the local PC for modification, adding a modified document to the repository, and other related tasks.

CHALLENGES

Riege (2005) found 17 individual barriers and 14 organizational barriers to knowledge sharing and also found that different combinations of knowledge-sharing barriers would be found in organizations. Much like Riege's findings, the challenges to implementing and using this new KM system stemmed from leadership, cultural, and language issues. When the new KM system was implemented, several of the tax managers and partners expressed trepidation at the transparency the new system provides. Their concerns included:

- Managers and partners see the research as their own work and not something that someone else in or out of the company should be able to benefit from without appropriate remuneration or compensation.
- The leaders were concerned about what others might think of their own work/research, possibly because they have poor research skills or are shy and do not want others to see or share their research.
- The managers do not want to be responsible for mistakes that propagate beyond the initial opinion letter. Even though there is a review by the partner in charge of the team, there is always the possibility of an error. If the error were not discovered, it could affect more than just a few clients. If the error were discovered, it would bring shame upon the entire team.

At the time of implementation, the KM system only handled English text; thus the language challenges included:

- For several team members, translating their research and opinion letters into English was quite challenging. Many team members were embarrassed by their poor English skills and did not want to even try to translate their work, even though this is why they hired an English editor.

- Developing English language metadata was also deemed too difficult by many team members. For several, there appeared to be no acceptable English translation for some words, ideas, and metadata.

The greatest challenges came from the cultural environment. These challenges included:

- The KM system provides more transparency for each partner's team so a spirit of competition entered into the group. Japan is quite team oriented, and competition among teams in this firm was a new experience.
- As teamwork is the norm, a manager or partner with more opinion letters than the others made them feel like they would stand out above the rest. Though the goal was to have the entire team succeed, if one team was deemed to have contributed much more than the others, team members would feel uncomfortable.
- The work culture was one of staying as late as possible, many times catching the last train home. Team members often went to dinner together and returned to the office afterward to finish up work. The practice of checking your work into the KM system at the end of each day resulted in the date and time stamps on documents showing who stayed late and who left early.

In spite of these challenges, the project received approval mainly on its financial merits. The cost savings of not printing multiple copies of each opinion letter, the time savings of not performing redundant research, and the idea of becoming one large team instead of several small teams convinced the senior partners to approve the project.

RESULTS AND CONCLUSION

Ultimately the KM system was successfully installed and implemented. However, the project was a failure because the challenges listed previously defied resolution. Specifically, the managers and partners didn't like to share their research with others. Their knowledge domain can be specialized, and it was also a validation of their worth and importance in the firm when they are asked for input or advice from other partners or managers. Furthermore, many were shy and didn't want others to see their research skills or lack thereof. The biggest challenge for the leaders, though, was the fear of making a mistake that was then propagated to other teams and clients. This was a fear that we were unable to overcome.

Additionally, the language challenges proved to be more difficult than anticipated. The firm was unwilling to hire a professional translator to help the English editor (who was not bilingual), and thus translating documents into English and developing the English metadata for ease of indexing and searching was not able to be accomplished.

Finally, the cultural challenges proved the most difficult. The competition that had entered into the team as a whole was not something that the leadership was comfortable with continuing. Moreover, conformity and not standing out in the crowd are valued characteristics in this culture. Having more opinion letters in the KM system than other teams would be a cause for embarrassment and make some employees feel uncomfortable and self-conscious. And knowing that your boss was able to see what time you checked in a document, which could point to what time you finished your work on a given night, was something employees were reluctant to encounter.

Riege (2005) found that "knowledge sharing practices often seem to fail because companies attempt to adjust their organizational culture to fit their KM or knowledge sharing goals and strategy, instead of implementing them so that they fit their culture." Clearly this tax organization did not attempt to consider all the cultural barriers before designing and implementing the KM system, which resulted in the ultimate rejection of the system. Due to the inability to overcome the challenges and the cultural environment, the KM system was scrapped less than a year after implementation.

CASE STUDY 2: BUILDING A BETTER KNOWLEDGE MANAGEMENT AND CUSTOMER SERVICE SYSTEM
INTRODUCTION

The customer on the phone was not happy. His service ticket for maintenance on his server was a few days old. The technician assigned to his case was on vacation, and there were no status updates to give him. Another technician was assigned, but it would be hours before he would be familiar enough to provide adequate service. Becky, the customer support manager at Acme Solutions, thought "There must be a better way."

This case study will detail the challenges encountered and successfully overcome in designing, implementing, and using a knowledge management system as the basis for a customer service solution.

BUSINESS SETTING

Acme Solutions provides the backend hardware and software for cable and internet companies providing video-on-demand. Acme is based on the West Coast of the United States, with customers spread throughout the United States and in various countries.

The customer service team worked normal office hours for the West Coast, as well as providing on-call service during evenings and weekends. The team used an internal help desk ticketing system to track customer service and maintenance issues. The ticketing system also produced reports, which gave management an idea of the time it took to respond to calls for service, which customer support technicians handled each service issue, and the length of time to resolution for each issue. Customers had access to a small but growing collection of technical articles and white papers on the company's website.

BUSINESS PROBLEM

Based on customer comments about recent service issues, Becky knew a new system or solution was necessary. The current help desk ticketing system was sufficient for internal purposes, but the customers wanted more information about their service issues and more timely status updates.

Nätti et al. (2006) found that insufficient communication channels among experts and subgroups of service providers can cause problems in relation to knowledge transfer, which can result in difficulties combining expertise creating innovative service concepts for customers. Becky also knew that a repository of issues and problems and their associated solutions would be necessary to satisfy the needs of the company and the wants of the customers. The employees generally kept solutions to common issues to themselves, usually because they did not know if anyone else needed the information, but also because the knowledge made them more valuable to the company.

Beyond the help documentation and online information, Becky needed an incentive to encourage support personnel to add issues and their solutions to the knowledge base part of the KM system she had planned.

GOALS

The overall goal for the KM and customer service system was simple: differentiate Acme Solutions' product and service offerings by providing a repository of information that internal and external stakeholders can access, modify, and add to if necessary. Breaking down this goal to more achievable and measurable units, the list of goals included:

1. More timely information for customers.
2. Repository for issues and solutions, accessible by both internal and external stakeholders.
3. Customers can access and add information to service tickets.
4. Internal only area in the help desk ticket system for customer service technicians.
5. Provide an incentive for customer support persons to add issues and solutions to the knowledge base.

SYSTEM IMPLEMENTATION

The system was implemented in phases. The first phase involved modifying the help desk ticket system into a customer service system. Phase two involved implementing a KM system that would be accessible both internally and externally. Phase three included devising an incentive to encourage employees to add to the KM system.

As the new system will be customer facing, the system creation methodology included the customers in the planning, development, and implementation stages, basically following the Agile programming methodology. This methodology also followed the company's method of adding features to the video-on-demand systems Acme provides to its customers, an adaptation of Agile programming.

HELP DESK TICKET SYSTEM

It was decided that in addition to customer support technicians, systems analysts, and management having access to the system, the customers would also be able to add information to the service tickets. This interactivity would allow the customers to participate more on the resolution of their issue(s), serving also as a way to educate the customers. The customers were quite enthusiastic about this idea, and had many requests for features they wanted in the system. After implementing and testing each feature, the customers were contacted and asked to try it out and give their feedback. The feedback was then incorporated into the feature(s).

There were some challenges that were encountered, including:

- Requested features that could not be implemented. For example, near the beginning of building the system, all of the entries added by the customer support technicians were visible by customers. Unfortunately, some of the entries concerned bugs in the program and other proprietary information. The system had to be modified to allow the customer support analysts to flag which entries were not to be seen by customers and which were visible by customers.
- Customer support technicians and customers were not able to access the most up-to-date information needed. Part of the reason for this is that the customers often performed system maintenance and restarts in the middle of the night and would report the results the next day. It helped the customer support technicians to be able to arrive at work in the morning with an update from the customer in the system. Conversely, the customers appreciated not having to wait until the support technician was available so they could report the results of the maintenance and have it entered into the ticketing system; they could enter the results and information themselves. This sped up the resolution of service issues.
- Customers wanted the ability to do some things that the company was not ready for. For example, several customers wanted the ability to open a service ticket, and assign their preferred technician.
- The customer service system was situated in the DMZ on the company's website. This required setting up an extranet and potentially exposing some proprietary information to public view. This challenge was overcome by requiring each customer to register each of their employees who needed access to the system. Security logs were kept and reviewed in order to ensure that customers only tried to view their own service tickets and information.

KM SYSTEM

Implementing the KM system was easier than first imagined. A simple online knowledge base was created and populated with initial articles and white papers. All articles were fully indexed, searchable, and viewable by both internal and external stakeholders. The knowledge base was also situated in the DMZ on the company's website. Beyond the security challenges that were shared with the help desk ticket system, there were no real challenges encountered.

During the investigation of each issue, the help desk employees were able to mark entries in each ticket as private or not shareable with the customers. This was important because some bugs in the programs or issues with the video-on-demand systems were not to be publicized. The KM system could not only be accessed via the company's website, but also each help desk ticket included links to any appropriate knowledge base article. When working on an issue, help desk employees would refer to appropriate knowledge base articles related to the issues. If none existed, but the employee deemed one or more were necessary, then the employee could create an article and link to it in the help desk ticket, allowing the customer to see where the solutions to their issues were found.

INCENTIVE PROGRAM

As with many programs, getting support from all levels of employees can be challenging. Morris and Empson (1998) found that "when a company has a KM system that is technology-based, as most currently are, it is imperative to have the right combination of personal incentives and cultural norm of cooperation." In this case, the management and leadership of the company supported the new customer service system and KM system fully. Unfortunately, however, the help desk employees were reluctant to contribute to the knowledge base; it appeared to be just extra work for them. This caused the content of the knowledge base to stagnate, and slowed its growth.

To encourage help desk employees to contribute content to the knowledge base, an incentive was devised. For each ten technical articles, white papers, issue and solution papers, or help-type articles, an employee was rewarded with a gift card from a local merchant, chain store, restaurant, or grocery store.

Upon implementation of this incentive, several employees started to participate. Soon there were a few hundred articles in the knowledge base, but another challenge presented itself. The quality of several knowledge base articles was very low, and in some cases, the content of the articles were wrong.

To overcome this challenge, a peer review system was implemented whereby two coworkers reviewed each article in the knowledge base before it was flagged for indexing, searching, and viewing by external stakeholders.

RESULTS AND CONCLUSION

Riege (2005) states that "the main reason … why most companies do not reach their knowledge-sharing goals seems to be due to the lack of a clear connection between the KM strategy and overall company goals, possibly because knowledge sharing time and again is perceived as a separate activity." After a while, Acme Solutions' employees discovered the connection between the KM and the company goals of great customer service. As a result, shortly after implementation of the new KM and customer service system, the goals were quickly realized:

- The timeliness of information on service issues provided customers with better and quicker service. The transparency provides motivation to customer support technicians to resolve issues quicker, which is facilitated by more active participation by the customers.
- The knowledge base became a wonderful repository of not only an online user and technical manuals, but also was accessible from the customer service system. As issues are resolved, the service tickets link to relevant information in the knowledge base. Service ticket information remained available only to customers who own the issue.
- Active contributions to the knowledge base increased. Some employees contributed for the incentive, some contributed in spite of the incentive, and a small group even began a contest of sorts to see who contributed the most articles.
- As more and more customers access the knowledge base for information including user manuals, the user manuals are no longer printed, saving thousands of dollars a year.
- One manager thought the prolific contributors were spending too much time writing knowledge base articles and not doing enough service tickets. Fortunately, the customer service system logged which employee handled each ticket, and we found that part of the reason some employees contributed more articles is because they handled and resolved more issues, and wrote articles to help the customers resolve issues without calling for help.
- Customers love being able to add information to service tickets and often times found issue resolution information in the knowledge base before the need to open a ticket. This created more loyalty among customers who were thinking of switching to a competing provider.
- Non-customers were invited to try out the customer service system and knowledge base, and as a result several customers switched to Acme's products and services.
- Because "customers don't always know how to express what they really need" (Koplowitz, 2014), several features were implemented that were later eliminated from the system after a period of time. Many of these were requested by customers, but after a while they found they did not need the feature or functionality after all.
- Customers continue to request new features or modification to current features. These are always taken under consideration, and if possible, implemented.

As a result of implementing the new customer service and KM system, Acme is retaining customers in a volatile market, competitor's customers are starting to switch to Acme's services and products, and employees feel more able to research and resolve issues more quickly, thus strengthening the customers' loyalty.

REFERENCES

Hall, H., 2001. Input-friendliness: motivating knowledge sharing across intranets. J. Inform. Sci. 27 (3), 139–146.

Jarvenpaa, S.L., Staples, D.S., 2001. Exploring perceptions of organizational ownership of information and expertise. J. Manage. Inform. Syst. 18 (1), 151–183.

Koplowitz, R., 2014. It's time to talk about customers, May 28, 2014 Available from: http://www.kmworld.com/Articles/Editorial/Features/Its-time-to-talk-about-customers-97040.aspx

Morris, T., Empson, L., 1998. Organization and expertise: an exploration of knowledge bases and the management of accounting and consulting firms. Account. Org. Soc. 23 (5/6), 609–624.

Nätti, S., Halinen, A., Hanttu, N., 2006. Customer knowledge transfer and key account management in professional service organizations. Int. J. Serv. Ind. Manage. 17 (4), 304–319.

O'Leary, D., 2002. Technologies of knowledge storage and assimilation. Handbook on Knowledge Management 1 Knowledge Directions. Springer-Verlag, Heidelberg, pp. 29–46.

Porter, M., 1979. How competitive forces shape strategy. Harv. Bus. Rev. 57, March–April, p. 138.

Riege, A., 2005. Three-dozen knowledge-sharing barriers managers must consider. J. Knowl. Manage. 9 (3), 18–35.

Shen, C.C., Ogiwara, N., Nair, P., Young, R., 2009. Knowledge Management: Case Studies for Small and Medium Enterprises. Asian Productivity Organization, Tokyo, Japan.

van den Hooff, B., de Ridder, J., 2004. Knowledge sharing in context: the influence of organizational commitment, communication climate, and CMC use on knowledge sharing. J. Knowl. Manage. 8 (6), 117–130.

Wong, C., Yuen, C., Yee, C., Chan, C., Lin, Y., Chan, E., Ling, Y., Cheng, S., Leong, L., 2014. Knowledge management cases in Asia/a case study on the effects of implementing a customer knowledge management system to a public transport corporation. Available from: http://en.wikibooks.org/wiki/Knowledge_Management_Cases_in_Asia/A_Case_Study_on_the_Effects_of_Implementing_a_Customer_Knowledge_Management_System_to_a_Public_Transport_Corporation

Zetie, C., 2003. Machine-to-machine integration: the next big thing? Available from: www.informationweek.com/story/showArticle.jhtml?articleID=8900042

Social Knowledge: Organizational currencies in the new knowledge economy

10

K.E. Russell*, R. La Londe**, F. Walters**

*Wichita State University, USA; **iTalent Corporation, USA

THE ODOMETER READING: EVOLUTION OF SOCIAL KNOWLEDGE MANAGEMENT

Social Knowledge simply stated is the information created through interaction. When people communicate to formulate ideas or solve problems, valuable knowledge is generated. This is not new; it has been around forever. However, with the emergence of social networking there is a new convergence of technologies, capabilities, human behaviors, and expectations that are changing the landscape and how we interact with each other, our customers, our partners, and especially our business colleagues and peers. Social Knowledge Management™ (SKM) as a practice works to facilitate and demonstrate how knowledge assets can be (re)used effectively and contributes to the success of communicating within connected organizations. It has and will continue to reshape how we live, work, and play. Our social knowledge, then, is a key factor in a larger *social knowledge economy* that governs our approach to working together, how we go to market, and how we exist in a collaborative society powered by interactive technologies—making social knowledge critical in the vocabulary of today's thought leaders. But why is social knowledge so valuable and so different from established knowledge management practices? A brief evolutionary history will provide the backdrop for why social knowledge is so important and relevant in today's fast-paced enterprise.

CONVERSATIONS BUILD COMMUNITIES

Social Knowledge emerges out of both formal (company meetings, portals, and email), as well as informal (office communications and reliance on chance encounters), conversations and the incidental sharing of information commonly known as *tribal knowledge*. Whether formal or informal, Social Knowledge has, at its core, the very basic elements of human interaction: the conversation. Think about what a conversation is: it is *bidirectional*, it is *participatory*, and it is *informational*. Social Knowledge is all of these things plus a bit of technology that enables conversations to take place between different individuals, whether they are across the building or across the world. There is a synergy that occurs through the *culmination of these ideas* that work together to create and build communities.

Isn't social knowledge the same as everyday conversation? Isn't participating and sharing information just *what we do*?

Think about your everyday life.

Most conversations occur in our lives without specific thought or consideration regarding the essential elements of Social Knowledge Management: sharing, tracking, crediting, and retaining. These elements hint at an *organizational currency* (currencies, actually), and each contributes to making Social Knowledge a relevant, influential, and valuable asset within an organization. Following are short definitions of each of the five organizational currencies. These are the key elements that represent organizational value in today's *Social Knowledge Economy*:

- *Content (knowledge assets)*: Provides a way for teams to capture knowledge naturally, thereby creating a *content* creation cycle where content is created, evolved, and shared globally.
- *Contribution (credit tracing)*: Provides a way for organizations to track *contributions* back to the origin of a knowledge asset.
- *Enhanced human experience*: Provides a solution that inspires people to participate, create, and socialize.
- *Collaboration (engagement/sharing)*: Provides opportunities for teams to connect, capture conversations, and *collaborate* to solve business challenges together.
- *Competence acceleration (expert)*: Provides for the ability to accelerate *competence* in the organization by fast-tracking the learning process and helping teams expand the number of subject matter experts quickly.

MORE THAN AN IDEA, IT'S A PRACTICE

Social knowledge is challenging boundaries as organizations are being pushed to be more creative and innovative. The resulting activities can lead to ambiguity and chaos as social knowledge capabilities begin to emerge organically across the enterprise. The path to the destination of a thriving SKM practice is transformational; however, it can be treacherous, bumpy, and crowded! Organizations that can harness the practice of Social Knowledge Management effectively will drive exponential value back into the business.

SKM delivers a distinct practice that provides the framework and method to capture, create, iterate, and share social knowledge assets across organizations. It is the demand to unlock the value that Social Knowledge provides that propels an SKM practice. SKM is the vehicle, Social Knowledge is the engine, and people are the fuel.

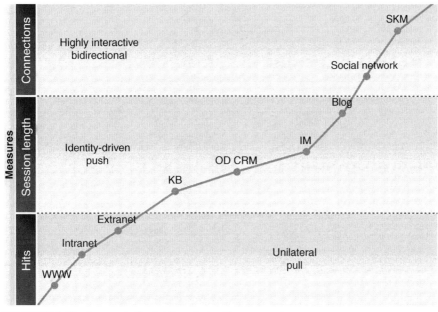

FIGURE 10.1 The journey to Social Knowledge Management

AN EVOLUTIONARY ROAD

Social Knowledge Management has evolved as part of the advances we have experienced since the proliferation of the World Wide Web (WWW) in the early 1990s. The journey, however, to connect the knowledge workforce has been dramatic, as shown in Fig. 10.1.

Consider the last 20 years:

- *Web, intranet, extranet, and portals*: These platforms focused on community but did not promote the use of knowledge and had minimal collaboration.
- *Knowledge bases (KBs)*: These platforms focused on content but did not focus on user-driven communities, limiting collaboration.
- *Early on-demand customer relationship management (OD CRM)*: Captured problems and tracked issues but lacked robust reuse opportunities.
- *Email*: Fostered collaboration and *individual* knowledge bases, but remained locked up in email folders with limited external access.
- *Early instant messaging (IM/web support chat)*: These have collaboration, but limited retained knowledge.
- *Blogs*: A step forward in online collaboration but with limited creativity or retention of structured knowledge assets.
- *Social network (enterprise and mobile collaboration)*: Real-time, anywhere, dynamic collaboration with limited ability to retain and reuse. Enabled creation of robust communities but limited ability to evolve the valuable interactions into knowledge assets.

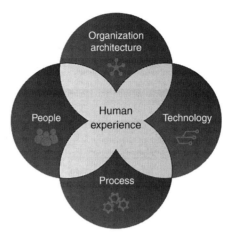

FIGURE 10.2 Influence of Social Knowledge Management

- *Social Knowledge Management: (SKM)*: This practice converges collaboration, communities, content management, and traditional knowledge management enabling the capture, publication, and reuse of the organization's Intellectual capital/property.

MANAGING SOCIAL KNOWLEDGE: PEOPLE, PROCESS, TECHNOLOGY, AND THE HUMAN EXPERIENCE

For business solutions, we historically focus on *people, process*, and *technology*. Many organizations spend a great deal of time on *process* and even more on the *technology*, but very little time on the most important component, the *people*. The *human experience* within an organization is significant, and when enabled by technology, it is a leading factor in the success or failure of any effort or project. An underpinning of the *human experience* is the *organization architecture*, and contributes to the way in which resources are organized to optimize an SKM practice, as shown in Fig. 10.2.

Without the *people* component, *processes* are not pursued and *technology* is not used, and most importantly, knowledge is not created.

SHOWING VALUE WITH SKM (PUTTING MILES ON THE ODOMETER)

Social Knowledge Management (SKM) contributes to the organization in a number of ways. These contributions have measurable value (currency) and can be used as guideposts that help mark progress and maximize the access and benefits of shared knowledge. These include:

- *Meaningful content*: Creation and capture of valuable collaborative knowledge.
- *Refine and reuse*: Dynamic interactions to capture, (re)use, iterate, evolve, and share knowledge.
- *Expert acceleration*: Faster development of expert knowledge workers.
- *Acknowledgement*: Enabling the ability to track, recognize, and give accolades.
- *Adoption*: Increasing usage resulting in a more productive, effective, and satisfying environment.

Organizations have never been better equipped to maximize the value of knowledge. SKM provides a method, a technique, and an approach to working with human capital in new and more meaningful ways … all while turning *normal* collaboration into knowledge that can be captured, shared, and reused. The practice of SKM enables an organization to harness of the value of knowledge from what was once ambiguous and chaotic by leveraging new and emerging technologies, expanded capabilities, and a better understanding and application of the human experience.

Quick List: Are you prepared for the SKM journey? You will know you are ready for SKM when:

- You can't remember why a particular solution was implemented.
- Your organization solves the same problem, over and over again.
- Your inability to develop experts quickly inhibits the scalability of your organization.
- What knowledge you do have seems to age quickly and is highly perishable.
- You finally realize there needs to be a destination to your journey (not just a constant road trip).
- You leave meetings with lots of notes, but no knowledge.
- You spend a lot of time on process improvement but realize it wasn't the process (or the technology) after all … it is the people.

Step by step: Want to try something today? Follow these steps to kick off the SKM process:

1. Make a list of all of the *notes* outside your knowledge management system to remind yourself of processes and tasks (check around you as well to see what others are doing).
2. Make sure all processes have a *human element*. Many people tend to skip the need for human participation in a value chain. This is a key element of SKM.
3. Make sure you are on at least two different social media platforms and understand how to use them.

MERGING INTO TRAFFIC: TRUSTING THE RULES OF THE ROAD IN THE NEW SOCIAL ECONOMY

As we've stated earlier, Social Knowledge begins with the conversation. Remember: *Conversations build communities*. Going a bit deeper, companies considering a Social Knowledge Management effort should pay special attention to other *traffic* within the organization to determine the impact of the effort on the rest of the organization, as well as the impact on the expectations of a particular community. With so many initiatives competing for attention, traffic jams can be common, with the organizational will ebbing and flowing within a given organization.

As popular Social Knowledge tools and mobile applications have proliferated in the market over the last several years, the change in the way we work has accelerated. The knowledge workforce, once dominated by the Baby Boomer generation, is now impacted heavily by Millennials and Generation Z. They all come to the workplace with vastly different expectations on how to work, when to work, where to work, and with whom to work.

A GENERATIONAL SHIFT

Millennials (and even younger Generation Z workers) expect technology and collaborative interaction to be a fundamental part of their job, while older workers may be more comfortable with traditional communication tools rather than learning new ways of working. Moreover, the older workers may even discount social capabilities and activities as *not working*. To some degree, Gen Xers expect these to be part of the job as well, particularly those already in some sort of digital workforce.

Generational challenges include a total transforming workforce, and not just the *older* versus the *younger*. There are also variations of technology agility, expectations, and arrogance within generations. Two examples are: the stigma of *job hopping* has evolved into *portability of workers*, and the meaning of cultural diversity continues to change as technology makes communication instantaneous and without *filters*.

Also, generational gaps can occur when attempting to communicate. Finding ways to convey or interpret tone in the written word can be difficult. For example, eliminating idioms that do not translate well into another language or culture will help make your content more understandable by all parties.

The world is getting smaller with global events and technology bringing us closer together. An example is watching news events unfold on Twitter, such as uprisings in Egypt and the Malaysia airline plane disappearance, and hearing news on social sites first before it hits the traditional news sources. Other examples are being able to stay in touch with family and friends across the world instantly, and connecting the workforce across time zones.

THE EMERGING SOCIAL (KNOWLEDGE) ECONOMY

We are facing enormous societal and economic pressures, and how we deal with them will depend heavily on our ability to gather, store, analyze, and model large and disparate amounts of data. The interesting thing about all of this is that many organizations have accumulated mountains of data from different sources but have difficulty

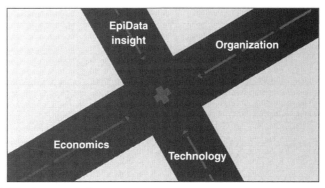

FIGURE 10.3 Kinetic crossroads

figuring out what to do with it or how to draw any insight (or the message/story) from it all. Financial service and large biotech organizations have a leg up on this type of thing due to their history and experience with large transactional data sets, but driving the activities surrounding this data requires a focus at the *intersection*, what we have labeled the "kinetic crossroads."

The key elements that represent the "kinetic crossroads" are shown in Fig. 10.3. Economic models include global or local impacts, market models, and complexity.

- EpiData insight includes dynamic data, impact of environment on data expression, and value from disparate data sets.
- Organizational change includes organizational structures, transformation, geopolitical changes, and leadership.
- Technology includes high-performance computing, smart controls and processes, and nanotechnology.

Our capabilities around high-performance computing and integrated processes finally are beginning to intersect with evolving trends in data management and insight, organizational changes, and global economic and geopolitical impacts. A technology-enabled, forward-thinking, and collaborative organization will be able to take advantage of this convergence and create new business models and opportunities.

WHAT HAS WORKED? WHERE TO START?

Forward-thinking organizations may want to consider how new Social Knowledge Management Environments (SKMEs) emerge and how they are quickly beginning to transform the way employees and customers create, consume, iterate, and reuse knowledge across an enterprise. Through collaboration with platform specialists such as Lithium, Salesforce, and Jive, organizations (and their clients) can jointly address innovative opportunities and challenges. Leveraging new technology methods including cloud-based delivery and dynamic data, organizations and their customers can capture, transform, and evolve intellectual capital across boundaries (real and manufactured) into knowledge assets, while keeping stake-holders informed at all stages of the process with real-time collaborative articles and communication.

Capturing and transforming institutional knowledge can occur by not only changing business processes and outcomes, but also by changing the way people think about social knowledge and collaboration. Users can collaborate to solve problems and quickly identify solutions as knowledge assets. An evolving workflow helps as well, integrating content and knowledge management dynamically. Processes are transformed, and talent throughout the organization feels free (and confident) to create and collaborate with each other in such a way that others can reuse and improve upon it later.

We must push the limits and nature of collaboration, not only to extend and grow our capabilities by providing a comprehensive view of our team activities to various stakeholders, but also to promote knowledge sharing and a foundational approach to extend the thinking of new groups looking to use SKM. It is about the dynamic, collective nature of social collaboration coupled with knowledge management that signifies the value of the activities, the producing, retaining, iterating, and reusing our intellectual capital in *innovative ways*.

So what's different? People are *connecting* who hadn't been connected before and are *removing barriers* to cross-functional and cross-industry *knowledge through collaboration.* It's about leveraging business processes and workflow and establishing integral relationships with our technology that impacts the value of social knowledge collaboration.

Organizations are creating entirely new models that are showcased in everyday business processes that can be leveraged within any business function. Given the dynamic nature of collaboration, experts can be connected with users anywhere and anytime, where before they would have never known others existed. Moreover, an expert can provide mentoring and coaching to many virtually, rather than one or two in person.

It all starts with conversations, which lead to communities, which in turn lead to relevant connections. As word spreads, more people hear about it and want to be involved. A Social Knowledge Management Environment grows naturally and organically. This produces reusable knowledge, in part, because of the ownership, participation, and passion community members have in making it a success. By measuring, for example, the number of accepted solutions to questions, the activity of discussions and knowledge bases, and the overall user activity within the social knowledge management environment, it is possible to improve customer satisfaction and employee effectiveness.

A Social Knowledge Management success story is probable if your organization has two or more of the elements as shown in Fig. 10.4.

Let's review the elements that represent an SKM opportunity here:

- *Highly interactive*: The resources in your organization actively work together to address issues, solve problems, and create new ideas. *There is an*

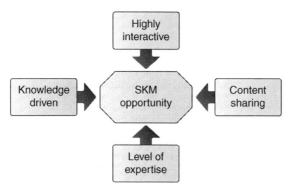

FIGURE 10.4 Necessary elements for success of Social Knowledge Management

opportunity for SKM if you are struggling with the ability to capture value from collaborative activities.

- *Levels of expertise*: There are various pockets or degrees of expertise that can be drawn upon to help others that may have less experience in a given discipline or topic area. *There is an opportunity for SKM if the experts in your organization do not optimally contribute to the growth of others or share their knowledge effectively.*

- *Content sharing*: Materials are shared among resources that represent "reusable assets." *There is an opportunity for SKM if this material could benefit from iterative updates from daily operational activities to stay current or if much of your content tends to be obsolete soon after it is published.*

- *Knowledge driven*: The individual and team's performance is based on and dependent upon knowledge. *There is an opportunity for SKM if complexity inhibits the individual ability to scale to an expert quickly across multiple disciplines.*

Quick list: How do you know it is time for the Social Knowledge path in your organization? You know it is time for Social Knowledge when:

- You can't afford to lose anymore knowledge.
- You are trying to change your processes.
- You must become more transparent.
- Too many things get lost in email.
- You want to cut down on noise.
- It's time to encourage collaboration instead of hoarding.

Step by Step: Want to try something today? Follow this process:

- Set your goal. What do you want to accomplish?
- Articulate the benefits. How will you sell it to your team/company?
- Define what success looks like. How will you decide if you are successful, and how much time can you give the project to succeed?

- Relate to history. Has this (or something similar) been done before? Was it successful? Know the environment, the history, and the culture going into any initiative.

ACKNOWLEDGMENT

Excerpted with permission from *Social Knowledge: Organizational Currencies in the New Knowledge Economy by* Kenneth E Russell, PhD, Renée La Londe, and Fred Walters. Copyright 2014 by iTalent Corporation and Spencer House Publishing, September 2014. ISBN: Hardback 978-0-692-28477-3; paperback 978-0-692-28478-0.

Knowledge management and analytical modeling for transformational leadership profiles in a multinational company

11

T. Ha-Vikström, J. Takala

University of Vaasa, Vaasa, Finland

INTRODUCTION

It is widely understood that leadership is one of the most critical success factors of knowledge management (KM). Leadership also plays a crucial role in employee performance and organization effectiveness. Especially in a seemingly weak economic environment, it is important that organizations should concentrate more on good leadership as well as KM intelligent to maintain employee's well-being and to increase the company's productivity.

Transformational leadership was first introduced theoretically by Burns (1978, 2003), and developed and conceptualized by Bass as well as many other researchers (Bass and Avolio, 1994; Avolio, 1999; Bass and Riggio, 2006). They explain that transformational leaders influence followers by inspiring followers to think differently and critically, involving followers in decision-making processes and inspiring loyalty, while recognizing and appreciating the different needs of each follower to develop his or her personal potential. Burns (1978, 2003) also explains transformational leadership as a process through which leaders and followers help each other to advance to a higher level of morality and motivation. Takala and Uusitalo (2012) argue that transformational leaders survive best from the challenges because they have the will to forecast and to prepare the organization to the changes fast enough. However, according to Pandey and Pandey (2013), a strategy for the success of organization is how to execute the KM and transformational leadership in organization. Because KM refers to efforts that are done systematically to find, create, access, and apply the intangible capitals of organization and to strengthen the culture of continuous learning and knowledge sharing in organization (Monavarian and Asgari, 2009).

During the recent years, the transformational leadership has been well studied and has become more popular in practice. A recent research shows that many case studies reveal a trend that 80% of the total sample size represents transformational leadership management style (Kazmi et al., 2015). Surprisingly in a real business environment, for example, in a multinational company, the term of transformational leadership still seems to be unknown to many middle level leaders.

Earlier researchers describe theories and techniques to show the correlations between different leadership styles and performance (Podsakoff et al., 1990; Nissinen 2001; Schaubroeck et al., 2007). In parallel with that, Nissinen (2001) introduces a model of deep leadership that analyzes the relationships between different leadership factors based on a large-scale data collection. Later on, Takala et al. (2005, 2006a) constructed and developed a new conceptual theoretical sand cone model, which can evaluate the direction of outputs, the leadership behavior, as well as the resource allocation of transformational leadership. However, as Takala et al. (2008a) conclude in their studies "in spite of the fact that the promising results from the longitudinal, more than 3 years, study period, it still needs a lot more empirical studies to validate, verify and apply in practice in different leadership situations within dynamic environments."

Due to the absence of that, in this study we investigate the company management's transformational leadership skills and examine the analytic transformational leadership indexes reflecting from this unique analytic model. By utilizing descriptive and normative approaches, the findings support a view that the sand cone model is a simple holistic analytic concept to visualize a clear transformational leadership profile. Beside a novel layout for the sand cone model, this study also provides an insight of transformational leadership for the company as well as a new total leadership index and three separate indexes (outcomes index, resource index, and leadership index) that can be utilized further in the sustainable competitive advantage research field. Last but not least, the cutting-edge "specific index" in the findings signify the current status for each certain leadership behavior capability.

In order to surface these results, it is essential to understand the three instruments that we utilize in our theoretical framework, that is, the transformational leadership model, the sand cone model, and the analytic hierarchy process tool, which we present in the next section.

THEORETICAL FRAMEWORK
TRANSFORMATIONAL LEADERSHIP MODEL

Transformational leadership model (TLM) is a tool that has been developed from the basis of transformational leadership (Nissinen, 2001; Takala, 2002; Takala et al., 2005, 2006a; Tommila et al., 2008). This theoretical framework we use has been adopted from educational psychology and leadership training based on the four dimensions of transformational leadership (Bass, 1985) because the model has been designed to enhance leadership coaching in any operational environment (Takala et al., 2008b, 2013; Takala and Uusitalo, 2012). Fig. 11.1 is the transformational leadership model which is adapted from the original research of Takala et al. (2006a),

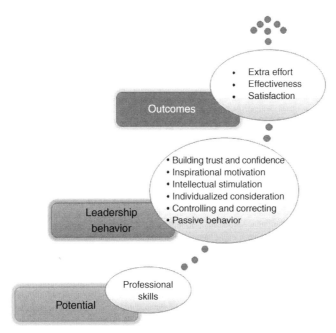

FIGURE 11.1 Transformational leadership model (TLM)

Adapted from Takala et al. (2008b)

which explains that coaching applies to the model as a bridge between theory and practice (Takala et al., 2008b).

Professional skills is the foundation (potential) for leaders. Leadership behavior consists of two main groups of behaviors—passive and controlling behavior—and the four behavioral components that originate from Avolio (1999) and Bass (1985, 1998): first, individualized consideration—connecting with each individual, understanding their needs, drawing out their strengths, and developing and satisfying their personal goals; second, intellectual stimulation—challenging followers to think differently and innovate new solutions to old problems; third, inspirational motivation—communicating a compelling vision and inspiring followers to reach their fullest potential; and fourth, building trust and confidence, which is developed from the original behavior of idealized influence—being a role model and involving followers to accomplish more than what they would do otherwise.

SAND CONE MODEL

Sand cone model is a specific concept that has multidimensional or hierarchical aspects to visualize the structure of leadership behaviors that was developed by Takala et al. (2005, 2008b) as shown in Fig. 11.2. In the following paragraphs in this section, green refers to the numerals that are underlined, yellow refers to those in ital, and red refers to those in boldface.

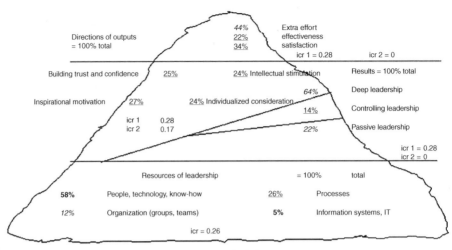

FIGURE 11.2 Sand cone model (Takala et al., 2008b)

We utilize this practical model as the second theoretical framework in this study because the model has a dynamic characteristic with cumulative layers for different performance dimensions. This multifocused concept is simple and also visual, which assists the identification and evaluation of leadership behaviors or leadership performances.

The model consists of four main parts: first, resources are at the ground level of the model; the next level is shared with cornerstones (left) and transformational leadership (right); and the highest level is the directions of outputs. The values of these variables are colored by using the traffic light technique defined by Takala et al. (2008b). The green stands for strength in the current variable, the yellow stands for possibility for development, and the red stands for focus in the development potential. In the black and white printed version, the green color is signified with blank, yellow with dots and red with dashes. The sand cone traffic light values can be found in the appendix 1.

Takala et al. (2008b) defines the optimal balance of transformational leadership as follows: directions of outputs (each 33%), cornerstones (each 25%), and resources (each 25%) are equalized, while the results with dynamic leadership (82%), passive and controlling (each 9%). Fig. 11.2 is adapted and we reillustrate it with a more comprehension view in Fig. 11.3.

The transformational leadership sand cone model in Fig. 11.3 is supported by the foundation resources (similar to arms and legs) that consists of processes (PC), information systems (IT), organizational groups, teams (OR) and people, technology, and know-how (PT). Next, the results level (like the body) shows three categories of leadership that is, dynamic, passive- and controlling; where dynamic plays a significant role, as Progen (2013) defines dynamic leadership is a dual-focused form of adaptive leadership that allows a leader to react to changes by being proactive. The third level is the cornerstones (like the heart) where the group of three I's: intellectual stimulation (IS), individualized consideration (IC), inspirational motivation

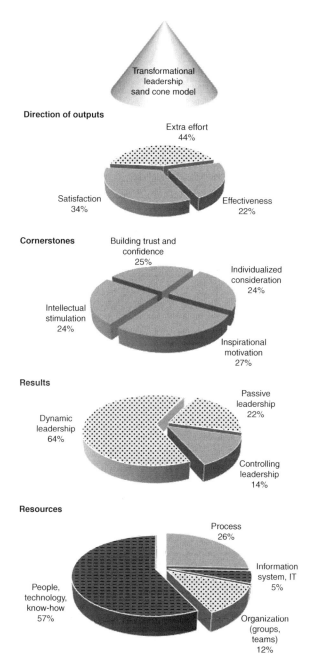

FIGURE 11.3 Transformational leadership sand cone model. In this traffic light model, the portions left blank indicates the areas in green, those filled with dots refer to yellow, and those with dashed lines refer to red.

(IM), and building trust and confidence (BT) was built. Finally, the fourth level of the sand cone model, the direction of outputs (like the eyes), is divided into three types of performances: effectiveness (EF), satisfaction (SA), and extra effort (EE). Above all, the top level direction of outputs and the dynamic leadership performance play an important role in this transformational leadership sand cone model.

ANALYTIC HIERARCHY PROCESS (AHP)

The third theoretical framework we use in this study is the analytic hierarchy process (AHP), which is a multicriteria decision method based on mathematics and psychological concepts through pair-wise comparisons. AHP was innovated and developed by Saaty in 1970 and has been widely studied and developed since then. The evaluation among different factors help us in making decisions in complex situations. The model has been used around the world in a wide variety of decision situations, in fields such as business, industry, healthcare, education, and government (Saracoglu, 2013). In this study, Expert Choice software (which implements AHP) was used for the calculation, where qualitative objects are converted to quantitative values (Saaty, 1982, 2008a, 2008b). Qualitative objects are 30 pair-wise comparison questionnaires that were originally invented by Takala et al. (2008a), which are based on the 10 dimensions of deep leadership (Nissinen, 2006) and have been comprehensively improved since then. In the three sections that follow, we address research environment and methods first, followed by the results, then the discussion, and finally the conclusions.

RESEARCH ENVIRONMENT AND METHODS

This study is a cooperative venture between the University of Vaasa and the Learning & Development department of a multinational energy company. Due to confidentiality matters, the real name of the company as well as the different departments will not be revealed.

Regarding the method, we utilize the descriptive research approach, which means we gather the facts from participants and try to describe them in an accurate way. The primary data of this study for examining and analyzing the leadership profiles and total leadership indexes was gathered through a questionnaire. Sample and procedures for data collection were: a total of 30 email invitations to complete a web-based questionnaire were sent out to the selected respondents, that is, middle managers who are working in four business units; each of these managers/leaders has at least 10 subordinates or more. Higher level managers (general managers and directors) were excluded from this study because their responsibilities and decision-making behavior sometimes differed from the middle managers.

The survey resulted in an overall response rate of 87% (26/30); 77% of the participants were men (20/26) and 23% of participants were women (6/26). In terms of different cultures in this global company, 64% of these managers have subordinates from other nationalities, and 26% have subordinates with the same nationality.

In terms of working condition steadiness, 32% of these leaders have recently or during this year had some significant responsibility changes (such as position, work conditions, or location). This last factor was taken into account because it may have some impact on the leaders' decision-making behavior, which might reflect on the responses.

In this case study, only matrixes with the inconsistency ratio (icr) value of 0.3 or lower can be considered as reliable answers and can be used to analyze further. Conclusively, 73% (18/26) responses were usable, and 27% (8/26) responses were discarded due to high icr. Finally, the quantitative results calculated by the AHP tool will be applied to the concept and will be further analyzed in order to form a unique profile for each respondent (Fig. 11.3 for an example of a TL profile).

TRANSFORMATIONAL LEADERSHIP INDEX (TLI)

In order to get TLI, the following four equations have been used and calculated in Excel (Takala et al., 2008b, 2013).

Outcome index (OI):

$$\mathbf{OI} = 1 - MAX(ABS((1/3) - (EF/100)); ABS((1/3) - (SA/100)); ABS((1/3) - (EE/100)))$$

EF, effectiveness; SA, satisfaction; EE, extra effort.

Leadership index (LI):

$$\mathbf{LI} = (DL/100) \times (1 - (MAX(PL;CL)/100)) \times (1 - ABS((1/4) - (MAX(IC;IM;IS;BT)/100)))$$

DL, dynamic leadership; PL, passive leadership; CL, controlling leadership; IC, individualized consideration; IM, inspirational motivation; IS, intellectual stimulation; BT, building trust and confidence.

Resource index (RI):

$$\mathbf{RI} = (1 - (PT/100)) \times ((3 \times MIN(PC; IT; OR))/100)$$

PT, people, technology, know-how; PC, processes; IT, information systems; OR, organization (groups, teams).

Transformational leadership index (TLI):

$$\mathbf{TLI} = OI \times LI \times RI$$

RESULTS
TRANSFORMATIONAL LEADERSHIP PROFILES

A similar profile as Fig. 11.3 is calculated for each leader. Despite the fact that each leader has a unique profile and a specific TL index, consolidation results can be visualized based on the color (light gray, white, and dark gray). These colors provide a good overview for the common strengths or weaknesses of the whole group. Tables 11.1–11.4 (in the appendix) demonstrate a results' consolidation, where column "group 1" to "group 7" shows the values calculated by the AHP tool converted from the qualitative responses. The four columns with colors are the four main parts of the sand cone model: cornerstones, resources, outputs, and results. The last column shows the values of four indexes: OI, LI, RI, and TLI. In the black and white printed version, the colors in the five tables (11.1 to 11.5) are changed as follows: the green color is signified with a check mark, yellow with an exclamation mark, and red with an x mark.

Table 11.1 (in the appendix 2) indicates that the strength of this department is in controlling leadership (CL) because 100% (5/5) are in green, that is, their behavior in current controlling is good. Second strength of this group is on satisfaction (SA) with 80% (4/5) in green and 20% (1/5) in yellow. However, the most weaknesses of this group of leaders are in dynamic leadership (DL) and passive leadership (PL), with 80% (4/5) in red.

Table 11.2 (in the appendix 3) shows the consolidated results for department 2, similarly as in consolidation 1, the strength of this group of leaders is in CL; 100% (4/4) are in green. However the important weaknesses are on PL and individualized consideration (IC), that is, 100% (4/4) and 75% (3/4) respectively.

Table 11.3 (in the appendix 4) shows the consolidated results for department 3. The strength of this group is on effectiveness (EF) and CL with 80% (4/5) in green for both. However the common weaknesses of this department are on PL and people and technology (know-how, PT) at 80% (4/5) and 60% (3/5) respectively.

Finally, Table 11.4 (in the appendix 5) is a consolidation of department 4, similar to the three previous departments, where the strength is also at CL, 100% (4/4) in green. Yet, the improvement should focus on PL, 75% (3/4) in red.

To summarize, the total general results reveal the transformational leadership *strengths* of these participation leaders are 95% (17/18) in controlling leadership and the *weaknesses* are 72% (13/18) in passive leadership.

In the following section we utilize the normative research approach, which means we try to point out particular details in which the object of the study can be improved as well as general conclusions that derive from the results.

TOTAL LEADERSHIP INDEX—REEXAMINATION

Two graphs of total leadership index (TLI) for all respondents follow:

Fig. 11.4 shows the TLI graph for all responses that was calculated according to the four existing equations.

Fig. 11.5 shows the TLI graph calculated based on the absolute value (ABS), which means every value of a piece of pie in the sand cone model will be compared with the optimal value. By using ABS we will always get the number as positive (or zero), but never negative. The reason for utilizing ABS was because the TLI index obtained from four previous equations was not compatible with its profiles. For example, the profile picture of E16 has more green color than the profile of M7, but the TLI index of M7 is higher than the TLI index of E16 (M7 and E16 are the codes of two respondents). This discrepancy can be easily recognized when comparing S8 versus S10, Su19 versus E5, etc.

As TLI = OI × LI × RI, a careful test through each separate index shows that the equation of OI is most likely correct because there is no deviation between the profile

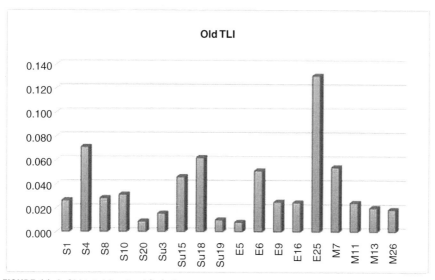

FIGURE 11.4 Old total leadership index

color and the OI index; if we place EF = 33, SA = 33, and EE = 33 in the OI equation 1, we will get the optimal values OI = 0.996.

Next, the leadership index (LI) calculation requires both values from cornerstones and results; if we place the optimal value for IC = IM = IS = BT = 25; and optimal value for PL = 9, CL = 9, and DL = 82; in the LI equation, we will get LI = 0.746.

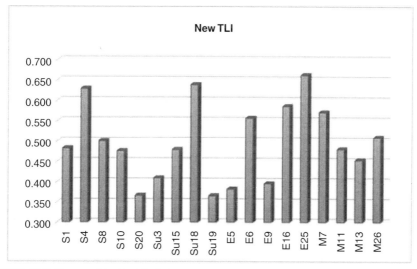

FIGURE 11.5 New total leadership index

Table 11.5 Leadership Index (LI), Respondent S8 Versus S10

S8				S10			
CORNERSTONES		RESULTS		CORNERSTONES		RESULTS	
IC, IM, IS, BT		PL, CL, DL		IC, IM, IS, BT		PL, CL, DL	
!	11	✖	41.6	!	17	✖	45.8
!	30	✔	12.6	!	18	✔	6.3
✔	25	✖	45.8	!	32.7	✖	47.9
!	34			!	32.5		
LI = 0.24				**LI = 0.24**			

In comparison between responses S8 and S10 in Table 11.5, for print version, three symbols to replace the colors as follows: a cross (X) stands for red; an exclamation mark (!) stands for yellow; and a tick or check mark stands for green. The green color of S8 already reveals that S8 performance is better than S10; however, the calculation with the LI equation will give discrepancy results: LI of S8 is equal to LI of S10.

Finally, to the resource index (RI), if we place PC = IT = OR = PT = 25 in the RI equation, we will get the optimal RI = 0.562.

In comparison between responses E1 and M2 versus Optimal in Table 11.6, the optimal of RI is 0.562, while the RI for E1 = 0.547, although the profile of E1 has IT and PT on red. Moreover, the largest discrepancy here is the RI of M2 = 0.565, which means the RI index of M2 is *higher than* the optimal index (0.562).

In most cases, the correctness can sometimes be violated because the equations of OI and LI utilizes MAX and the equations of RI utilizes MIN, which means the best values (or the variable in the optimal array) may be taken into account while the worst were ignored, or vice versa. For example, between three values—6, 45, and 49—the MAX result is 49 and this will be taken into account, but 6 and 45 will be ignored. Or with the MIN in an equation, for example, with the same three values 6, 45, and 49, the MIN result is 6 and this will be taken into account while 45 and 49 will be ignored. Therefore, this study suggests a more accurate TLI by using the "absolute value" (ABS) instead of MAX or MIN. By using the absolute value for every weight, we will always acquire the precise value of how far the current performance is from the optimal performance.

Table 11.6 Resource Index (RI), E1 and M2 Versus Optimal

Optimal	E1	M2
RESOURCES	RESOURCES	RESOURCES
PC, IT, OR, PT	PC, IT, OR, PT	PC, IT, OR, PT
25	29.2	27.8
25	46.5	48.7
25	19.2	19.6
25	5	3.9
RI = 0.562	RI = 0.547	RI = 0.565

Table 11.7 New Transformational Leadership Index

TL factors	Optimal	Result	Abs(Opt. - Result)
IC	25	30.4	5.4
IM	25	29	4
IS	25	20.3	4.7
BT	25	20.3	4.7
PC	25	13.4	11.6
PT	25	48.4	23.4
IT	25	15.5	9.5
OR	25	22.8	2.2
EF	33.3	12.2	21.1
SA	33.3	32	1.3
EE	33.3	55.8	22.5
PL	9	26	17
CL	9	11	2
DL	82	63	19
	400		**148**
		1- (148/400)	**0.63**

Table 11.7 shows an example of a new transformational leadership index calculation.

The column "optimal" shows the optimal values, the column "result" points out the results from responses, and the column "ABS" contains absolute values (comparing optimal values and result values). In this example, 148 is the sum of ABS values and 0.630 is the total leadership index. The higher the index, the better the performance.

Following new equations for TL indexes are proposed:

$$\mathbf{TLI} = 1 - \frac{\Sigma\,\text{ABS values}}{\Sigma\,\text{Optimal values}} \qquad (11.1)$$

$$\mathbf{Specific\ index} = 1 - \left(\frac{\text{Absolute difference}}{\text{Maximal difference}} \right) \qquad (11.2)$$

$$\textit{New OI} = \text{Mean (Specific index \{EF, SA, EE\})} \qquad (11.3)$$

$$\textit{New LI} = \text{Mean (Specific index \{IC, IM, IS, BT, PL, CL, DL\})} \qquad (11.4)$$

$$\textit{New RI} = \text{Mean (Specific index \{PC, PT, IT, OR\})} \qquad (11.5)$$

Table 11.8 demonstrates an example of how to calculate these new indexes, that is, new TLI, specific index, new OI, new LI, and new RI. All acronyms mentioned here were explained in the previous transformational leadership index section.

Table 11.9 illustrates a consolidation of old TLI versus new TLI. A verification of these two indexes with the profile pictures reveals that the new indexes are accurate and compatible with the profile, that is, the closer the results to the optimal values, the higher the TLI index. And the highest or the best index is always equal to 1. In addition, the *specific index* (as shown in Table 11.8) is the actual result for every certain behavior (specific index traffic light values can be found in the appendix 6). Furthermore, the new TLI is also practical and can be used with one or two decimals, while the old index has to use three decimals or more because the old TLI was smaller, for example, 0.003; see Figs. 11.4 and 11.5 for graphs of old and new TLI, respectively.

DISCUSSION

This study supports the empirical evidence that "Leadership behavior can be effectively visualized in a holistic way by using a Sand Cone model" (Takala et al., 2006a, 2006b). The sand cone model is definitely simple to use; the common traffic light defined in the sand cone model could help leaders easily recognize what they should put more focus on. The colorful profile is a guideline for a leader to follow and improve their behavior as well as their decision making in order to get maximal results of the outcomes.

Regarding the transformational leadership capability for the participating leaders in this multinational company, the results show that 72% of total respondents (13/18) have passive leadership in red; this should be further investigated inside the company. Because recent findings of Harold and Holtz (2014) research proved that passive leadership is associated with lower perceived support, weaker organizational identity, less citizenship behavior, and greater workplace incivility. As mentioned previously, leadership or especially transformational leadership is the most fundamental key success factors of KM; researchers believe that this factor will support the organization's IQ, it will make the organization smarter. However, the toughest issue is how to make leaders change KM, how to get leaders to think differently. As Nancy Dickson, president, Common Knowledge Associates, expresses at the KMWorld 2015 conference "What we've wanted is the support of top management to provide the resources, to encourage people to share their knowledge and so forth. We've never asked the top of the organization themselves to do knowledge management." In a turbulent business world, in case of complexity issues the leaders' roles in KM are to share knowledge, to get people involved, to keep people informed, to wake their interest, and make them feel part of the journey, "on the move together."

Although the findings of this study are based on responses from high experienced managers from four different business units, and each of them has at least 10 or more subordinates, one limitation is the relatively small sample of respondents compared with the total amount of managers in a large company.

Table 11.8 Specific Index, New Outcome Index, New Leadership Index, New Resource Index

TL components and factors	Optimal values	Response values	Absolute difference	New TLI	Specific index	New OI	New LI	New RI
Directions of outputs								
Effectiveness EF	33.3	12.2	21.13		0.68			
Satisfaction SA	33.3	32	1.33		0.98			
Extra Effort EE	33.3	55.8	22.47		0.66			
Cornerstones								
Individualized consideration IC	25	30.4	5.40		0.93			
Inspirational motivation IM	25	29	4.00		0.95			
Intellectual stimulation IS	25	20.3	4.70		0.94			
Building trust and confidence BT	25	20.3	4.70		0.94			
Results								
Passive leadership PL	9	26	17.00		0.81			
Controlling leadership CL	9	11	2.00		0.98			
Dynamic leadership DL	82	63	19.00		0.77			
Resources								
Process PC	25	13.4	11.60		0.85			
People, technology, know-how PT	25	48.4	23.40		0.69			
Information systems, IT	25	15.5	9.50		0.87			
Organisation (groups, teams) OR	25	22.8	2.20		0.97			
Total	400		148.43	0.629		0.78	0.90	0.84

*Maximal difference (in Eq. 11.2) is the worst case scenario
Maximal difference EF = SA = EE = (100 - 33.3) = 66.7
Maximal difference IC = IM = IS = BT = (100 - 25) = 75
Maximal difference PL = CL = 91
Maximal difference DL = 82
Maximal difference PC = PT = IT = OR = (100 - 25) = 75

Table 11.9 Old TLI Versus New TLI

Respondents	Old TLI	New TLI
S1	0.026	0.482
S4	0.072	0.629
S8	0.028	0.500
S10	0.031	0.476
S20	0.010	0.366
Su3	0.019	0.409
Su15	0.046	0.479
Su18	0.062	0.638
Su19	**0.010**	**0.365**
E5	**0.008**	**0.382**
E6	0.059	0.556
E9	**0.025**	**0.395**
E16	0.024	0.586
E25	0.130	0.662
M7	0.054	0.571
M11	0.024	0.480
M13	0.020	0.453
M26	**0.027**	**0.509**

CONCLUSIONS

This is one of the first studies to empirically examine participants' transformational leadership profile and TL indexes in a global company. Additionally, this study's uniqueness is the new proposal layout of the sand cone model and the new equation of TL indexes as well as the specific index that provides accurate assessments to the respondents.

Generally, results show that every individual leader has a unique profile; depending on the leaders' responsibilities in their current situation, each of them has one or more specific areas that they should focus on to improve their own leadership styles. Nevertheless, the results clearly support the view that the sand cone model is beneficial in analyzing the transformational leadership profile. The common traffic light colors give clear indications to the leader of good areas and areas to improve.

We expect that this new approach with new accurate transformational leadership indexes will significantly increase the use of this analytic modeling concept for transformational leadership profiles. It will improve the self-awareness from each leader and to help the organization to having better understanding of their current transformational leadership capabilities. The results may convey to the company new insights into developing training programs to support leaders in improving their transformational leadership behaviors as well as to develop their own profession. In addition, this simple evaluation concept can also be utilized further in recruitment, selection, or promotion purposes.

Finally, as self-awareness is the first step of successful knowledge management, we also expect that this finding may contribute to the company a better perspective into improving KM because transformational leadership capability and knowledge management have reciprocal effects. In a good KM business environment, when transformational leaders make decisions, they are always well informed with the latest research, which contributes to faster and better decisions. This implies that knowledge management is getting the right intelligence, from the right person, at the right time, and to make the right decision (Leondes, 2005).

As mentioned earlier, one limitation of this study is the relatively small sample compared with the total amount of leaders in a multinational company. Therefore, further research with a larger sample of respondents/leaders who are located in Finland as well as in other countries would be needed. More research to prove the new transformational leadership indexes as well as to compare the transformational leadership trend among different areas, for example, private industries versus public sectors and profit versus nonprofit organizations, is also suggested.

REFERENCES

Avolio, B., 1999. Full Leadership Development: Building the Vital Forces in Organization. Sage Publications, Thousand Oaks.

Bass, B.M., 1985. Leadership and performance beyond expectations. Free Press, New York. Hum. Res. Manage. 25 (3), 481–484.

Bass, B.M., 1998. Transformational Leadership: Industrial, Military, and Educational Impact. Lawrence Erlbaum Associates, Mahwah, New Jersey, London.

Bass, B.M., Avolio, B.J. (Eds.), 1994. Improving Organizational Effectiveness Through Transformational Leadership. Sage Publications, Thousand Oaks, CA.

Bass, B.M., Riggio, R.E., 2006. Transformational Leadership, second ed. Lawrence Erlbaum Associates, Inc, Mahwah, NJ.

Burns, J.M., 2003. Transforming Leadership: A New Pursuit of Happiness. Atlantic Monthly Press, New York.

Harold, C., Holtz, B., 2014. The effects of passive leadership on workplace incivility. J. Org. Behav. 36 (1), 16–38.

Kazmi, S.A., Takala, J., Naaranoja, M., 2015. Sustainable solution for competitive team formation. J. Global Strateg. Manage. 17.

Kinnunen, T., 2013. Simply Leadership and Coaching Effectiveness. Aldus Oy Lahti.

Leondes, C.T., 2005. Intelligent Knowledge-Based Systems: Business and Technology in the New Millennium. In: Leondes, C.T. (Ed.). Kluwer Academic Publishers, Boston.

Monavarian, A., Asgari, N., 2009. Organization in Industry, Information and Wisdom Era. Tehran University Publications, Tehran.

Nissinen, V., 2001. Military Management: Development of Leadership Behavior in the Finnish Defence Forces. Publication Series. 1, Research reports.

Nissinen, V., 2006. Deep leadership. Talentum oyj.

Nissinen, V., 2004. Deep Leadership. Talentum Oy, Hämeenlinna, Finland, second print in 2006.

Pandey, N., Pandey, A., 2013. Knowledge management through transformational leadership. Int. J. Adv. Res. Manage. Social Sci. 2 (9).

Podsakoff, P.M., MacKenzie, S.B., Moorman, R.H., Fetter, R., 1990. Transformational leader behaviors and their effects on followers trust in leader, satisfaction, and organizational citizenship behaviors. Leadership Q. 1, 107–142.

Progen, M.D., 2013. Dynamic Leadership. Leadership Writing Contest entry. MarineCorps Association & Foundation. Available from: https://www.mca-marines.org/gazette/dynamic-leadership.

Saaty, T.L., 1982. Decision Making for Leaders. The Analytical Hierarchy Process for Decisions in a Complex World. Wadsworth, Belmont, CA. Latest edition, revised (2000), RWS Publications, Pittsburgh.

Saaty, T.L., 2008a. Decision making with the analytic hierarchy process. International Journal of Services Sciences. 1 (1), 83.

Saaty, T.L., 2008b. Decision Making for Leaders: The Analytic Hierarchy Process for Decisions in a Complex World. RWS Publications, Pittsburgh, PA.

Saracoglu, B.O., 2013. Selecting industrial investment locations in master plans of countries. Eur. J. Ind. Eng. 7 (4), 416–441.

Schaubroeck, J., Lam, S.S.K., Cha, S.E., 2007. Embracing transformational leadership: team values and the impact of leader behavior on team performance. J. Appl. Psychol. 92, 1020–1030.

Takala, J., 2002. Analyzing and synthesizing multifocused manufacturing strategies by analytical hierarchy process. Int. J. Manuf. Technol. Manage. 4 (5), 345–350.

Takala, J., Hirvelä, H., Hiippala P., Nissinen, V., 2005. Management and Deep Leadership Sand Cone model for human resource allocation, the first phase of the study. In: Fourth International (Automation & Manufacturing) Conference, ATDC (Advanced Technologies for Developing Countries), September 21–24, 2005, Slavonski Brod, Croatia. University of Vaasa, Department of Production, Vaasa, Finland.

Takala, J., Hirvelä, H., Hiippala P., Nissinen, V., 2006a. Management and deep leadership sand cone model for human resource allocation, the second phase of the study. In: The Eleventh International Conference on Productivity and Quality Research, ICPQR'2005, December 12–15, 2005, New Delhi, India. International Conference on Multinational Enterprises— Multinational Enterprise in the Global Economy, March 14–16, 2006, Taipei, Taiwan. University of Vaasa, Department of Production, Vaasa, Finland.

Takala, J., Leskinen, J., Sivusuo, H., Hirvelä, J., Kekäle, T., 2006b. The sand cone model: illustrating multi-focused strategies. Manage. Decis. 44 (3), 335–345.

Takala, J., Koskinen, J., Liu, Y., Tas, M.S., Muhos, M., 2013. Validating knowledge and technology effects to operative sustainable competitive advantage. Manage. Prod. Eng. Rev. 4 (3), 45–54.

Takala, J., Kukkola, A., Pennanen, J., 2008a. Prospector, analyzer and defender models in directions of outcome in transformational leadership. In: The 17th International Conference on the Israel Society for Quality, ISAS 2008, November 18–20, 2008, Jerusalem, Israel. The 10th Management International Conference, MIC 2009, November 25–28, 2009, Sousse, Tunis. University of Vaasa, Department of Production, Vaasa, Finland.

Takala, J., Pennanen, J., Hiippala, P., Maunuksela, A., Kilpiö, O., 2008b. Decision maker's outcome as a function of transformational leadership. In: Kinnunen, T. (Ed.), Simplify Leadership and Coaching Effectiveness. Deep Lead Oy, Aldus Oy, Lahti, 144 pages, pp. 67–86. University of Vaasa, Department of Production, Vaasa, Finland.

Takala, J., Uusitalo, T., 2012. Resilient and proactive utilization of opportunities and uncertainties in service business. In: Proceedings of the University of Vaasa. Reports 177.

Tommila, H., Takala, J., Jokitalo, J., Penttinen, R., 2008. Effectiveness of transformational leadership training programme. University of Vaasa, Department of Production. In: The 17th International Conference on the Israel Society for Quality, ISAS 2008, November 18–20, 2008, Jerusalem, Israel.

APPENDIX 1: SAND CONE TRAFFIC LIGHT VALUES IN THE BLACK AND WHITE PRINTED VERSION, THE GREEN COLOR IS SIGNIFIED WITH A CHECK MARK, YELLOW WITH AN EXCLAMATION MARK, AND RED WITH AN X MARK.

Directions of outputs/optimal 33%

    50–100 (✖)
    40–50 (!)
    20–40 (✓)
    10–20 (!)
    0–10 (✖)

Cornerstones/optimal 25%

    40–100 (✖)
    30–40 (!)
    20–30 (✓)
    10–20 (!)
    0–10 (✖)

Dynamic Leadership/optimal 82%

    70–100 (✓)
    50–70 (!)
    0–50 (✖)

Controlling and passive leadership/optimal 9%

    25–100 (✖)
    15–25 (!)
    0–15 (✓)

Resources/optimal 25%

    40–100 (✖)
    30–40 (!)
    20–30 (✓)
    10–20 (!)
    0–10 (✖)

APPENDIX 2

Table 11.1 Consolidation 1

S1

	Group 1	Group 2	CORNERSTONES IC, IM, IS, BT	Group 3	RESOURCES PC, PT, IT, OR	Group 4	Group 5	OUTPUTS EF, SA, EE	Group 6	Group 7	RESULTS PL, CL, DL	
	36.8	18.2	↑	22	✓	70.1	16.3	↕ 43.2	23.8	52.8	✗ 38.3	OI 0.86817
	20	5.5	✗	57.4	✗	19.3	54	↕ 36.65	13.7	9.1	✓ 11.4	LI-1 0.26349
	67	36.2	↕	9	✗	10.6	29.7	✓ 20.15	62.5	38.1	↕ 50.3	RI 0.11502
	36.4	40.1	✗	11.6	↕							S1 0.02631
	CR = 41.7%	CR = 8.2%		CR = 26.1%		CR = 26.8%	CR = 26.8%		CR = 1.9%	CR = 11.3%	TLI	

S4

	Group 1	Group 2	CORNERSTONES IC, IM, IS, BT	Group 3	RESOURCES PC, PT, IT, OR	Group 4	Group 5	OUTPUTS EF, SA, EE	Group 6	Group 7	RESULTS PL, CL, DL	
	12.5	48.4	↕ 30.4	13.4	↕ 13.4	12.2	13.5	↕ 12.2	16	35.7	26	OI 0.77533
	38.3	19.8	✓ 29	48.4	✗ 52.7	32	28.1	✓ 32	14.9	7.5	11	LI-1 0.44103
	27.3	13.2	✓ 20.3	15.5	↕ 20.7	55.8	58.4	✗ 55.8	69.1	56.7	63	RI 0.20743
	21.9	18.6	↕ 20.3	22.8	↕ 16.1							S4 0.07093
	CR = 7.9%	CR = 3%		CR = 8.9%		CR = 1.9%	CR = 14.1%		CR = 0.6%	CR = 5.6%	TLI	

S8

	Group 1	Group 2	CORNERSTONES IC, IM, IS, BT	Group 3	RESOURCES PC, PT, IT, OR	Group 4	Group 5	OUTPUTS EF, SA, EE	Group 6	Group 7	RESULTS PL, CL, DL	
	9.6	11.5	↕ 11	10.5	↕ 10.5	10	12.6	↕ 11.3	41.6	24.7	✗ 41.6	OI 0.77967
	55.1	5.6	↕ 30	52.7	✗ 52.7	43.3	41.6	↕ 42.5	12.6	13.1	✓ 12.6	LI-1 0.24340
	8.8	40.8	✓ 25	20.7	✓ 20.7	46.6	45.8	↕ 46.2	45.8	62.2	✗ 45.8	RI 0.14900
	26.5	42.2	↕ 34	16.1	↕ 16.1							S8 0.02827
	CR = 9.7%	CR = 9.5%		CR = 17.6%		CR = 0.6%	CR = 1%		CR = 1%	CR = 22.7%	TLI	

S10

	Group 1	Group 2	CORNERSTONES IC, IM, IS, BT	Group 3	RESOURCES PC, PT, IT, OR	Group 4	Group 5	OUTPUTS EF, SA, EE	Group 6	Group 7	RESULTS PL, CL, DL	
	6.4	27.8	↕ 17	13.3	↕ 13.3	7.7	11.7	↕ 10	23.5	45.8	✗ 45.8	OI 0.76667
	27.1	8.4	↕ 18	24.6	✓ 24.6	46.2	26.8	✓ 36	11.3	6.3	✓ 6.3	LI-1 0.23963
	21.4	44	↕ 32.7	7.5	✗ 7.5	46.2	61.4	✗ 54	65.2	47.9	✗ 47.9	RI 0.16965
	45.1	19.9	↕ 32.5	54.7	↕ 54.7							S10 0.03117
	CR = 5.6%	CR = 7.6%		CR = 19.1%		CR = 0%	CR = 7.7%		CR = 14.1%	CR = 0.2%	TLI	

S20

	Group 1	Group 2	CORNERSTONES IC, IM, IS, BT	Group 3	RESOURCES PC, PT, IT, OR	Group 4	Group 5	OUTPUTS EF, SA, EE	Group 6	Group 7	RESULTS PL, CL, DL	
	28.5	13.6	↕ 13.6	17.1	↕ 17.1	32.7	16	✗ 24.4	46.6	46.6	✗ 46.6	OI 0.78133
	22.7	22.4	↕ 22.4	61.8	↕ 61.8	26	14.9	✓ 20.4	10	10	✓ 10	LI-1 0.16301
	37.3	54.5	✗ 54.5	15.2	↕ 15.2	41.3	69.1	✗ 55.2	43.3	43.3	✗ 43.3	RI 0.06761
	11.5	9.5	✗ 9.5	5.9	✗ 5.9							S20 0.00861
	CR = 41.1%	CR = 12.5%		CR = 12.3%		CR = 5.6%	CR = 0.6%		CR = 0.6%	CR = 0.6%	TLI	

APPENDIX 3

Table 11.2 Consolidation 2

Su3	Group 1	Group 2	CORNERSTONES IC, IM, IS, BT	Group 3	RESOURCES PC, PT, IT, OR	Group 4	Group 5	OUTPUTS EF, SA, EE	Group 6	Group 7	RESULTS PI, CI, DI		
Group 1	7.5	7.3	× 7.5	5.7	5.7 ×	27.2	17.4	↕ 17.4	12.5	48.1	× 303	OI	0.69933
	44.5	9.1	× 44.5	63.5	63.5 ×	9.3	19.2	↕ 19.2	7.9	5.6	✓ 6.8	LI-1	0.35292
	14.1	58.5	↕ 14.1	22.3	22.3 ✓	63.5	63.4	× 63.4	79.6	46.3	¿ 62.9	RI	0.06242
	33.8	25	↕ 33.8	8.5	8.5 ×							TU	Su3 0.01540
CR=1,7%	CR=27,8%		CR=25,9%		CR=30,8%	CR=1%		CR=5,6%		CR=0,2%			

Su15	Group 1	Group 2	CORNERSTONES IC, IM, IS, BT	Group 3	RESOURCES PC, PT, IT, OR	Group 4	Group 5	OUTPUTS EF, SA, EE	Group 6	Group 7	RESULTS PI, CI, DI		
Group 1	7.1	16.1	× 7.1	28.5	✓ 28.5	18.4	14.3	↕ 14.3	20.2	47.2	× 47.2	OI	0.80967
	61	8.6	× 61	32.5	32.5 ↕	6.3	42.9	↕ 42.9	• 9.7	8.4	✓ 8.4	LI-1	0.15004
	24.9	48.6	✓ 24.9	18.6	18.6 ↕	75.3	42.9	↕ 42.9	70.1	44.4	× 44.4	RI	0.37665
	7.1	26.8	× 7.1	20.3	20.3 ✓							TU	Su15 0.04576
CR=11,7%	CR=55,8%		CR=7,9%		CR=30,8%	CR=0%		CR=14,1%		CR=0,4%			

Su18	Group 1	Group 2	CORNERSTONES IC, IM, IS, BT	Group 3	RESOURCES PC, PT, IT, OR	Group 4	Group 5	OUTPUTS EF, SA, EE	Group 6	Group 7	RESULTS PI, CI, DI		
Group 1	3.7	9.6	× 6.6	10.3	↕ 10.3	66.5	33	✓ 33	23.5	33.5	¿ 23.5	OI	0.99333
	18.3	9.5	↕ 13.9	50.3	50.3 ×	9	33	✓ 33	11.3	7.1	✓ 11.3	LI-1	0.40451
	17.5	53.8	↕ 35.6	16.1	16.1 ↕	24.5	34	✓ 34	65.2	59.5	¿ 65.2	RI	0.15357
	60.5	27.2	× 43.9	23.2	23.2 ✓							TU	Su18 0.06171
CR=7,5%	CR=3,9%		CR=4,3%		CR=15,9%	CR=0%		CR=14,1%		CR=29,2%			

Su19	Group 1	Group 2	CORNERSTONES IC, IM, IS, BT	Group 3	RESOURCES PC, PT, IT, OR	Group 4	Group 5	OUTPUTS EF, SA, EE	Group 6	Group 7	RESULTS PI, CI, DI		
Group 1	5.6	49.8	× 49.8	13.6	↕ 13.6	19.6	11.4	↕ 11.4	27.4	65.7	× 46.5	OI	0.78067
	66.2	14.5	↕ 14.5	67.1	67.1 ×	49.3	40.5	↕ 40.5	7.7	8.3	✓ 8	LI-1	0.18306
	4.9	10.1	↕ 10.1	12.3	12.3 ↕	31.1	48.1	↕ 48.1	64.9	26.1	× 45.5	RI	0.06909
	23.3	25.6	✓ 25.6	7	7 ×							TU	Su19 0.00987
CR=27,6%	CR=11,4%		CR=5,3%		CR=22,7%	CR=3%		CR=29,2%		CR=22,7%			

APPENDIX 4

Table 11.3 Consolidation 3

E5

	Group 1	Group 2	CORNERSTONES IC, IM, IS, BT	Group 3	RESOURCES PC, PT, IT, OR	Group 4	Group 5	OUTPUTS EF, SA, EE	Group 6	Group 7	RESULTS PL, CL, DL		
	15.5	38.1	38.1	11.7	11.7	48.1	10.5	29.3	64.4	46.7	55.6	OI	0.88133
	44.3	6.2	6.2	59.2	59.2	11.4	39.6	25.5	8.5	6.7	7.6	LI-1	0.13414
	10.8	12.8	12.8	5.4	5.4	40.5	49.9	45.2	27.1	46.7	36.8	RI	0.06610
	29.4	42.9	42.9	23.7	23.7						TLU	E5	0.00781
	CR=73,7%	CR=3,9%		CR=8,2%		CR=3%	CR=5,6%		CR=5,6%	CR=0%			

E6

	Group 1	Group 2	CORNERSTONES IC, IM, IS, BT	Group 3	RESOURCES PC, PT, IT, OR	Group 4	Group 5	OUTPUTS EF, SA, EE	Group 6	Group 7	RESULTS PL, CL, DL		
	5.9	20.5	13.2	17.2	17.2	77.2	22.6	22.6	18.8	68.2	18.8	OI	0.65933
	40.4	7.6	24	41.8	41.8	5.3	10.1	10.1	8.1	4.8	8.1	LI-1	0.46536
	38.3	55	46.6	9.5	9.5	17.5	67.4	67.4	73.1	27.1	73.1	RI	0.16587
	15.4	16.9	16.2	31.5	31.5						TLU	E6	0.05039
	CR=16,2%	CR=7,8%		CR=21,4%		CR=38,4%	CR=9%		CR=6,8%	CR=22,7%			

E9

	Group 1	Group 2	CORNERSTONES IC, IM, IS, BT	Group 3	RESOURCES PC, PT, IT, OR	Group 4	Group 5	OUTPUTS EF, SA, EE	Group 6	Group 7	RESULTS PL, CL, DL		
	25.8	43.7	43.7	35.1	35.1	12.6	11.7	12.2	19.2	57	38.1	OI	0.78867
	31	8	8	47.8	47.8	45.8	26.8	36.3	17.4	9.7	13.6	LI-1	0.24307
	14.5	8.8	8.8	8.3	8.3	41.6	61.4	51.5	63.4	33.3	48.3	RI	0.12998
	28.7	39.5	39.5	8.8	8.8						TLU	E9	0.02492
	CR=53,4%	CR=0,4%		CR=2,3%		CR=1%	CR=7,7%		CR=1%	CR=2,6%			

E16

	Group 1	Group 2	CORNERSTONES IC, IM, IS, BT	Group 3	RESOURCES PC, PT, IT, OR	Group 4	Group 5	OUTPUTS EF, SA, EE	Group 6	Group 7	RESULTS PL, CL, DL		
	6.1	6.2	6.2	29.2	29.2	42.9	26	34.5	10.1	49.9	30	OI	0.90167
	38.9	13.6	26.3	46.5	46.5	42.9	41.3	42	22.6	10.5	16.5	LI-1	0.33780
	11.8	53.7	32.7	19.2	19.2	14.3	32.7	23.5	67.4	39.6	53.5	RI	0.08025
	43.2	26.5	34.8	5	5						TLU	E16	0.02444
	CR=3,9%	CR=16,3%		CR=5,2%		CR=0%	CR=5,6%		CR=9%	CR=5,6%			

E25

	Group 1	Group 2	CORNERSTONES IC, IM, IS, BT	Group 3	RESOURCES PC, PT, IT, OR	Group 4	Group 5	OUTPUTS EF, SA, EE	Group 6	Group 7	RESULTS PL, CL, DL		
	21.5	9.2	15.3	42.5	42.5	62.2	38.7	38.7	15	16	15	OI	0.83567
	10.6	10.6	10.6	27	27	24.7	44.3	44.3	10.6	6.7	10.6	LI-1	0.49390
	18.9	35.5	27.2	14.4	14.4	13.1	16.9	16.9	74.4	77.3	74.4	RI	0.31536
	49	44.7	46.9	16.1	16.1						TLU	E25	0.13016
	CR=4,3%	CR=4,5%		CR=1,7%		CR=22,7%	CR=1,9%		CR=12,4%	CR=27,4%			

APPENDIX 5

Table 11.4 Consolidation 4

	CORNERSTONES			RESOURCES			OUTPUTS			RESULTS		
M7 Group 1	IC, IM, IS, BT	Group 2	Group 3	PC, PT, IT, OR	Group 4	Group 5	EF, SA, EE	Group 6	Group 7	PL, CL, DL		
25.9	17.9	10	35.7	35.7	17.8	5.9	5.9	9.1	44.4	26.7	OI	0.72567
24.4	16.4	8.4	39.4	39.4	30.4	45.1	45.1	9.1	8.4	8.8	LI-1	0.43402
39.8	33.2	26.5	15.6	15.6	51.9	49	49	81.8	47.2	64.5	RI	0.17089
10	32.5	55.1	9.4	9.4							M7	0.05382
CR = 8,9 %		CR = 3,2 %	CR = 7,6 %		CR = 30,8 %	CR = 0,7 %		CR = 0 %	CR = 0,4 %	TLI		
M11 Group 1	IC, IM, IS, BT	Group 2	Group 3	PC, PT, IT, OR	Group 4	Group 5	EF, SA, EE	Group 6	Group 7	PL, CL, DL		
20.4	20.4	17.3	8.6	8.6	52.4	22.1	37.2	22.9	47.4	35.1	OI	0.85367
33.9	33.9	14.4	66.8	66.8	7.6	31.9	19.7	7.5	5.3	6.4	LI-1	0.32765
38.7	38.7	39.8	11	11	40	46	43	69.6	47.4	58.5	RI	0.08566
7	7	28.5	13.7	13.7							M11	0.02424
CR = 6,5 %		CR = 29,8 %	CR = 1,5 %		CR = 7,7 %	CR = 14,1 %		CR = 8 %	CR = 0 %	TLI		
M13 Group 1	IC, IM, IS, BT	Group 2	Group 3	PC, PT, IT, OR	Group 4	Group 5	EF, SA, EE	Group 6	Group 7	PL, CL, DL		
4.6	13.9	23.3	59.9	59.9	58.4	11.3	34.8	8.8	61.4	35.2	OI	0.85167
11.4	12.2	12.8	24.5	24.5	13.5	23.5	18.5	13.9	117	12.8	LI-1	0.23655
20.6	19.1	17.7	11.3	11.3	28.1	65.2	46.6	77.3	26.8	52	RI	0.09966
63.4	54.8	46.3	4.4	4.4							M13	0.02008
CR = 11,9 %		CR = 17,8 %	CR = 12,9 %		CR = 14,1 %	CR = 14,1 %		CR = 5,6 %	CR = 7,7 %	TLI		
M26 (end) Group 1	IC, IM, IS, BT	Group 2	Group 3	PC, PT, IT, OR	Group 4	Group 5	EF, SA, EE	Group 6	Group 7	PL, CL, DL		
3.7	6.5	9.2	27.8	27.8	13.5	9.1	9.1	9.1	6.2	9.1	OI	0.51533
26.6	28.4	30.3	48.7	48.7	28.1	9.1	9.1	9.1	13	9.1	LI-1	0.59708
51	44.7	38.4	19.6	19.6	58.4	81.8	81.8	81.8	80.8	81.8	RI	0.06002
18.7	20.4	22.1	3.9	3.9							M26	0.01847
CR = 21,5%		CR = 19,1 %	CR = 11 %		CR = 58,5 %	CR = 0 %		CR = 0 %	CR = 14,1 %	TLI		

APPENDIX 6: SPECIFIC INDEX TRAFFIC LIGHT VALUES IN THE BLACK AND WHITE PRINTED VERSION, THE GREEN COLOR IS SIGNIFIED WITH A CHECK MARK, YELLOW WITH AN EXCLAMATION MARK, AND RED WITH AN X MARK.

Direction of outputs

   0–0.7 (✘)
   0.7–0.85 (!)
   0.85–1 (✓)

Cornerstones

   0–0.8 (✘)
   0.8–0.93 (!)
   0.93–1 (✓)

Results
Dynamic leadership

   0–0.5 (✘)
   0.5–0.7 (!)
   0.7–1 (✓)

Controlling and passive leadership

   0–0.75 (✘)
   0.75–0.85 (!)
   0.85–1 (✓)

Resources

   0–0.8 (✘)
   0.8–0.93 (!)
   0.93–1 (✓)

Success and failure in improvement of knowledge delivery to customers using chatbot—result of a case study in a Polish SME

12

B. Filipczyk*, J. Gołuchowski*, J. Paliszkiewicz**, A. Janas[†]

*University of Economics, Katowice, Poland; **Warsaw University of Life Sciences, Warsaw, Poland; [†]Podhale State College of Applied Sciences, Nowy Targ, Poland

INTRODUCTION

Proponents of new information and communication technology are convinced that chatbots (also known as conversational systems, virtual assistants, virtual agents, dialog systems, chatterbots, artificial conversation entities), which use knowledge recorded formally in a knowledge base, are a valuable ICT tool. Chatbots are computer applications that imitate human personality (Allison, 2012). Previously, chatbots only responded to written text. In the last few years, "chatbots became more versatile and included speech synthesis and recognition, and affective state detection and responses" (van Rosmalen et al., 2012, p. 526–527).

Chatbots enable enterprises to manage the collection of knowledge and communicate interactively with customers and in this manner to share knowledge collected in a chatbot's knowledge base. Despite the significant increase of the interest in those tools, their usage in small and medium enterprises (SMEs) faces many limitations caused by the quality of the developed knowledge bases and the difficulties encountered during improving them.

The processes of developing and improving the chatbot's knowledge base are expensive and time consuming. They involve the most highly paid employees in the enterprise (knowledge workers).

The conversation logs of chatbots seem to be a valuable source of knowledge for customers, as well as for perfecting the chatbot's knowledge base automatically. However, extracting knowledge from the content of conversations requires smart supporting tools, as the sets of chatbots' dialogs with customers tend to constitute large amounts of data.

In this chapter, results of a case study for improvements of knowledge delivery to an SME's customers using chatbot are described. The conclusions for SMEs from the case study show the possibilities and limitations of improving the process of knowledge delivery to the clients via chatbots.

THE NEEDS AND DIFFICULTIES IN MANAGEMENT OF KNOWLEDGE DELIVERY TO CUSTOMERS IN THE SELECTED SME

The information gap interferes with people's ability to make rational decisions (Forlicz, 2001). This applies to both managers and customers. Therefore, filling an existing gap in knowledge is one of the most important tasks of the enterprise in their relationship with customers. The selection of the strategy of knowledge delivery to customers and knowledge acquisition from them are significant tasks of knowledge management (Paliszkiewicz, 2007).

The case study took place in a Polish company. The Janas company is an SME operating since 1993 in the meat processing industry. There are more than 180 people employed in the Janas company, working in the meat processing plant in Nowy Targ, and in three distribution centers, plus a chain of branded outlets. The company has frequently been rewarded for dynamic growth. It also implements projects co-financed from European funds. In 2013, quality control and food safety certificates, International Food Standard (IFS), and the British Retail Consortium Global Standard—For Food Safety (BRC) were implemented, which all guarantee meeting international nutrition standards.

The customers' knowledge gap is minimized at the Janas company through the process of communication. A call center is used to ensure good communication between customers and the enterprise. It requires efficient knowledge management to deliver information at the right time to the right customers.

At Janas there is an awareness that the delivery of information to customers requires not only the right strategy but also the correct tools for its implementation. It determines the reliability of the company and, as a consequence, satisfaction in cooperation with the enterprise and the loyalty of existing customers, as well as attracting new ones.

Knowledge codification was adopted at the Janas company as a knowledge management strategy. In addition, technology for knowledge acquisition and its delivery to customers in the process of communication with customers (via the Internet) are constantly improved. For that purpose, the customer relationship management (CRM) system used by the call center and a corporate portal has been developed. Improvement of customer service was enriched with an application for which the main goal is to reach a broad array of potential new customers, supplying them with high-quality service and starting to build a relationship with them. According to McNeal and Newyear (2013), these user-friendly implementations of artificial intelligence have enjoyed remarkable success in different sectors, like in industry or government, and are projected to continue to grow in popularity. Making the decision on the broader application in customer service of the codification strategy consists of collecting information and knowledge in an extensive computer base (Paliszkiewicz, 2007). To build a knowledge management strategy (knowledge for, from, and about customers) in the Janas company, the following assumptions were made:

- the user needs to be able to place questions through the chatbot and receive expert knowledge related to the case;
- codification and storing all information in computer databases, from which it will be possible to quickly and easily draw from every customer and improve in an automated way by a company employee;
- once encoded information can be used many times, by many customers, as long as it proves helpful or needed;
- information and telecommunication systems dedicated to various access devices will be developed at the company;
- particular emphasis—in regard to the company's employees—will be placed on the ability to use existing patterns and solutions, as well as care for contributing to the development of the already functioning databases;
- in relation to the possibility of applying ready-made solutions and projects, the duration of servicing a customer will be reduced, and as a consequence the costs of labor and financial outlays will be reduced.

While developing a codification strategy, Janas company assumed that it was important to place emphasis on the creation of databases and knowledge bases that would be accessible for both employees and customers. To improve knowledge delivery, it was decided to develop and use an interactive tool relatively new to Polish SMEs, a chatbot called SAGA (available from: http://firmajanas.pl). It was decided at the Janas company that it will be an important part of the CRM system, which relieves the call center employees of the recurring questions. Communication with customers carried out by that system should be useful both for the company and for the customers. It enables relatively inexpensive communication without the involvement of a large number of employees. It offers the possibility to communicate synchronically and have an individual approach to each customer, but with a massive reach. It also enables collecting knowledge for and from customers, as well as supervision over its delivery and monitoring of obtaining it by the company's customers.

When deciding to use the chatbot at Janas, it was taken into account that the use of tools for analysis of conversations may have some limitations, basically stemming from the quality of chatbot knowledge. The development of special knowledge base requires the involvement of experts and is time and work consuming, thus often exceeds the financial possibilities of SMEs. There was a huge expectation for the analysis of knowledge base quality and the process of knowledge delivery to customers through the use of an intelligent system that improves the chatbot's knowledge base.

One of the approaches that enables automation of improvement of collecting knowledge for customers is an analysis of the conversations from chatbot's logs. During conversations, users provide a lot of valuable information, eg, personal data, opinions about the company, the offered products or services, or the competition. During the conversation logs analysis, it is possible to determine whether the data obtained from the chatbot's users are valuable or useless. For that purpose, an automatic log analyzer of the knowledge base improvement would be useful.

In the chatbot's conversation log analyzer, called Zuza, the following methods were used:

- Methods of preliminary analysis, aimed at reducing linguistic defects, to limit the set of analyzed cases in the business conversation logs to relevant statements, worthy of analyzing, and for the data collected from conversation partners, to the reliable ones.
- Methods of detecting and elimination of irregularities that occur in the chatbot's knowledge base, based on analysis of conversation logs.
- Methods of detecting related categories, which are aimed at reducing the possibility of the occurrence of conflicts between categories in the chatbot's knowledge base.
- The method of reducing the number of analyzed cases, ie, user questions, chatbot answer pairs, operating by inference from the base of cases.
- Methods of assessing the quality of the chatbot's knowledge base based on statistical analysis of conversation logs.

ZUZA extracts data from the chatbot's knowledge base (AIML) and the conversation logs (where the content of conversations is recorded) to the relational database (Fig. 12.1). This enables the creation of precise inquiries (in SQL), and most significantly, searching for information contained directly in both source sets. An additional information layer is the template of the analyzed chatbot.

IMPROVEMENTS OF KNOWLEDGE BASES AND DELIVERY PROCESSES USING CHATBOTS

An analysis of the conversations with Polish chatbots has indicated that many problems occurred during the users' conversations with the chatbots (Janas, 2015, unpublished data, p. 63–68). The most frequent were repeated chatbots' responses (answers) and lack of response to questions. Another problem was inadequate answers of the chatbot to users' questions and the chatbot's problems with referring to prior statements (failure to take the context of the conversation into account). However, what seems to be the most important, the same defects appear (even after an interval of 6 months), which leads to the conclusion that the chatbot had not been improved over that time in the scope of the examination. The defects influence the decrease of the customers' interest in this application, which could mean that chatbot does not fulfill its functions.

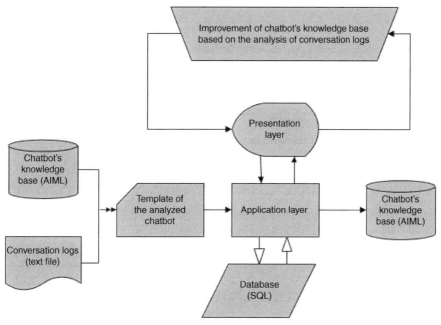

FIGURE 12.1 Model of a ZUZA system (Janas, 2015, unpublished data)

THE IMPROVEMENTS OF KNOWLEDGE DELIVERY TO CUSTOMERS IN JANAS COMPANY

Improving the knowledge base of SAGA, three databases containing the logs of conversations of the SAGA users were used, collected in the periods: 1.04.2014–17.04.2014, 19.04.2014–9.05.2014, 1.07.2014–14.07.2014, and 15.10.2014–12.11.2014, containing 390, 397, and 377 users' questions and the chatbot's responses respectively, three versions of the SAGA's knowledge base (resulting from the performed improvement processes). In addition, the statistics of visits to the website of the Janas company and the statistics of the logs of SAGA conversation were used, as well as an interview with one of the co-owners of Janas company was carried out.

Conversation logs form a set of dialogs (conversations) between chatbot and its users, recorded in a text file. While analyzing the quality of the knowledge base improvement and its impact on knowledge delivery to customers, it was assumed that each iteration would consider the same number of conversations (100). Analysis of the dialogs recorded in conversation logs should provide relevant knowledge about the processes of delivery knowledge to customers and its acquisition by them. The knowledge obtained during the analysis of the conversation logs may concern:

- the conversation process—the duration, number of user's questions per conversation, the number of conversations, etc.;
- conversation irregularities—that is, chatbot's failure to refer to prior questions, failure to respond (submission of an evasive reply), failure to provide an

adequate reply, recurrence of replies in a conversation, lack of cohesion in the conversation, etc.;

- results of conversation—that is, whether the conversation system displayed correct answers, consistent with the user's expectations, if it performed the user's instructions, if the chatbot managed to reach the objective of the conversation (eg, the sale of a specific product, a change of the opinion on a given topic, obtaining personal data, etc.);
- user's questions—that is, finding out how and what about chatbot's users ask most often, what topics they bring in most frequently and how they build their messages, etc.

To assess how the presence of SAGA and its improved versions of the knowledge base are influenced by the number of visitors to the website, the decision was made to use the statistics of visits to the service before implementation of the conversation system and after subsequent implementation of the improved chatbot's knowledge base and conduction of the interviews with the company management.

Between 1.04.2014 and 17.04.2014, data for the first stage (iteration) of improvement were compiled. To assess the capacity (potential) for the proposed solution to reduce the number of defects in the chatbot's knowledge base. The chatbot's knowledge base underwent a process of improvement based on analysis of the collected conversation logs using the ZUZA. The improved knowledge base was reused and the same questions were asked to the SAGA, with the use of an automatic tool, which took question after question from the previously examined dialogs. The new conversation logs were reanalyzed and then obtained data were compared to the results obtained before the improvement process. For further improvements of the chatbot's knowledge base, the second and third iterations were made (iterations II and III). The logs of conversations between the chatbot and its users of 19.04.2014–9.05.2014 (iteration II), 1.07.2014–14.07.2014, and 15.10.2014–12.11.2014 (iteration III) were used.

RESULTS OF IMPROVEMENTS OF KNOWLEDGE DELIVERY TO CUSTOMERS USING SAGA

The results of the three iterations of improvements to SAGA's knowledge base, conducted by acquiring new knowledge from analysis of the conversation logs (iterations I, II, and III), are presented in Table 12.1. It represents the way in which a number of knowledge base irregularities were detected by the system during the analysis of conversation logs, such as inadequate chatbot responses, lack of response, recurring responses, or failure of the chatbot to refer to prior questions. After each improvement iteration, the quality of the knowledge base improved gradually—which is testified to be the lower proportion of irregularities occurring during the conversations (see Table 12.1).

An analysis of the graphs reveals that after the implementation of the chatbot on the Janas company website, as well as after implementing the improved versions

Table 12.1 The Results of Improving Chatbot's Knowledge Base in Three Successive Iterations (Janas, 2015, unpublished data)

Measure	*i* = 1	*i* = 2	*i* = 3
Number of analyzed conversations	100	100	100
Average daily number of conversations	5.88	4.76	3.22
Number of analyzed pairs: user's message—chatbot's response	390	397	377
Number of insignificant messages from the perspective of design assumptions	22	32	23
Number of recognized templates	235	276	273
Number of adequate responses (answers)	194	237	244
Adequate response rate (answers)	49.74%	59.70%	64.72%
Adequate response rate (answers)—absolute increase	—	9.95%	5.02%
Adequate response rate (taking into account design assumptions)	52.72%	64.93%	68.93%
Adequate response rate (taking into account the design assumptions)—absolute increase	—	12.21%	4.00%
Adequate response rate (responses)—only recognized patterns	82.55%	85.87%	89.38%
Adequate response rate (responses) (only recognized patterns)—absolute increase	—	3.32%	3.51%
Number of missing responses to user question	155	121	104
Nonresponse to question rate	39.74%	30.48%	27.59%
Nonresponse to question rate—absolute increase	—	−9.27%	−2.89%
Nonresponse to question rate (taking into account design assumptions)	36.14%	24.38%	22.88%
Nonresponse to question rate (taking into account design assumptions)—absolute increase	—	−11.76%	−1.50%
Number of chatbot recurring responses	72	40	35
Chatbot response recurrence rate	18.46%	10.08%	9.28%
Chatbot response recurrence rate—absolute increase	—	−8.39%	−0.79%
Chatbot response recurrence rate (taking into account the design assumptions)	19.57%	10.96%	9.89%
Chatbot response recurrence rate (taking into account design assumptions) absolute increase	—	−8.61%	−1.07%
Number of inadequate responses (answers) of the chatbot	41	39	29

(Continued)

Table 12.1 The Results of Improving Chatbot's Knowledge Base in Three Successive Iterations (Janas, 2015, unpublished data) (*cont.*)

Measure	$i = 1$	$i = 2$	$i = 3$
Inadequate chatbot's response (answer) rate	10.51%	9.82%	7.69%
Inadequate chatbot's response (answer) rate—absolute increase	—	−0.69%	−2.13%
Inadequate chatbot response (answer) rate (taking into account design assumptions)	11.14%	10.68%	8.19%
Inadequate chatbot response (answer) rate (taking into account design assumptions)—absolute increase	—	−0.46%	−2.49%
Inadequate chatbot response rate (only recognized patterns)	17.45%	14.13%	10.62%
Inadequate chatbot response rate (only recognized patterns)—absolute increase	—	−3.32%	−3.51%
Number of missing references	28	15	11
No reference rate	7.18%	3.78%	2.92%
No reference rate—absolute increase	—	−3.40%	−0.86%
No reference rate (taking into account design assumptions)	7.61%	4.11%	3.11%
No reference rate (taking into account design assumptions)—absolute increase	—	−3.50%	−1.00%
Response rate	63.86%	75.62%	77.12%
Response rate—absolute increase	—	11.76%	1.50%

of the knowledge base of SAGA, the increase in the number of visits to the Janas website were noticed. However, there are doubts to link the growth directly to the results of the improvement of knowledge base (see Figs. 12.2 and 12.3). There is no clear trend related to visits on the website after the last implementation of the improved chatbot's knowledge base. After launching the chatbot on the Janas company website, there was no recorded increase in the number of users of the conversation system, but on the contrary, the daily number of users of SAGA was gradually falling (see Table 12.1). Conclusions that the implementation of the system had an impact on the company's call center are not clear. The initial high interest in conversations with SAGA, right after its deployment on the website, could be explained by the company's promotional campaign.

The interview conducted with a manager of the Janas company (in charge of sales, promotion, and IT), has shown that SAGA implemented on the company's website constitutes a marketing tool related to the company's innovation. The management of the company received positive feedback from the company's customers and employees on the presence of SAGA and was satisfied with the implementation of the system on the website.

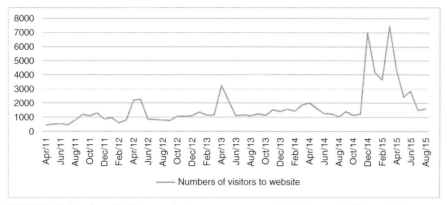

FIGURE 12.2 Number of visitors to the Janas company website (Janas, 2015, unpublished data)

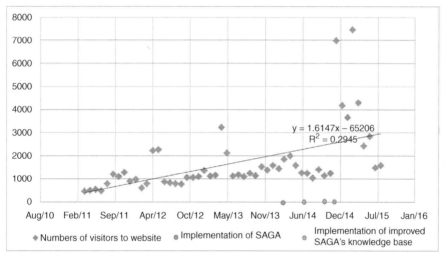

FIGURE 12.3 Trend line for the number of visitors to the Janas company website (Janas, 2015, unpublished data)

DISCUSSION

Some researchers design chatbots with the intention of obtaining a more natural conversation, closer to a talk between humans. Others, on the other hand, are focused on facilitating the processes of developing and improving a chatbot's knowledge base. Chat is a more efficient way to provide customer support and sales assistance. Chatbot conversation threads contain valuable information saved in conversation logs. However only few research reports' dedicated log analysis could be found on the Internet (eg, Kelemen, 2015).

An analysis of the literature shows that there is a lack of research on the quality of knowledge delivered to customers via chatbots and on improvements of the chatbot's knowledge base used as the company's virtual assistant. Actual research related mainly to improvement of dialogs quality, coherence of the knowledge base, and anthropomorphization of chatbots.

There is research conducted on dialog modeling to increase the efficiency of conversations held by a chatbot (Montero and Araki, 2005) and efficient, automatic feeding of a chatbot's knowledge base with knowledge (see Abu Shawar and Atwell, 2003a, 2003b, 2004; Huang et al., 2007; Whetsel, 2009). Moreover, there is research related to increasing the validity of responses given by a chatbot and improving dialog management, including maintenance of cohesion and the context of the dialog [see Zdravkova (2000), Hung (2002), and Branting et al. (2004) in: Kuligowska, 2012] and learning from conversation partners (eg, the Jabberwacky project, written by programmer Rollo Carpenter). Then, there is a group of researchers (eg, Walker et al., 1997; Walker et al., 2000) who dedicated their work to issues related to the assessment of dialog systems and comparison of the effectiveness of various strategies for conducting dialogs.

Many studies have turned toward anthropomorphization of chatbots (eg, Cassell et al., 2000; Cavalluzzi et al., 2003; De Angeli and Brahnam, 2008; De Boni et al., 2008; Mućko, 2009). Other research has focused on recognition of the emotions of conversation partners and the expression of chatbot's emotions (Heuft et al., 1996; Cowie and Douglas-Cowie, 1998; Ball and Breese, 2000; Cavalluzzi et al., 2003), or attempts to add elements of humor (De Boni et al., 2008) and mechanisms of memorizing the course of conversation (Mućko, 2009) so that the conversation system would offer the possibility of referring to prior messages of its own and its users. To improve the chatbot for a "more humanlike" effect, the inclusion and adjustment of personality features as well as a mechanism for maintaining a relationship with the conversation partner were used (De Boni et al., 2008). Furthermore, a lot of attention in research on anthropomorphic chatbots has been paid to speech synthesis and recognition. With respect to the first issue, spectacular success was enjoyed by the speech synthesizer called IVONA—considered at the international science competition Blizzard Challenge in 2006 to be one of the best synthesizers in the world (IVONA, 2012).

During the last 15 years, many tools that facilitate the development of chatbot's knowledge bases have been proposed. Unfortunately, they have mainly used specialized programming languages (AIML, VHML, RiveScript), interpreters of those languages, and relatively unsophisticated knowledge base editors, such as AutoAIML. Tools that enable not only development of a chatbot's knowledge base, but also the automatic publication of the chatbot on the website and ongoing testing of the results of work on the knowledge base are also available (eg, GaitoBot, Chatbot4You, Pandorabots). Furthermore, the programs used to create chatbot make it possible to build reasoning chatbots (eg, AI Pioneer) or chatbot messages with emotional characteristics (eg, The Personality Forge).

There are studies related to improvement of the knowledge base of intelligent systems that discuss the issue in a systematic manner (eg, Owoc et al., 1999; Owoc and Galant, 1999). However, the main research problem was the coherence of the knowledge base. Another, no less important issue is filling the knowledge base with valuable information, later sought by chatbot users. Another research effort was related to improvement of communication carried out in natural language between people and computers. The last 15 years have abounded in publications concerning the improvement of communication between a chatbot and its users.

CONCLUSIONS AND DIRECTIONS FOR FUTURE RESEARCH

In this chapter, the case study from the Janas company, which showed that improvement of the chatbot's knowledge base conducted using the analysis of conversations between chatbots and customers is presented. Improvements of the knowledge delivery to customers with the use of a chatbot is possible, but still is limited by lack of reliable methods and tools.

Analysis of chatbot's conversations with users undoubtedly provides important knowledge, useful for those who manage the company's knowledge base. However, the adapted solution did not bring expected improvements of the knowledge base in a short period of time. It turned out to be not fully effective; three iterations failed to provide an improvement of the knowledge base and an increase in the customers' interest in that form of contact. The growth of interest was only temporary.

The most significant effects of the improvements are:

- Achieving facilitation of improving the chatbot's knowledge base using automatic analysis of conversation logs, as it enabled detection of irregularities in the chatbot's knowledge base. This reduced the number of analyzed cases by the knowledge engineer, who supported their decisions on improvement of the chatbot's knowledge base and ensured more convenient ways of editing the chatbot's knowledge base.
- Subsequent iterations in the improvements of the knowledge base led to enhancement of the quality of the knowledge base of the SAGA, measured by the number of instances of nonresponse of the chatbot, recurring chatbot's responses during a conversation, or lack of chatbot's reference to prior messages. The numbers of these irregularities decreased along with the subsequent improvement process through elimination of all irregularities present in the chatbot's knowledge base, important from the perspective of the design assumptions, which were detected during the analysis of the conversation logs between the chatbot and users. This means that the system no longer makes those errors during subsequent conversations.

Beyond doubt, the analysis of chatbot's conversations with customers, performed with the use of a specialized IT tool, facilitates delivery of knowledge to customers using a chatbot, as well as management of knowledge collected in the chatbot's knowledge base and its delivery using an intelligent system. The quality of the process must depend on the initial quality of the knowledge base, and as a consequence, its improved version could have a significant impact on the improvement process. However, the results of improvements are not satisfactory. Long-standing customers did not treat the improved chatbot as a good source of valuable knowledge. This might have resulted from the convenience related to direct contact with the call center. Three iterations of the improvement process by conversation logs turned out to be insufficient for those customers. Also, defects remained; the efficiency of their removal did not exceed 60%. Perhaps, it will be possible to obtain additional explanations of this phenomena through interviews with selected customers. The task was entrusted to the call center.

The results of the three iterations indicate that the process of improvement is more difficult than expected. To overcome the obstacles that appear in the knowledge base, it is not enough to carry out analysis of the knowledge saved in the conversation logs. The expectations that the automatically improved knowledge base of the examined chatbot would be a valuable source of knowledge turned out to be too optimistic. The knowledge base requires much more work and time to be improved in the long term, and not only by knowledge obtained from automatic conversation analysis.

The most important limitations are:

- Chatbot's users still encounter problems during the conversation, as only some of the knowledge base irregularities have been detected and eliminated.
- Analysis of logs did not provide permanent users any new knowledge or did not facilitate its acquisition, a traditional phone call to the call center may take less time.
- After implementation of improved versions of the chatbot's knowledge base on the website, there was no recorded increase in the number of users of the conversation system; to the contrary, the daily number of SAGA's users was gradually decreasing (see Table 12.1). The expectations of customers are, therefore, much higher than the possibilities of the knowledge base of the chatbot.

Despite facilitation of the improvements of the chatbot's knowledge base using results of an automatic analysis of conversation logs is still work and time consuming. And the benefits obtained from the process of improvements of the knowledge delivery to customers are uncertain.

To conclude, it may be stated that a chatbot's knowledge base is undoubtedly a valuable approach to collecting knowledge for customers and its delivery to them in an attractive way. Thus facilitation of the knowledge management especially knowledge delivery to customers.

A case study in Janas company, of course, does not legitimize making far-reaching conclusions, yet it shows that the process of improvements of a knowledge base by analyzing the conversations cannot be the only method of improvement.

So the process is still cost and time intensive, which seems still a long way from becoming a good tool for cooperation between an SME and customers. The current state of knowledge management and skills in this area for creating and improving the knowledge base of chatbots are still too expensive and laborious to be a competitive solution to other forms of communication between customers and a small company. Insufficient progress in the improvements of knowledge bases will discourage users who encounter problems in the course of a conversation with a chatbot from using this form of contact with the company and obtaining the desired knowledge.

The described case study in Janas leads to the conclusion that the proposed approach to improve the chatbot's knowledge base must be complemented with obtaining new knowledge for the knowledge base, rather than only improving the existing one. Analysis of conversation logs via computer analyzers (such as ZUZA) is a good approach. Other methods of improving the knowledge base are needed, such as gathering knowledge during direct contact with customers (inquiry), plus the knowledge of those who manage contact with customers, as well as knowledge from the marketing automation system and analysis of social media used by the company.

Methods of improvements of the chatbot knowledge base need to be more sophisticated. Also improvement of analysis is required, mainly in the area of higher or even complete automation of detecting inadequate responses of chatbots, which is related to the application of new and better methods of analyzing of unstructured data (such as semantic methods). Despite many improvements, the process of knowledge base analysis is still work intensive and discourages people from using the analyzer in the long term.

Many chatbots have the same problems, such as difficulty of a relevant search, the complexity of available information, and bandwidth limitations. But the main arguments in favor of developing the tools are the preference for real-time events. People like real-time information flow. They like dialogs instead of monologs (e-mails). Future research should be conducted to improve dialog quality and further refinement of the emotions module.

As a future direction, further techniques could be involved to conduct a more detailed conversation log analysis with the goal of understanding underlying processes and analyzing the behavior of chatbots. Defects in chatbot conversations are not (and probably cannot be) fully eliminated as new problems arise with new users' questions.

REFERENCES

Abu Shawar, B., Atwell, E., 2003a. Using dialogue corpora to train a chatbot system. In: Archer, D., Rayson, P., Wilson, A., McEnery, T. (Eds.), In: Proceedings of the Corpus Linguistics conference (CL2003). Lancaster University, UK.

Abu Shawar, B., Atwell, E., 2003b. Using the Corpus of Spoken Afrikaans to generate an Afrikaans chatbot. South. Afr. Linguist. Appl. Language Stud. 21, 283–294.

Abu Shawar, B., Atwell, E., 2004. Accessing an information system by chatting. In: Meziane, F., Metais, E. (Eds.), In: Proceedings of 9th International conference on the Application of Natural Language to Information Systems, NLDB 2004. LNCS Lecture Notes in Computer Science, Springer, Salford, UK, pp. 396–401.

Allison, D., 2012. Chatbots in the library: is it time? Library Hi Tech 30 (1), 95–107.

Ball, G., Breese, J., 2000. Emotion and personality in a conversational agent. In: Cassell, J., Sullivan, J., Prevost, S., Churchill, E. (Eds.), Embodied conversational agents. The MIT Press, Cambridge, Mass.

Cassell, J., Sullivan, J., Prevost, S., Churchill, E. (Eds.), 2000. Embodied conversational agents. The MIT Press, Cambridge, Mass.

Cavalluzzi, A., De Carolis, B., Carofiglio, V., Grassano, G., 2003. Emotional Dialogs With an Embodied Agent. User modeling '03. Springer-Verlag, Berlin.

Cowie, R., Douglas-Cowie, E., 1998. Automatic statistical analysis of the signal and prosodic signs of emotion in speech. Proceedings of ICSLP, Philadelphia.

De Angeli, A., Brahnam, S., 2008. I hate you! Disinhibition with virtual partners. Interact. Comput. 20 (3), 302–310.

De Boni, M., Richardson, A., Hurling, R., 2008. Humour, relationship maintenance and personality matching in automated dialogue: a controlled study. Interact. Comput. 1 (20), 342–353, May.

Forlicz, S., 2001. Niedoskonała wiedza podmiotów rynkowych [Imperfect knowledge market participants]. PWN, Warszawa.

Heuft, B., Portele, T., Rauth, M, 1996. Emotions in time domain synthesis. Proceedings of ICSLP, Philadelphia. Available from: http://citeseerx.ist.psu.edu/viewdoc/download?doi=10.1.1.16.6101&rep=rep1&type=pdf.

Huang, J., Zhou, M., Yang, D., 2007. Extracting chatbot knowledge from online discussion forums. Proceedings of the Twentieth International Joint Conference on Artificial Intelligence. IJCAI '07. Morgan Kaufmann Publishers Inc., San Francisco, California.

IVONA, 2012. Home page of IVO SOFT. Available from: http://www.ivona.com/technology.php.

Kelemen, Z.D., 2015. Fundamental analysis of a developer support chat log for identifying process improvement opportunities. Available from: http://arxiv.org/ftp/arxiv/papers/1503/1503.05533.pdf.

Kuligowska, K., 2012. Wirtualny asystent na stronach WWW. Zasady działania, implementacja, koszty i korzyści wdrożenia [A virtual assistant on the web. Principles of operation, implementation, costs and benefits of implementation]. BonNote, Warszawa.

McNeal, M.L., Newyear, D., 2013. Introducing chatbots in libraries. Library Technol. Rep. 49 (8), 5–10.

Montero, C.S., Araki, K., 2005. Enhancing computer chat: toward a smooth user-computer interaction. In: Knowledge-Based Intelligent Information, Engineering Systems, vol. 3681, Lecture Notes in Computer Science. Springer-Verlag, Berlin.

Mućko, A., 2009. Antropomorfizacja systemów sztucznego rozmówcy [Anthropomorphize artificial systems caller]. Master's thesis, Electrical Department, Warsaw University of Technology, Warsaw. Available from: http://www.ee.pw.edu.pl/~czajewsw/studenckie/magisterskie/praca_pM_WE_PW_2012_Mucko_Aleksandra_197729.pdf.

Owoc, M., Galant, V., 1999. Validation of rule-based systems generated by classification algorithms. In: Zupancic, J., Wojtkowski, G., Wojtkowski, W., Wrycza, S. (Eds.), Evolution and Challenges in System Development. Kluwer Academic/Plenum Publishers, New York, pp. 459–468.

Owoc, M., Ochmanska, M., Gladysz, T., 1999. On principles of knowledge validation. In: Vermesan, A., Coenen, F. (Eds.), Validation and Verification of Knowledge Based Systems: Theory, Tools and Practice. Kluwer Academic Publishers, Boston.

Paliszkiewicz, J., 2007. Zarządzanie wiedzą w małych i średnich przedsiębiorstwach. Koncepcja oceny i modele [Knowledge management in small and medium-sized enterprises. The concept of assessment and models]. wyd. SGGW, Warsaw.

van Rosmalen, P., Eikelboom, J., Bloemers, E., van Winzum, K., Spronck, P., 2012. Towards a game-chatbot: Extending the interaction in serious games. European Conference on Game Based Learning. Available from: http://search.proquest.com/docview/1326330162?accountid=48272.

Walker, M., Hindle, D., Fromer, J., Fabbrizio, G.D., Mestel, C., 1997. Evaluating competing agent strategies for a voice email agent. Proceedings of Fifth European Conference on Speech Communication and Technology. Available from: http://arxiv.org/pdf/cmp-lg/9706019.pdf.

Walker, M.A., Kamm, C.A., Litman, D.J., 2000. Towards developing general models of usability with PARADISE. Nat. Lang. Eng. 6 (3–4), 363–377, Available from: http://users.soe.ucsc.edu/~maw/papers/nle-4.pdf.

Whetsel, R., 2009. Improving human-like qualities of chatbots—draft. Available from: http://robertwhetsel.com/?series=the-state-of-chatbots.

Don't neglect the foundation: how organizations can build their knowledge architecture and processes for long-term sustainability

13

S. Earley

Earley Information Science, Inc., USA

Knowledge is about context. What information do you need right now? What answers are you seeking? What are you trying to accomplish, and what will help you accomplish that goal? Knowledge management is continually evolving. In most organizations, there is no longer a dividing line between structured and unstructured information as there was in prior years. Previously, knowledge artifacts were considered documents and content. However the definition of "content" has been broadened to include rich media assets and structured data along with unstructured data. Increasingly, knowledge management also entails a spectrum of activities from knowledge creation and collaboration to knowledge access and reuse. Business leaders and managers are continually synthesizing information to answer questions, solve problems, and creatively differentiate their products and services in the marketplace.

DIVERSE, FAST-CHANGING INFORMATION SOURCES

To make meaningful decisions, employees need information from diverse sources. Those sources are continually changing and evolving with new information and information sources being updated, enhanced, and added to the enterprise information ecosystem. It is not possible to stay ahead of the changes in the information environment or anticipate all the sources that users need. A marketer might interact with dozens of systems to help plan, execute, and analyze campaigns. In order to understand the impact of a marketing campaign, they need to know what the results were and what caused those results—insights that require synthesis of multiple information sources. Are social media campaigns impacting pay-per-click effectiveness? Are particular customer segments responding differently to incentives? Are dealers seeing more customers in showrooms? Developing and fine tuning strategies requires continual evaluation, combination, and synthesis of new information. Knowledge processes run at faster clock speeds and knowledge management programs seek to increase the information metabolism of the enterprise. Knowledge management is adding order to the information chaos. In order to do this correctly, KM technologies become the synthesis, integration, and access layer across multiple systems, processes, and technologies and require an architectural scaffold on which to organize that information. This is the core information architecture of the system.

KNOWLEDGE THAT SERVES THE CUSTOMER

Internal systems and processes ultimately have one purpose—to serve external customers. Those customers now have greater access to information sources, and come armed with more knowledge than ever before. The role of knowledge management in serving customers is in contextualizing and surfacing solutions, services, and products to meet the needs of the user at that particular point in time.

The competitive environment is also changing at a faster pace. The arms race of technologies and tools to serve customers is causing massive changes in the enterprise. This is causing organizations to rethink every system and process that serves customers directly or helps employees serve customers. Digital transformation used to mean taking paper out of a process. It now means transforming processes, creating new value streams, changing supply chains and creating new capabilities—both digital and physical. Digital transformations are knowledge transformations because knowledge is at the heart of all value in the enterprise. KM is more important than ever; it reaches into every aspect of the enterprise. The principles of contextualization are the same as those for personalization. Creating a seamless customer experience is about getting customers access to answers, services, product information, and solutions faster and more conveniently. Personalization is about anticipating the needs of a customer and serving up the right information at the right time for the right person—the mantra of knowledge management. Contextualization is enabled by information structures and those structures need to be built on a consistent and comprehensive, harmonized information architecture.

INCORRECT ARCHITECTURE REDUCES ORGANIZATIONAL AGILITY

Not having the correct architecture slows the ability to get to the correct information. It prevents systems from being easily integrated and slows down the adaptability of those systems. Adaptability and agility are what is required in the hypercompetitive marketplace; adding friction to the process in the form of brittle integrations, manual transformations and integrations, and information disconnects creates a competitive disadvantage. The organization that adapts most quickly to changes in the marketplace, competition, and customer needs, and gets products and services out to market more quickly is the winner. A faster information metabolism means a more competitive and successful organization. The key to this speed and agility is having a foundational architecture and evolving that architecture in a coherent, controlled fashion.

Many organizations embark on KM initiatives without understanding the role of a harmonized, integrated content and knowledge architecture. Or they attempt to develop a KM program without the necessary skills, personnel, or approaches. Projects are initiated in silos or, when established with an enterprise view, fail to develop and socialize the organizing principles that are required as infrastructure. In the cases where they do make an attempt, organizations get some of the pieces right but fail to correctly validate, or they validate their design and terminology decisions in too narrow a context. Just because someone has a woodworking shop does not mean they are a fine furniture craftsman. The difference between success and failure lies in numerous details that may be overlooked due to short-term budget constraints or a lack of attention due to short executive attention spans and type 1 thinking.[a] All of this is solvable, but leadership needs to face the challenges head on and understand the complexity of the solution. Successful KM is very attainable. It is complex but not mysterious—meaning there are many steps to the process, but they are understandable and can be accomplished in a sustainable way that is cost effective and achieves the desired outcome.

Organizations have been attempting to leverage knowledge processes using computer technology for decades. In the 1990s, collaborative technologies such as Lotus Notes came to the fore. Lotus Notes was a breakthrough product connecting disparate networks and operating systems together. Having Apple computers and Microsoft compatible computers sharing email across different network protocols was quite a feat in the early days of corporate messaging. This innovation ushered in the era of networked PCs, collaboration, and knowledge management. It used to be said, "Notes did poorly what nothing else can do at all." This statement summed up nicely the challenges that enterprises face even today when it comes to new technology. In some ways, the structure of those pioneering applications resembles structures that we see today on smartphones: icons representing knowledge bases or applications organized on different pages in a workspace. In that world of collaboration, all of those applications were disconnected and developed with organizing principles (metadata, taxonomies, and content models) that were developed on the fly by the system designers with no consideration of how others in the organization might name these elements or how inconsistencies would impact the ability to find information.

---

[a]http://www.scientificamerican.com/article/kahneman-excerpt-thinking-fast-and-slow/

ARCHITECTURAL PROBLEMS ACROSS THE INFORMATION ECOSYSTEM

Similar problems arise with web content management tools, business intelligence applications, transaction systems, ERP tools, marketing automation, CRM, and so on. One large nationwide retailer reported operating over 600 applications that it used to run its day-to-day operations. The vast majority of them had varying definitions of everything from product descriptors and attributes to vendor classifications, document types, employee job functions, financial reports and charts of accounts, and location information.

No matter what the tool or application, the challenge seen time and again is deployment of technology without foundational elements such as governance processes, consistent enterprise architecture, and ongoing curation of data and content. The root causes are:

- thinking about foundational architecture as a project rather than a program,
- taking a parochial view of the application being developed or deployed,
- not balancing centralized standards with distributed decision making,
- passing on data and content quality issues rather than addressing them upstream,
- cutting corners or checking the boxes rather than fully validating design decisions,
- incorrect development and application of use cases and scenarios,
- lack of understanding of user types and the needs of users,
- lack of appreciation of the value of unstructured information,
- lack of meaningful metrics to tie business value to information,
- lack of maturity in enterprise architecture, user experience, and governance.

FOUNDATIONAL ARCHITECTURE AS A PROJECT RATHER THAN A PROGRAM

Successful enterprises have achieved results by being intentional about maintaining a long-term frame of reference to applying taxonomy and information architecture approaches to their problems and challenges. In each case the organizations had the necessary ingredients to stay the course, build competencies, and develop organizational capabilities in content and information structure, management, and curation processes. They achieved a level of maturity and operational excellence by planning for the long term, not simply funding a standalone project with limited duration. Many companies have succeeded but many others have fallen short of their aspirations.

The first consideration is that successful taxonomy, search, IA, and content management initiatives are programs and not simply projects. Of course programs are broken down into projects, and projects need to be aligned with the organization's goals. What is interesting about taxonomy projects and programs specifically is that they span multiple areas: business units, departments, processes, functional areas, applications, technologies, projects, and programs. A well-managed taxonomy and metadata program affects all projects that the enterprise undertakes. Not everything that an enterprise does can be subsumed under taxonomy, but all projects need to have a seat at the taxonomy table and vice versa in order for an effective information architecture to be developed.

PAROCHIAL VIEW OF THE APPLICATION

Most information management projects are funded as stand-alone initiatives, or the span of integration is limited to the applications and processes immediately upstream or downstream. Even in the case of ERP systems, issues relating to product information quality or unstructured system integration are usually deferred for a later phase. However, all too often that phase either never comes or is given minimal attention and funding. As a colleague has said "there is no funding for the greater good." In other words, projects are funded with a view toward getting minimal functionality stood up without consideration of other parts of the enterprise. One aerospace manufacturer spent over $100 million on an ERP deployment without considering the supporting knowledge and content systems. When it came time to fund the knowledge initiative, a mere $300K was devoted to the project, when relative to its value, a much larger expenditure would have been justified. Without considering the entire ecosystem of information, new tools and applications will be developed with built-in friction to their information processes.

BALANCING CENTRALIZED VERSUS DISTRIBUTED CONTROL

Perhaps one of the toughest challenges in information governance is the need to balance the knowledge and expertise that resides in the business units throughout the enterprise with a centralized authority for maintaining standards and control. A KM system that is too highly centralized does not make sufficient use of that expertise, while a system that is too distributed can fail to provide a cohesive, enterprise-wide view of information that might be valuable throughout the organization.

Other tough questions focus on assigning responsibility for enterprise information. Decisions need to be made about whether information resides with IT or the business units, and how ownership is assigned. Myriad information owners, stewards of information compliance, and stakeholders must be aligned. If a centralized authority is established for information management and governance, what is the best way for the stakeholders to participate constructively? Organizations that do not have a clear roadmap for resolving these issues are unlikely to have successful KM initiatives.

PASSING ON DATA AND CONTENT QUALITY ISSUES

Rather than work with upstream stakeholders to remediate poor data and content quality, many organizations pass along the problem to the downstream user. Unfortunately, leadership does not take a sufficiently proactive role to ensure an enterprise view and mandate certain processes or allocate costs and resources appropriately. The costs and benefits of content and data quality are therefore not evenly distributed, and one part of the organization that could address issues frequently does not have the incentive—or might have a disincentive—to do so. Rather than make the additional investment in content curation or additional tagging at the source, or pushing data quality responsibility to a vendor or supplier, the problem is passed down the line because there is not responsibility or funding to fix the issues. The problems multiply and become more costly, and can end up costing the organization an order of magnitude more downstream as it would upstream.

CUTTING CORNERS OR CHECKING THE BOXES

Though practices for developing appropriate architectures, validating requirements, testing, and iterating are reasonably well established, organizations seemingly have little appetite to correctly apply them. One global professional services firm with over 100,000 employees routinely sent out spreadsheets of terms to managers to approve, rather than applying rigorous testing through use cases, and failed to develop and monitor metrics to measure fitness to purpose. The result was though it appeared the organization had a high level of maturity because it had well-established processes, people still could not find their assets. The problem was revealed upon closer examination to be due to a failure to correctly validate and measure appropriateness of the architecture underlying the user experience. Though the organization had the correct tools and techniques, it was not applying them appropriately.

One example of a situation in which the right steps were taken but the outcome was not effective is a B2B manufacturer that implemented a new change management process for product data and content. Changes were implemented through an appropriate governance process with greater oversight, and approval required for major changes such as a new top-level category, versus a minor change to a list of values to accommodate a new product.

The process worked well and prevented category sprawl and inconsistencies in attributes. However, the process did not tell the organization what they needed to do to make customer purchases more seamless and to improve crosssell, or make product content more effective to improve conversions. Improved processes were a good start, but more was needed to reach the ultimate goal of producing greater value for customers by improving their access to product information and the manufacturer's solutions.

INCORRECT DEVELOPMENT AND APPLICATION OF USE CASES AND SCENARIOS

One of the most powerful tools to validate any approach and to continue to evolve systems and processes and ensure that the needs of users are met is development of granular use cases. These should be built over time until the organization has libraries that cover various jobs, tasks, and processes. Use cases and scenarios should be developed based on job role, function, and user type. Use cases tell the designer what users need to do their jobs. Testing these use cases on an ongoing basis provides foundational metrics as a baseline and allows the capture of hard data to show improvement. Use cases need to be specific. In many organizations the use cases are very high level and lack meaningful context. An example might be something along the lines of "Locate and download information about customers." This objective lacks specificity, cannot be measured, and says very little about the specific types of information needed.

LACK OF UNDERSTANDING OF USER TYPES AND THE NEEDS OF USERS

Along the same lines of ambiguous use cases is a lack of understanding of user requirements. This is closely related to use case development and is based on considering users as a homogenous group rather than developing user types and personas and understanding how those users go about their jobs. An ambiguous requirement might be along the lines of "User must be able to quickly find needed information." This requirement is even more ambiguous than the previous example. Who is the user? What type of information? Conducting what task? With what additional supporting information and contextual clues?

LACK OF APPRECIATION OF THE VALUE OF UNSTRUCTURED INFORMATION

Every organization has an accounting function, and its value is undisputed. There is an inherent understanding that the financial data of the organization is essential and that this information needs to be kept up to date and be accurately inputted and manipulated. Unstructured information, however, does not have the same perceived value. Not all information is of equal value; organizations need to differentiate between low-value and high-value unstructured content, and treat high-value content appropriately. This is done to varying degrees in most organizations. Many understand that help desk content or content that serves customers is very valuable. However internal content processes are not seen in the same light. By understanding and differentiating according to process and lifecycle, the correct resources can be applied to managing high-value unstructured content.

LACK OF MEANINGFUL METRICS OR INTERPRETATION TO TIE BUSINESS VALUE TO INFORMATION

Data and content quality can be measured in isolation, but this metric is not meaningful by itself. Knowledge and collaboration processes are notoriously difficult to map and measure. The correct approach is to consider what process the information under consideration supports and determine the baselines of that process. After an intervention, the performance of the process can be measured again, and compared with the baseline. The key is to illustrate the connection of the content to a process. For a sales process, the time to develop proposals might be a good measure when installing a new proposal management and reuse platform. The important thing is to measure the quality of content and align that content with a measurable business process.

Multiple elements contribute to business outcomes, including the platforms on which the digital programs are running, the quality of the search function, information architecture elements such as taxonomy, metadata, and tagging, as well as the quality of the content. Often, though dashboards are put into place to provide valid and useful metrics, process owners need guidance regarding the meaning and impact of each metric that relates to their particular area. If a metric appears on the dashboard with a particular trend or outside of a prescribed range, the user should know what to do to get the customer experience back on track. Even if the metrics are intrinsically useful, they will not be useful from a business viewpoint if the process owners do not know how to use the knowledge that is generated.

LACK OF MATURITY IN ENTERPRISE ARCHITECTURE, USER EXPERIENCE, AND GOVERNANCE

Lack of maturity is a catch-all bucket to describe the inability to correctly derive, apply, and deploy information management processes. Most organizations have pockets of maturity in these areas and do not devote enough funding and attention to addressing deficiencies until a problem becomes unmanageable or disaster strikes. This happened with a large construction engineering firm when its knowledge management infrastructure collapsed due to heavy reliance on search that was running on outdated software and infrastructure. When the organization could not access critical knowledge for 2 weeks, the CEO took notice. A project was deployed that was very successful. However, the organization did not continue supporting updates to terminology, architecture, and workflow including content tagging and curation. The system gradually deteriorated and the organization cycled back to crisis mode. A better approach is to apply consistent resourcing and discipline to ongoing governance processes. Governance entails changing the ways that people do their jobs. Change management is a necessary component of every successful project or program, and the level of change management can range from short-term training on an application to long-term application of Kotter's eight steps to organizational change[b] or other enterprise change approaches. The point is that the organization will do something differently at the end of the day. It will no longer be business as usual.

---

[b]http://www.kotterinternational.com/the-8-step-process-for-leading-change/

OWNERSHIP AND SPONSORSHIP

All projects need to be owned and all projects need to have a sponsor. The broader the span across the enterprise, the more senior the sponsor needs to be. However, ownership and sponsorship involve different roles and responsibilities. In the case of a program, longer-term activities span the various work streams that require ownership. The ownership role and responsibilities of that role need to be carefully defined and assigned. For example, an enterprise taxonomist may own the taxonomy. This individual needs to interact with the owners and sponsors of all of the other work streams and projects, and ultimately be responsible for the correct application and exploitation of the taxonomy. That role is very important, as it helps align interests, handle different requirements and conflicting needs of different groups, and ensure the long-term integrity of the taxonomy. Governance issues can be complex and convoluted but need to be adapted to the specific needs of the enterprise.

SHORT-TERM OBJECTIVES WITH LONG-TERM VISION

Since projects typically comprise a program, and programs by their nature are longer term, projects that are undertaken in the short term need to be aligned with the goals of the longer-term program. A good example of this is illustrated by the need to be expeditious with e-commerce taxonomy while the rest of the enterprise is building a longer-term view of enterprise master data management (MDM). The short-term project will not be perfect, as it needs to meet fast turnaround goals. But future iterations can begin to align with the enterprise considerations of the MDM program.

GOALS OF PROCUREMENT VERSUS NEEDS OF THE PROGRAM

The procurement function is needed in an enterprise to negotiate the best prices and terms from vendors. This makes sense and is how an organization remains competitive. However, some in the consulting world do not like to think of themselves as "vendors." They want to be perceived as trusted partners in a transformative project. Even assuming that they are trusted partners in a transformative project and not "vendors," procurement still has to do its job, which is to negotiate the best prices and terms from "trusted partners in a transformative project." Sometimes procurement can go overboard, though, and either leave a well-qualified resource (perhaps the only qualified resource) out of the picture or reduce the pricing or resources needed to the point where the partner either cannot execute the project with the correct resources or may not want to put their best resources on the project. Organizations should keep in mind that trying to save money on a project with a value that is many multiples of its cost can backfire if the service provider walks away or relegates the project to a lower-level team.

FOCUS ON THE OUTCOME VALUE, NOT THE COST OF THE ENGAGEMENT

The program should receive the resources needed to effect change or impact the organization. Having a well-constructed, well-tested, integrated, and aligned taxonomy can provide orders of magnitude greater impact than one produced by a low-cost hourly resource. The contrast is dramatic, between a generic way of organizing information versus a personalized adaptive, informed, anticipatory approach that understands the way you do your job and can anticipate what you need. The first is worth very little. The second is a work of thoughtful execution with meaningful approaches. It is important to keep the desired outcome in mind. Of course the value has to be there, but that is intrinsic in the approach, not the price.

Along with this issue is the need to project out all of the success factors and program requirements and associated funding over the term in which benefits will accrue. These will be higher early on, and will decline over time, but may still be significant. If one does not budget appropriately, then the long-term program goals will not be achieved.

SOCIALIZATION

Socialization is needed on projects of any size—from informing stakeholders and getting buy-in on small projects to long-term opportunities for improving how people do their jobs. Socialization needs to be undertaken no matter how large or small the project. People want to know what is going on in the organization, how it impacts them, what is needed from them, and how longer-term changes will affect how they do their jobs. The level of effort around socialization can be low-touch and a small part of the project, or a major work stream in a large, longer-term initiative.

There are several characteristics of successful program journeys that improve knowledge processes as compared with shorter term projects as shown in Table 13.1. It is important to communicate goals and set expectations of shorter term versus longer term initiatives. Stakeholders will frequently expect the benefits of a program while only funding and supporting a short term project.

SUMMARY

What makes your knowledge management project worthwhile? Why should yours be funded, not only in the short-term but on an ongoing basis? Organizations have many different drivers and initiatives that require time, attention, and funding. The question is one of resource allocation. For example, an organization may have a problem with its customer service web content—customers are unable to locate content on the website and therefore are spending time with customer service reps in the call center or simply abandoning the site. There are a number of root causes for this problem and a variety of potential approaches to solving them. It may be considered a web content management issue where the core content management infrastructure needs to be

Table 13.1 Project Versus Program Perspectives

	Project	Program
Nature of outcome	Capability	Competency
Focus of outcome	Task focused or component of larger project	Multiple processes with broader business impact
Ownership	Short term—PM	Long term—business leadership
Timeline/funding	Short-term project 3–12 months	Long-term program 1–3 years
Alignment	Project plan	Business objective
Change management	Short-term training	Ongoing engagement with stakeholders
Span of impact	Project work streams	Business processes
Socialization	Department	Cross department, business unit or enterprise
Vision	Shorter-term outcome	Long-term transformation

PM, project manager

reworked. Or perhaps the core system is constrained due to connection to legacy applications. In that case, it might be considered a search problem. Or, the challenge may be that content is incorrectly tagged. Too much out-of-date content may result from a content curation problem. Many causative factors are possible, and each of these will require a short-term fix placed into a bigger picture program parameter. Perhaps the taxonomy is also handling digital assets or marketing assets. E-commerce systems may be involved, or search applications. People may want to include their pet projects around search or customer experience or collaborative content in your project.

Taxonomy and metadata can be the über project in all of this. But the participants need to understand how all the pieces fit together as well as how to manage and govern the pieces and justify the ongoing efforts. Taxonomy, IA, metadata, and search programs yield enormous benefits when well managed and integrated. If knowledge management initiatives are well-conceived and well-constructed in terms of looking at the full enterprise architecture, then synergistic results should accrue as the whole will be greater than the sum of its parts. Ongoing curation and evolution of the knowledge architecture supported by metrics-driven governance processes ensure long-term viability and effectiveness of knowledge management programs and form the basis for an adaptable, agile enterprise information ecosystem—a requirement in today's constantly connected, fast-changing, hyper-competitive digital environment.

Semantic technologies for enhancing knowledge management systems

14

V. Sugumaran

School of Business Administration, Oakland University, Rochester, MI, USA

INTRODUCTION

Typically, knowledge management (KM) focuses on managing the knowledge assets of an organization and the processes that act upon them (Earl, 2001; Massaro et al., 2016). Knowledge networks facilitate interactions with external stakeholders, such as suppliers, customers, and business partners (Gold et al., 2001; Wu, 2001; Sedlačko and Staroňová, 2015). Some of the advantages of implementing a KM infrastructure are: (1) providing effective and timely access to corporate knowledge at all levels so that efficiencies and competitive advantages are realized, (2)) transforming the diverse members of the organization into a knowledge work community, and (3) enabling evidence/knowledge-based decision making to improve the quality and timeliness of the decisions made (Offsey, 1997; Anupan et al., 2015).

While several organizations have successfully implemented KM initiatives, there are many cases of unsuccessful KM projects (Barth, 2000; Fahey and Prusak, 1998). Some of the pitfalls of KM projects (Davenport, 1997; Gibbert et al., 2011) are lack of: (1) alignment between strategic objectives and KM objectives, (2) identification and standard representation of knowledge assets to be managed, (3) routine processes to support KM life cycle, (4) infrastructure and key personnel in charge of KM activities, (5) access to knowledge, and (6) knowledge-sharing attitudes and motivation. Fahey and Prusak (1998) also point out that the fundamental purpose of managing knowledge is to create a shared context between individuals, which is not always achieved. Organizations have to redesign their internal structure and external relationships and create knowledge networks to facilitate the creation and management of organizational knowledge that would improve back-office efficiency, greater customer intimacy, and flexible adaptation to market changes (Aguirre et al., 2001; Caldwell et al., 2000). Thus, it is imperative that organizations invest in appropriate tools and technologies and establish processes and the necessary infrastructure for creating and managing their organizational knowledge.

With the advent of the semantic web, semantic technologies are increasingly being utilized to provide machine interpretation and processing capability of existing knowledge. They help create an environment where information is given well-defined meaning (semantics), which better enables computers and people to work in cooperation and use intelligent techniques to take advantage of the underlying representations. Thus, semantic technologies create a universal medium for information exchange by giving semantics, in a manner understandable by machines, to the content of resources (Wu, 2001; Sriti et al., 2015). The objective of this chapter is to: (1) develop a knowledge management framework for capturing, manipulating, and disseminating organizational knowledge using semantic technologies, and (2) develop an architecture for such a system.

The remainder of this chapter is organized as follows. Following the introduction, some background material on knowledge management, intelligent agents, and XML technology is provided. The next section discusses various semantic technologies used to build a KM framework. The following section presents the architecture for a KM system and discusses the various components. The chapter concludes with some implementation ideas for the KM system and provides a summary.

BACKGROUND

This work relies on established theories from knowledge management (KM life cycle), intelligent agent systems (agency theory), and text representation and rendering (markup languages). These three areas are briefly described in following sections.

KNOWLEDGE MANAGEMENT

To a large extent, the design and development of a KM system depends on the type of knowledge it has to manage. Fowler (2000) presents the following knowledge taxonomy: *declarative* (facts and assertions), *procedural* (logic and methods), *explicit* (articulable, codeable, systematic), *tacit* (inarticulable, interpretive, conceptual), *specific* (localized, clear, inductive), *abstract* (generalizable, obtuse, deductive), and *logic* (concept, attribute, value). Several KM frameworks have been presented (Hahn and Subramani, 2000; Newman and Conrad, 2000; Nonaka and Takeuchi, 1995; Zack, 1999) that consider these different types of knowledge and the processes involved in conversion from one to the other. For example, conversion from tacit to explicit knowledge is called "externalization," whereas from explicit to tacit is called "internalization." Drawing from system development literature, several authors have proposed knowledge management life cycle models, which advocate a phased approach for knowledge management (Davenport and Prusak, 1998; Despres and Chauvel, 1999; Nissen et al., 2000). These models provide a high level view of the activities that should be part of knowledge management. However, they fall short of incorporating the processes, tools, and techniques that are necessary in each phase. Several enabling technologies are used that support organizational knowledge creation, use, and management. Two such technologies are intelligent agents and extensible markup language (XML), which are briefly discussed in the following section.

INTELLIGENT AGENTS

Intelligent software agents have the capability to learn and make recommendations regarding a particular course of action. They act on behalf of human users to perform laborious and routine tasks such as locating and accessing necessary information, resolving inconsistencies in the retrieved information, filtering away irrelevant and unwanted information, and integrating information from heterogeneous information sources. To execute tasks on behalf of a user, they are designed to be goal driven, that is, they are capable of creating an agenda of goals to be satisfied. Several types of intelligent agents have been proposed and implemented (Dasgupta et al., 1999; Eriksson et al., 1999; Maes et al., 1999; Wu, 2001). Agents are typically characterized as (Sycara et al., 1996): (1) taskable, (2) netcentric, (3) semiautonomous, (4) persistent, (5) active, (6) collaborative, (7) flexible, and (8) adaptive. The taskable property refers to being able to take directions from human agents as well as other software agents, whereas the netcentric property relates to agents being distributed over a network but are self-organizing. Agents are semiautonomous and perform tasks on their own. They are also persistent and do not require frequent attention. Agents are active and have the ability to initiate problem-solving activities. They are collaborative, that is, delegate tasks to other agents and work cooperatively. Agents are also flexible and adaptive in the sense that they can deal with heterogeneity of other agents and information sources, as well as accommodate changing user needs and task environments.

XML AND KNOWLEDGE MANAGEMENT

Extensible markup language (XML) is a fundamental enabling technology for content management and application integration. XML is a set of rules for defining data structures and thus making it possible for key elements in a document to be characterized according to meaning. It enables us to build a structure around the document's attributes, and RDF (resource description framework) allows us to improve search mechanisms using the semantics of annotations (Decker et al., 2000). RDF uses a simple data model for representing properties of resources such as images, documents, and the relationships between them. The content of documents can be described using semantic annotations, which can then be used in searching for documents with certain content. RDF provides many advantages, such as: (1) a standard way to represent semantics, (2) supporting human readable and machine processable vocabularies, (3) standardized vocabularies within a particular community, and (4) eliminating the need for a centralized registry. Thus, RDF provides an information architecture that can extend capabilities for networking resources and information retrieval. XML makes it possible to deliver information to agents in a form that allows automatic processing after receipt and therefore distribute the processing load over a federation of agents that work cooperatively in problem solving.

SEMANTIC TECHNOLOGIES

The semantic web provides a common framework to: (1) represent data on the Web or a database in a manner understandable by machines; and (2) allow data to be shared and reused across application, enterprise, and enterprise boundaries. If a computer understands the semantics of a document, it doesn't just interpret the series of characters that make up that document, it understands the document's meaning. Semantic technologies therefore help separate meanings from data, document content, or application code, using technologies based on open standards. Semantic technologies represent meaning using ontologies and provide reasoning through the relationships, rules, logic, and conditions represented in those ontologies (Davies et al., 2002). To represent knowledge on the semantic web, we use the following technologies: (1) RDF (a standard syntax for describing data); (2) RDF schema (a standard means of describing the properties of that data); and (3) ontologies—defined using OWL, the web ontology language (a standard means of describing relationships between data items).

RDF—RESOURCE DESCRIPTION FRAMEWORK

RDF is the underlying data model for representing semantics. The data model and XML serialization syntax is used for describing resources both on and off the web. RDF makes use of unique identifiers (URI, uniform resource identifier) for describing metadata. URIs are used to describe things, also called resources, that could be people, places, documents, images, databases, etc. All RDF applications adopt a common convention for identifying these things. A subset of URI, the uniform resource locator or URL, is concerned with the location and retrieval of resources, while URI is a unique identifier for things or resources that we describe but may not retrieve. However, RDF provides a consistent, standardized way to describe and query internet resources, from text pages and graphics to audio files and video clips.

RDF SCHEMA

RDF schema is a standard means to describe the properties of resources defined using RDF. For example, if a resource is of a particular type, has a certain relationship to another resource, or has some specified attribute, RDF uses URIs to uniquely identify these descriptive concepts. Since the assignment of URIs is decentralized, one can be sure that uniquely named descriptive properties don't get mixed up when we integrate metadata from multiple sources. RDF schema is a semantic extension of RDF and provides mechanisms to describe groups of related resources and the relationships between those resources (Brickley and Guha, 2002). Both RDF and RDF schema are based on XML and XML schema. The existence of standards for describing data or other resources (RDF) and data or other resource attributes (RDF schema) enables the development of a set of readily available tools to read and exploit data or other resource from multiple sources.

ONTOLOGY

Ontologies capture concepts and relationships between concepts in a domain. They provide shared semantics to metadata, enabling a degree of semantic interoperability (Maedche and Staab, 2001). The challenge is how to represent, create, manage, and use ontologies as shared knowledge representations as well as large volumes of metadata records used to annotate resources of different types. The aim of building ontologies is to share and reuse knowledge as well as describe semantically equivalent things. It is necessary to map elements of ontologies if one wants to process information across applications or domains.

W3C's OWL (ontology working language) web ontology language is a poplar language used to represent ontologies on the web. OWL facilitates greater machine interpretability of web content than that supported by XML, RDF, and RDF schema by providing additional vocabulary along with formal semantics. The basic components of OWL include classes, properties, and individuals. Classes are the basic building blocks of OWL ontology. A class is a concept in a domain. Classes usually constitute a taxonomic hierarchy (eg, a subclass–superclass hierarchy). Properties have two main categories: (1) Object properties, which relate individuals to other individuals; and (2) datatype properties, which relate individuals to datatype values, such as integers, float, and strings. OWL makes use of XML schema for defining datatypes. Individuals are instances of classes, and properties can relate one individual to another.

WEB SERVICES

Web services are "services" offered by one application to other applications via the web (Zhao and Cheng, 2005). Developers can aggregate the services to form an end-user application, enable business transactions, or create new web services. They are software components and applications that use internet technologies and standards, and they can be accessed through the internet, intranet, or extranet. Their applications are growing, and it has been projected that most of the next generation internet–intranet-based KM systems will be based on web services (Kreger, 2003). The popularity of web services is due to the fact that it is designed to allow enterprises to move to a more "plug-and-play" business IT infrastructure, which would provide tremendous flexibility in managing IT resources and budgets.

SEMANTIC TECHNOLOGIES–BASED KNOWLEDGE MANAGEMENT ENVIRONMENT

Organizations are beginning to explore the use of semantic web technologies within their knowledge management application development (Hagel, 2002). The integration of web services into the KM environment provides several benefits, such as improving application sharing, increasing flexibility, and including innovative knowledge representation mechanisms. However, there are a few obstacles that need to be overcome before widespread adoption of semantic web technologies into KM systems can happen (Tilley et al., 2004). They include searching for appropriate KM services, the availability of relevant services and their reliability, composition of these services, and performance of web services–based knowledge management. The semantic web technologies discussed in the previous section help to design a flexible, intelligent, and sophisticated KM environment. These technologies also help minimize the cognitive burden on the user.

The architecture of the proposed semantic KM environment is shown in Fig. 14.1. The two major subsystems that comprise the architecture are (1) internal components and (2) external components. The internal components subsystem contains modules or resources that are available and under the control of the organization as well as the components that typically constitute a KM system. The internal components

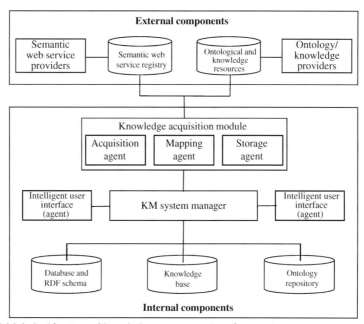

FIGURE 14.1 Architecture of knowledge management environment

subsystem is composed of: (1) intelligent user interface; (2) database and RDF schema; (3) knowledge base; (4) ontologies; (5) KM system manager; and (6) knowledge acquisition module consisting of acquisition, mapping, and storage agents. The external components consist of: (1) semantic web service providers, (2) semantic web service registry, and (3) ontological and knowledge resources. These components are briefly described in the next section.

INTERNAL COMPONENTS
Intelligent user interface
The user interface contains intelligent agents that can act on behalf of humans and assist them in executing complex tasks. They can be integrated into knowledge management tasks to shield the complexities and help novice users undertake KM activities. Development of multiagent systems is also increasing (He and Jennings, 2003; Wang et al., 2002), and these systems contain agents that are capable of acting autonomously, cooperatively, and collaboratively to achieve a collective goal. An agent by itself may not have sufficient information or expertise to solve an entire problem; hence mutual sharing of information and expertise is necessary to allow a group of agents to produce a solution to a problem. The interface agent provides mechanisms for the user to interact with the system. It enables the user to query, search, and retrieve appropriate knowledge from the KM system to support different activities. It also maintains user profiles and facilitates customization and parameterization of the tasks.

Database and RDF schema
The database component provides data support for the operations of the semantic KM environment. Data management component provides access to organizational data that could be attribute and spatial data. It may encompass traditional databases as well as GIS databases. Thus, the data management component provides easy access to large volumes of organizational data. The RDF Schema provides the underlying knowledge representation mechanism that is used to represent and store the organizational knowledge.

Knowledge base
The knowledge base contains domain-specific knowledge relevant to the organization. It also contains rules that enable the user to select appropriate knowledge elements to be used in a particular task. It may also contain organizational policies, procedures, business rules, and constraints that may be relevant for the problem at hand. This helps in ensuring that developers adhere to the organization-wide standards that need to be followed during application development.

Ontologies
Ontologies capture domain-specific or common sense knowledge about the real world and can be used to increase our semantic understanding for decision support.

An ontology generally consists of terms, their definitions, and axioms relating to them. For this research, the most relevant ontologies are domain ontologies that specify conceptualizations specific to a domain (Weber, 2002). Ontological resources may incorporate a combination of different lexical and ontological sources of knowledge. For example, different kinds of information can be gathered from WordNet (Fellbaum, 1998) and the DAML ontology library (http://www.daml.org/) that are useful for disambiguating terms and providing additional semantic information.

KM system manager

The KM system manager serves as the controlling unit that takes care of the communication between the collaborating modules and coordinates the various tasks that need to be executed in order to carry out various KM activities. This module essentially drives the user interaction. It maintains metadata about the other components within the system and facilitates the sharing of appropriate knowledge and information relevant to a particular task. It coordinates the results generated by other modules which carry out specific subtasks related to problems.

Knowledge acquisition module

The knowledge acquisition module is responsible for identifying, acquiring, and storing new knowledge that would be useful in decision making. This module contains the following agents: (1) acquisition agent, (2) mapping agent, and (3) storage agent. Based on their day-to-day activities, stakeholders may either identify new knowledge that needs to be gathered or create knowledge that could be used by others within the organization. Any knowledge that is generated needs to be represented and stored in such a manner that it is readily accessible and usable by others. The mapping and storage agents are responsible for generating the internal representation of the knowledge artifacts so that they can be stored, organized, disseminated, and used by other stakeholders and applications. The knowledge artifacts within the repositories can be organized based on subject or a specific taxonomy.

EXTERNAL COMPONENTS

Semantic web service providers

The semantic web service providers primarily consist of vendors that provide one or more web services that might be integrated into a KM application. These services may support specific functionalities with well-defined interfaces and extensive documentation as to how to use them in a particular application. The success of web service providers greatly depends on describing and advertising their services correctly and efficiently. Web service providers face the problem of how to publicize their services so that service seekers can easily find these services and evaluate their suitability.

Semantic web service registry

The semantic web service registry is a central repository that publishes the availability of web services. Web services are modeled using DAML-S or other ontology languages, which contains ServiceProfile, ServiceModel, and ServiceGrounding (Sycara et al., 2003). The ServiceProfile describes what a service can do and contains contact information about the service provider and an extensible set of service characteristics. This helps in advertising the service as well as being able to be spotted by service seekers.

Knowledge resources

The knowledge resources contain information about various web services, computational and model execution, which can be used by KM applications for reasoning and exhibiting intelligent behavior. Domain specific knowledge resources may contain knowledge that is relevant to a particular application domain that the organization specializes in. This knowledge would be of great help to semantics-based application developers.

The KM system architecture described previously is modular in nature and additional domain specific components can be easily added to the system as long as the interfaces are clearly defined. Using this environment, the entire KM life cycle can be supported for an organization. The system supports interoperability between internal and external components through ontologies and existing standards. It also improves communication with other existing applications.

SUMMARY

Organizations are investing heavily in creating centralized knowledge repositories to improve business processes, promote knowledge sharing, and retain expertise even after employees leave the organization. This chapter has presented a framework and architecture for supporting knowledge management activities within organizations. The unique contributions of this research are: (1) the knowledge management framework that takes into account different types of knowledge that exists within an organization, (2) client-server based architecture for implementing a system that supports various phases of the knowledge management life cycle, and (3) integrating enabling technologies such as intelligent-agents, XML and RDF, and ontologies and web services to create an environment that fosters cooperative knowledge work. Our future work will involve designing a knowledge management system that will facilitate ubiquitous access to information and decision support tools through the use of mobile tools, mobile e-services, and wireless protocols such as wireless applications protocol (WAP), wireless markup language (WML), and iMode.

ACKNOWLEDGMENT

This research has been supported by a 2014 School of Business Administration Spring/Summer Research Fellowship at Oakland University.

REFERENCES

Aguirre, J.L., Brena, R., Cantu, F.J., 2001. Multiagent-based knowledge networks. Expert Syst. Appl. 20 (1), 65–75.

Anupan, A., Nilsook, P., Wannapiroon, P., 2015. A Framework for a knowledge management system in a cloud computing environment using a knowledge engineering approach. Int. J. Knowl. Eng. 1 (2), 146–149.

Barth, S., 2000. KM horror stories. Knowl. Manage 3 (10), 36–40.

Brickley, D., Guha, R. (Eds.), 2002. Resource Description Framework (RDF) Schema Specification. W3C, Cambridge, MA, W3C Working Draft 30 April 2002. Available from: http://www.w3.org/TR/rdf-schema.

Caldwell, N., Clarkson, P.J., Rodgers, P., Huxor, A., 2000. Web-based knowledge management for distributed design. IEEE Intell. Syst. 15 (3), 40–47.

Dasgupta, P., Narasimhan, N., Moser, L.E., Melliar-Smith, P.M., 1999. MAgNET: mobile agents for networked electronic trading. IEEE Trans. Knowl Data Eng. 11 (4), 509–525.

Davenport, T.H., 1997. Known evils: the common pitfalls of knowledge management. CIO Magazine, June 15, 1997.

Davenport, T.H., Prusak, L., 1998. Working Knowledge: How Organizations Manage What They Know. Harvard Business School Press, Cambridge, MA.

Davies, J., Fensel, D., van Harmelen, F. (Eds.), 2002. Towards the Semantic Web: Ontology-Driven Knowledge Management. Wiley, New York, NY.

Decker, S., Melnik, S., Harmelen, F.V., Fensel, D., Klein, M., Broekstra, J., Erdmann, M., Horrocks, I., 2000. The semantic web: the roles of XML and RDF. IEEE Internet Comput. 4 (5), 63–74.

Despres, C., Chauvel, D., 1999. Mastering information management: part six—knowledge management. Financial Times, March 8, 1999, pp. 4–6.

Earl, M., 2001. Knowledge management strategies: toward a taxonomy. J. Manage. Inform. Syst. 18 (1), 215–233.

Eriksson, J., Finne, N., Janson, S., 1999. SICS MarketSpace—an agent-based market infrastructure. Lecture Notes in Computer Science, Issue 1571. Springer-Verlag, Berlin, pp. 42–53.

Fahey, L., Prusak, L., 1998. The eleven deadliest sins of knowledge management. Calif. Manage. Rev. 40 (3), 265–276.

Fellbaum, C., 1998. WordNet: An Electronic Lexical Database. MIT Press, Cambridge, MA.

Fowler, A., 2000. The role of AI-based technology in support of the knowledge management value activity cycle. J. Strateg. Inform. Syst. 9 (2/3), 107–128.

Gibbert, M., Probst, G.J.B., Davenport, T.H., 2011. Sidestepping implementation traps when implementing knowledge management: lessons learned from Siemens. Behav. Inf. Technol. 30 (1), 63–75.

Gold, A., Malhotra, A., Segars, A., 2001. Knowledge management: an organizational capabilities perspective. J. Manage. Inform. Syst. 18 (1), 185–214.

Hagel, J., 2002. Out of Box: Strategies for Achieving Profits Today and Growth through Web Services. Harvard Business School Press, Boston: MA.

Hahn, J., Subramani, M., 2000. A framework of knowledge management systems: issues and challenges for theory and practice. In: Proceedings Of International Conference on Information Systems, Brisbane, Australia, 2000, pp. 302–312.

He, M., Jennings, N.R., 2003. SouthamptonTAC: an adaptive autonomous trading agent. ACM Trans. Internet Technol. 3 (3), 219–235.

Kreger, H., 2003. Fulfilling the web services promise. Commun. ACM 46 (6), 29–34.

Maedche, A., Staab, S., 2001. Ontology learning for the semantic web. IEEE Intell. Syst. 16 (2), 72–79.

Maes, P., Guttman, R.H., Moukas, A.G., 1999. Agents that buy and sell. Commun. ACM 42 (3), 81–87, 90, 91.

Massaro, M., Handley, K., Bagnoli, C., Dumay, J., 2016. Knowledge management in small and medium enterprises: a structured literature review. J. Knowl. Manage. 20 (2), 258–291.

Newman, B.D., Conrad, K.W., 2000. A framework for characterizing knowledge management methods, practices, and technologies. In: Proceedings of the Third International Conference on Practical Aspects of Knowledge Management (PAKM2000), Basel, Switzerland, October 30–31, 2000, pp. 16.1–16.11.

Nissen, M., Kamel, M., Sengupta, K., 2000. Integrated analysis and design of knowledge systems and processes. Inform. Res. Manage. J. 13 (1), 24–43.

Nonaka, I., Takeuchi, H., 1995. The Knowledge-Creating Company: How Japanese Companies Create the Dynamics of Innovation. Oxford University Press, New York.

Offsey, S., 1997. Knowledge management: linking people to knowledge for bottom line results. J. Knowl. Manage. 1 (2), 113–122.

Sedlačko, M., Staroňová, K., 2015. From knowledge utilization to building knowledge networks. Cent. Eur. J. Public Policy 9 (2), 4–9.

Sriti, M.F., Assouroko, I., Ducellier, G., Boutinaud, P., Eynard, B., 2015. Ontology–based approach for product information exchange. Int. J. Prod. Lifecycle Manage. 8 (1), 1–23.

Sycara, K., Pannu, A., Williamson, M., Zeng, D., Decker, K., 1996. Distributed intelligent agents. IEEE Expert 11 (6), 36–45.

Sycara, K., Paolucci, M., Ankolekar, A., Srinivasan, N., 2003. Automated discovery, interaction and composition of semantic web services. J. Web Semant. 1 (1), 27–46.

Tilley, S., Gerdes, J., Hamilton, T., Huang, S., Miller, H., Smith, D., Wong, K., 2004. On business value and technical challenges of adopting web services. J. Softw. Maint. Evol. 16, 31–50.

Wang, H., Mylopoulos, J., Liao, S., 2002. Intelligent agents and financial risk monitoring systems. Commun. ACM 45 (3), 83–88.

Weber, R., 2002. Ontological issues in accounting information systems. In: Sutton, S., Arnold, V. (Eds.), Researching Accounting as an Information Systems Discipline. American Accounting Association, Sarasota, FL.

Wu, D.J., 2001. Software agents for knowledge management: coordination in multi-agent supply chains and auctions. Expert Syst. Appl. 20 (1), 51–64.

Zack, M.H., 1999. Developing a knowledge strategy. Calif. Manage. Rev. 41 (3), 125–145.

Zhao, J.L., Cheng, H.K., 2005. Web services and process management: a union of convenience or a new area of research? Decis. Support Syst. 40, 1–8.

Subject Index

Printed in the United States
By Bookmasters